PRAISE FOR MAVIS GALLANT

"Line by line, word by word, no one writes with more compression than Gallant."

—FRANCINE PROSE

"Gallant's talent is as versatile and witty as it is somber and empathetic."

—JOHN UPDIKE

"One of the great story writers of our time."

—MICHAEL ONDAATJE

"Gallant had a rare gift: a solid imagination."

—*The New Yorker*

"Relentlessly, charmingly witty."

—*The Vllage Voice*

"There is no writer in English anywhere able to set Mavis Gallant in second place."

—*Washington Post*

The Other Paris (1956)

Green Water, Green Sky (1959)

My Heart Is Broken (1964)

A Fairly Good Time (1970)

The Peignitz Junction (1973)

The End of the World and Other Stories (1974)

From the Fifteenth District (1979)

Home Truths (1981)

Overhead in a Balloon (1985)

In Transit (1988)

Across the Bridge (1993)

The Moslem Wife and Other Stories (1994)

The Collected Stories of Mavis Gallant (1996)

Paris Stories (2002)

Varieties of Exile (2003)

Going Ashore (2009)

The Cost of Living (2009)

PARIS NOTEBOOKS

PARIS NOTEBOOKS

ESSAYS & REVIEWS

Mavis Gallant

FOREWORD BY

HERMIONE LEE

BOSTON

GODINE NONPAREIL

2023

Published in 2023 by
GODINE
Boston, Massachusetts

These essays were originally published in the following periodicals: *The
Atlantic, The Canadian Forum, The New York Review of Books, The New York
Times Book Review, The New Yorker,* and *PMA.*

LIBRARY OF CONGRESS CATALOGING-IN-PUBLICATION DATA
Names: Gallant, Mavis, author. | Lee, Hermione, writer of foreword.
Title: Paris notebooks : essays & reviews / Mavis Gallant ; foreword by
    Hermione Lee.
Description: Boston : Godine, 2023.
Identifiers: LCCN 2023005862 (print) | LCCN 2023005863 (ebook) | ISBN
    9781567927894 (paperback) | ISBN 9781567927900 (ebook)
Subjects: LCGFT: Essays. | Literary criticism. | Book reviews.
Classification: LCC PR9199.3.G26 P37 2023 (print) | LCC PR9199.3.G26
    (ebook) | DDC 814/.54--dc23/eng/20230210
LC record available at https://lccn.loc.gov/2023005862
LC ebook record available at https://lccn.loc.gov/2023005863

First Printing, 2023
Printed in the United States of America

For Josie Peron

CONTENTS

PART TWO: REVIEWS

Foreword

"ALL LIVES ARE interesting; no one life is more interesting than another." "I simply followed events as they occurred from day to day, keeping track of conversations and things observed." "One of the hardest things in the world is to describe what happened next." There is the voice of Mavis Gallant: unblinkingly attentive and keen-eyed, making little of herself and much of others, tracking every nuance of human behavior, wise, dry, funny, and subtle.

One of the fascinating monsters she writes about in these essays (and she never flinches from monsters), the journalist and diarist Paul Léautaud, was asked why he went to observe his dreadful father's deathbed. He replied, spelling it out: "*Cu-ri-o-si-té.*" Gallant's own *Cu-ri-o-si-té*, as a novelist, short-story writer, diarist, critic, and reporter, is omnivorous. And it is never more acute than when writing about her adopted country and its people.

From her mid-twenties a naturalized Parisian and Fran-
cophile, she was also a Canadian-born outsider. As one of
her admirers and fellow-Francophiles Anita Brookner put
it in a 1988 article in the *Observer*: "For those who cannot
live in Paris she is an essential witness." Much of Gallant's
writing life was taken up with sending "translations" of
French affairs to readers of the *New York Times Book Review*, the *New York Review of Books*, and *The New Yorker*,
which was also—thanks to the legendary editor William
Maxwell—the home for her marvellous short stories.
Like Edith Wharton or Janet Flanner, both of whom
Gallant admired, she was an impeccable transcriber of
French life for North American readers. She did this with
the true fiction writer's combination of deep feeling and
estrangement, and out of a lifelong compulsion to turn
lived experience into memorable sentences. In the preface
to her *Selected Stories*, she cites with wry fellow feeling the
response of another exile-in-France, Samuel Beckett, on
being asked "a hopeless question from a Paris newspaper—'Why do you write?'" He said, "It was all he was
good for: 'Bon qu'a ça.'"

The longest piece in this selection (which dates from
the 1960s to the 1980s and was first published in 1986) is
the diary she kept during the "*événements*" of May '68, the
huge students and workers revolution that started in Paris,
spread all over the country, changed everyone's lives, and
was over within seven weeks. This account is written without what she calls "the irony of hindsight" or the "confused collective memory" that subsequently settled into
French consciousness, making a "*soixante-huitard*" into "a

nostalgic bourgeois" and, frequently, "a colossal bore, to whom, one feels, nothing else has ever happened." Gallant is reporting from the thick of things, clinging on to a traffic island as a sea of flag-waving students and workers bear down on her, her eyes smarting from tear gas leaking down into the Métro, sitting through the hectic and repetitive political debates in the occupied Sorbonne, glued day and night to the news reports, filled like everyone else with exhilaration, admiration ("How brave these kids are now!"), fear, bewilderment, and exhaustion. She tells us exactly how it felt to be there. It is bitterly cold. The "speaking clock" is on strike; in the "well-to-do suburbs" "they are stealing gas from each other's cars"; the trees of Paris are being cut down; there is panic-buying and hoarding, and the streets are full of leaflets, smashed signs, broken grilles, wrecked traffic lights, and rubbish:

> Garbage piled on curb of Rue de Sèvres. Cluster of pedestrians staring at something. Five plastic bags, each holding a kilo of peeled new potatoes rotting in the sun. Hoarder evidently didn't know that peeled potatoes in plastic bags rot quickly, have to be used almost the day you buy them. Five kilos!

Through this exact, close-range lens, all the big stories emerge, including the atrocious police violence, the shifting politics of left and right, the clash between generations, the suspense as to the outcome, and the sudden end. What was it all for, what did people want, she keeps asking and being asked. Even long afterward, she still finds something noble and "poignant" in the answer: "Quelque chose de propre." Something decent.

That mixture of emotion and detachment colors all the writing, notably in her report on a scandal that electrified France at the end of 1968 and which, as she shows us, is unintelligible without the context of the "*événements*," of the French judicial system, French prison conditions, French psychiatric practice, and French attitudes to women. The shocking and tragic story of Gabrielle Russier, an emotionally immature thirty-year-old divorced schoolteacher and mother of two, who had an affair with her nineteen-year-old student, was punitively treated by the boy's Communist parents and by the law, was sent to prison and committed suicide, is analysed with forensic care. Gallant presents the case in all its moral and social complexity, without passing judgment on the protagonists, but with strong words for a society where, intellectually, socially, and professionally, women are respected and accepted, but where in law, "women never have the last word."

You can feel Gallant itching to turn the Russier case into a novel or a short story, with the mysteries and perversities of human relationships at its heart. Every so often she opens it out: "The question of what people see in each other still defies analysis." "Even the most selfless and indulgent parents will seldom grant [their children] the right to a private life without a struggle." "One of the lessons of literature . . . is the hopeless folly of trying to separate lovers by force."

That experienced, ironical tone marks her fiction, which anyone coming to Gallant for the first time with this volume should certainly go on to read. It's the voice of a writer for whom nothing is alien and everything is possible. Her stories, like her essays, pay calm attention to extreme and often cruel events, peculiar types, irrational acts, loss and grief, "love, hate and desire." Her fictional characters are émigrés, war-survivors, refugees, divorcées, orphans, the homeless and the emotionally displaced, people "in transit" (the title of one of her collections) or who have "jumped out of a social enclosure." She herself is a kind of displaced person of the imagination, with an uncanny ability to make herself at home in other minds, and to ingest the lives of others as forms of "information."

That is what makes her accounts of the challenging, notable personalities she writes about here so compelling. Her brief, masterly pieces on Giraudoux, Yourcenar, Nabokov, de Beauvoir, Malraux, Céline, Colette, Simenon, and the wonderfully repulsive journalist and diarist Paul Léautaud are brilliantly poised between satire and inwardness, objectivity and fascination. She knows her French cultural icons like the back of her hand—"I am devoted to Giraudoux's writing in the way that some people are Gaullists or vegetarians"—and she is irresistibly sharp on their strangeness and peculiarities. Here she is on Yourcenar's fictional women: "the dismal ranks of scolds, harpies, frigid spouses, sluts, slatterns, humorless fanatics and avaricious know-nothings who people her work." Here on de Beauvoir's last volume of autobiography: "She is tired of everything and especially of us, her readers." Here on Céline's xenophobia: "He seems torn apart by an inner grenade of spleen." And here on the dangerousness of

Léautaud: "He was not a lovable old grump, a mixture of The Misanthrope and Father Christmas, but a literary snapping turtle who bit to wound."

In her nonfiction, as in her stories, she is at her wittiest when writing about her adopted country's prejudices, snobberies, customs, and "social enclosures." "You can't ask for a divorce at lunch. It has to be done by mail," says one Parisian to another in the story "Rue de Lille." Another, an art dealer (in "Speck's Idea"), has his premises in the Faubourg Saint-Germain: "The building had long before been cut up into dirty, decaying apartments, whose spiteful, quarrelsome, and avaricious tenants were forgiven every failing . . . for the sake of being the Count of this and the Prince of that." In the essays, we find these wonderful examples of knowing, amused satire on Parisian customs: "It must be borne in mind that no turn of phrase in French conversation is ever meant as a joke." "They [the children] observe one another with the brief, prudent, Parisian appraisal that takes in the unknown without acknowledging it." "A British dinner table of total strangers will spend a lively evening listening to one another's accents; in France, the guests perform a kind of whooping crane courtship dance as they try to establish, without asking directly, which guest is a graduate of which elite school." "It is distressing, at [Brasserie] Lipp to be sent upstairs. It means you have missed the dead-on tone of temperate confidence required for getting a table on the ground floor. (The food is the same.)"

As these examples show, Mavis Gallant is an unerring stylist. I might have spent the whole of this introduction rejoicing in the Frenchness of her aphorisms: "She was a quarrelsome pessimist, as women are apt to become when married to philandering optimists." "The truth remains that every artist causes absent-minded destruction and that a writer totally unselfish would never get anything done." And she hates bad writing. Her bête noire is the mangling of language that comes from over-literal translations from French to English, comprehensively described in one example as "a kind of bogus English that lurches from careless to pretentious to incomprehensible to barely literate." She is suspicious of style that doesn't ring true to what fiction, she thinks, is fundamentally about, which is "that something is taking place and that nothing lasts": "A loose, a wavering, a slipshod, an affected, a false way of transmitting even a fragment of this leaves the reader suspicious." Her sympathies go out to fine writers who live their life in a foreign language, like Nabokov or Yourcenar: "Writers who choose domicile in a foreign place . . . usually treat their native language like a delicate timepiece, making certain it runs exactly and that no dust gets inside." In the '68 diary, she is offended by a student who is tearing down a flag attached to a poster for an exhibition at the Louvre. "Ce n'est pas élégant," she bursts out at him. Gallant is never anything but.

Hermione Lee

2023

All stories cited in this introduction are from *The Selected Stories of Mavis Gallant*, McClelland & Stewart, 1996.

Introduction

IN THE EARLY spring of 1968, the Paris afternoon newspaper *Le Monde* ran on its back page a boxed paragraph about the threatened expulsion from France of a German-Jewish undergraduate, whose name was not disclosed. According to *Le Monde*, students at the suburban university of Nanterre—recently opened and already a hotbed of youthful Marxist activity—had taken to the streets to protest the measure. The very idea that French students would stop to consider the fate of a foreigner seemed so remarkable that I clipped the story and kept it. It did not occur to me that it had political significance; I simply saw a dent in the armor of French xenophobia, almost the sign of a mutation in the French national character.

By the end of April the foreign student was still in France. His name was Daniel Cohn-Bendit, aged twenty-four, a French-German binational who had opted for

German citizenship because he wanted no part of the Algerian war. He had bright red hair, a cherubic face, an insolent manner, and a gift for leadership. (Subsequent rumors had him engaged to marry a number of young women from wealthy or politically powerful French families, none of whom, probably, he had met in his life, and receiving the support and protection of the C.I.A., the K.G.B., Fidel Castro, East and West Germans, the President of the United States, and the Prime Minister of France.)

He and others from Nanterre were dubbed *les enragés*, because of their extreme leftist views. They carried their protest into the Latin Quarter, around the ancient Sorbonne, the heart of the University of Paris, and in the process clashed with their natural enemies—right-wing students from the law school on Rue d'Assas, and members of "Occident," a street-fighting radical far-right group that is now banned by law.

On May 3 a gang of Occident supporters, hanging about outside the Sorbonne, with their usual brass knuckles and iron bars, happened to watch the arrest of some Nanterre demonstrators, and immediately joined them in battling the police. The frontier of the nineteen-sixties, youth vs. authority, already clearly visible in North America, was now drawn in Paris. When the rector of the Sorbonne allowed the police to enter the university, students struck. The Sorbonne retaliated by closing down. The events of May, as they were called, had begun.

What developed next was a gigantic happening. To André Malraux, then Minister for Culture, it signified "a crisis of civilization." Now it seems to have been an extraordinary kind of make-believe, a collective dream in which an entire city played at being on the brink of civil war. The events did not start in France; student unrest, which is always contagious, spread from Italy to the United States and came back to Europe. The difference between rebellion at Columbia and rebellion at the Sorbonne is that life in Manhattan went on as before, while in Paris every section of society was set on fire, in the space of a few days.

The life of the capital blazed and stopped. In almost no time, Paris became a city where it was impossible to buy a newspaper, go to school, mail a letter, send a telegram, cash a cheque, ride in a bus, take the Métro, use a private car (doctors excepted), find cigarettes (the no-smoking campaign was not yet under way), sugar, canned goods, or salad oil, watch television or, towards the end, listen to a news bulletin. No garbage was collected; no trains left the city; there was no time signal, no weather report. Teachers stopped teaching, actors stopped acting. Discussion groups replaced professional activity. And yet there was no general strike order (power and water supplies were maintained, which did not prevent mass hoarding of candles, matches, and bottled mineral water) and no real direction to the protest. Young Jews occupied the Israelite Consistory ("The telephone switchboard is in their hands," announced *Le Monde*) and football players occupied their professional headquarters. It was as though people on every level of society intended to bring matters to a halt, pause, and set off in a different direction. Set off where?

What did they want? Nothing is easier to exercise than the irony of hindsight. The collective hallucination was that life can change, quite suddenly, and for the better. It still strikes me as a noble desire, and the answer I heard, when I asked one woman what she had expected to emerge out of all the disorder (*"Quelque chose de propre"*—something clean, decent), still seems to me poignant.

We know, now, from Prime Minister Georges Pompidou's posthumous memoirs, that President Charles de Gaulle was not as sure and farseeing as he appeared to be when the events were over. We have learned that when he vanished on May 30 (to French army headquarters at Baden-Baden, in Germany) it was without informing his prime minister that he was leaving the country. The man he went to Baden-Baden to consult, his old enemy General Massu, was astonished to see a lost and bewildered old man, ready to bring the army in on the side of the government, if need be. According to Massu, he turned the President around and sent him back to Paris, to the triumph of the great pro-Gaullist demonstration on May 31.

And so order was restored, elections were held, and a large conservative majority was chosen to govern the country. Alain Peyrefitte, Cabinet minister many times over, remarked, "If we don't do anything foolish, we're in power until the year 2000." (They held until 1981, and were restored in 1986.) Less than a year later, the same voters rejected de Gaulle—quietly, this time, without barricades—but accepted his successor, Georges Pompidou. Nothing was left but a confused collective memory, the

stuff of kitsch. Today, *un soixante-huitard* (a sixty-eighter)
means a nostalgic bourgeois, somewhere in his late thirties or early forties, still mourning his lost, adolescent ide-
als. It can also stand for a colossal bore, to whom, one feels,
nothing else has ever happened.

Readers of this journal should keep in mind that it
was never intended to be an historical document, or an
appraisal, or an overall view of a situation that even President de Gaulle called *insaisissable*. I simply followed
events as they occurred from day to day, keeping track
of conversations and things observed. If *The New Yorker*
had not asked to see the record, I might never have bothered to type my notes or put them into order. I began the
journal in London, in Heathrow Airport, as I sat waiting for a Paris plane, after reading the first description
of police action (lurid and fake, as it turned out) in an
English newspaper, and I kept a close record until June 17,
the day the police entered the Sorbonne for the last time,
to clear out the last of the rebels. The original document
is somewhat longer. I have restored a few of the cuts *The
New Yorker* made, and corrected mistakes committed by
their well-meaning but sometimes muddled checking department. The published journal does not go on to June
17: by that time, I had left Paris and was in the south of
France. My information was at second hand and, I think,
of no interest to a reader, who could obtain the same information from a newspaper file. Nothing has been added
except the full titles of groups and organizations I had
mentioned by their initials in my own notes—for example, Compagnies Républicaines de Sécurité is indicated at

least once as the name of the C.R.S., the riot police. I have maintained the privacy of friends and strangers quoted by first name or initial. Some are dead; others have changed their mind and opinions since those days. Now, eighteen years after the events, even the "I" of the journals seems like a stranger.

The account of the Gabrielle Russier case and its sad aftermath was written as an introduction to the American edition of her letters from prison. It is a story that today seems almost like fiction—perhaps because a somewhat silly film was made from it—and was inextricably bound up with the school and university climate of May 1968. The Communist Party was a much stronger force in French intellectual and academic life: the Communist vote fluctuated between nineteen and twenty-five per cent, year in and year out. Now the figure has dropped to less than ten. In "The Taste of a New Age," written in January 1981, the unemployment figures mentioned are about half the present number. The site of the old Halles, still a hole in the ground six years ago, has been filled in, and provides another example of the decline of French architecture and urban design. The restaurant just opposite the Georges Pompidou Centre, the talk of Paris that particular winter, has been replaced by a fast-food place. The Centre itself, which seemed used up, exhausted, a white elephant, has been considerably refurbished and is now run with taste and imagination. Finally, in the piece about Paul Léautaud, I quote his late friend and biographer, Marie Dormoy, and her assurance that she and Léautaud were never lovers. This information, volunteered by Mlle. Dormoy, unsolicited by me, was something I believed easily, given Léautaud's household and personality. Last winter, a journal Léautaud had kept in secret about their long affair was finally published. It is an explicit and often cruel document; but then, he was often unkind.

Mlle. Dormoy was in her forties and Léautaud considerably older when their *histoire* began. She was custodian and archivist of the Jacques Doucet Foundation, which included a private collection of rare manuscripts and books. Determined to obtain Léautaud's original manuscript diaries for the Foundation, she seduced him. (The seduction is Léautaud's unchallenged version of events.) At any rate, she did get the manuscripts, became his literary executor, and devoted whatever time she could spare from his quarrels and obsessions to transcribing them for publication. Léautaud was dirty, toothless, mean-tempered, and habitually unfaithful. He shared his bedroom with a colony of cats. He was both easily swindled and avaricious. One can only praise Mlle. Dormoy's patience and firmness of purpose. She provides a sterling example of the lengths to which a determined archivist may be ready to go. Among her merits is the fact that she did not destroy the "secret Journal," and no one can blame her for having kept quiet about it during her lifetime.

Mavis Gallant
Paris, April 1986

PARIS NOTEBOOKS

———

PART ONE: ESSAYS

The Events in May:
A Paris Notebook—I

MAY 3

Photographs, in newspapers, of students in front of the Sorbonne. Members of Occident, an extreme-right-wing student group, waiting in the street to beat up Nanterre *enragés*, start fighting with police when they see *enragés* arrested.

MAY 4

H. T. caught in traffic jam around Saint-Germain-Saint-Michel in midst of student disorders. Says this is "different"—they all seem very young. He sees a barricade made of parked cars they have moved away from the curb. Is very impatient—hates disorder.

Talk with M. B. She saw the police charge, outside the

Balzar Brasserie. Says their apartment full of tear gas—they live on the fifth floor! Wouldn't let her daughter talk on telephone in sight of windows. Police think nothing of throwing grenades into houses. Doubt if they could throw one up to fifth floor. Says gas makes it impossible to sleep at night.

Crowds, traffic jams. See a crowd. I feel the mixture of tension and curiosity that is always the signal of something happening, and I hear shouting and see police cars. I duck into Saint-Germain Métro. I hate these things. See more pictures in papers, and accounts, surprising, of how the students, far from fleeing, "regroup and charge."

MAY 6

In the night, hear that familiar wave of sound, as during the crisis in 1958. Get dressed, go out as far as Carrefour Raspail. All confusion. Students do not run—it is not 1958, after all. Attack in a kind of frenzy that seems insane. The courage of these kids! Don't get too near. See what is obviously innocent bystander hit on the ear by a policeman. Decide not to tell anyone, as friends would have fit. All night, shouts, cries, harsh slogans chanted, police cars, ambulances, cars going up and down my one-way street, running feet. I open a shutter and see that I am the only person on the street at a window. Are they scared, or respectable, or what? Scared of police, or of students?

MAY 7

Dined at the B.s', Quai Saint-Michel. No one takes a car now—not safe to park in the area. Students are marching all over Paris: "*Libérez nos camarades!*"—meaning those who were sentenced by a monkey court on Sunday. From the B.s' living room you see Seine, sunset, expanse of quais, very few cars, scarcely any traffic, many police. Christine (fifteen) says, "But is my *duty* to be out there with the students." Nothing doing. However, I notice she does not eat her dinner with us. Has it by herself in the kitchen. Almost seems like the heart of the matter—not with the adults, not with the kids. In Métro, find I have tears in my eyes. Astonished. Think: I must be tired—working too much? See everyone is dabbing and sniffling. It is tear gas that has seeped down. By Saint-Placide it is almost unbearable, prickling under the lids, but so funny to see us all weeping that I begin to laugh.

Out of the Métro, Rue de Rennes a wall of people. The end of the student march. They have been all over Paris. Quiet, grave, in rows straight across the road, linking arms, holding hands. Boys and girls. I find their grave young faces extremely moving. Perfect discipline, a quiet crowd. They are packed all the way up the street to the ruined Montparnasse Station—I can't see the end of them. They hold the banners of the C.N.R.S. (National Scientific Research Center) and a banner reading, "LES PROFESSEURS DE NANTERRE CONTRE LA REPRESSION." Behind a red flag, a tight cluster of non-identified, other than by the meaning of the flag. Ask if I can cross the street. Boy parts the rows so I can get through; girls begin chanting at me, "*Avec nous! Avec nous!*" Slogans start up, swell, recede as if the slogans themselves were tired: "*Li-bé-rez nos ca-ma-rades. Fi-ga-ro fa-sciste.*" Marchers look exhausted. The police bar their route up near the Hôtel Lutetia. Sometimes the marchers have to move back, the word is passed along: "*Reculez doucement!*" A number of good citizens of our neighborhood watch without commenting and without letting their faces show how they feel. A little girl, about four feet nine, collects from everyone "for the wounded." Notice that the non-identified lot behind the red flag give freely, the watchers around me a little less. At midnight, the news; someone has parked a minute car on the edge of the crowd with a portable radio on the roof. Touching narcissism of the young; a silence, so that they can hear the radio talk about *them*. When the announcer describes where we are—the Rue de Rennes—and says that there are about fifteen thousand left out of the thirty thousand who were earlier on the Champs-Élysées, a satisfied little ripple is almost visible. Something to do with looks exchanged. But then he says, "The police are simply hoping they will, finally, be tired and go home," and a new slogan is shouted, quite indignantly: "*Nous sommes pas fatigués!*" This is a good one—three beats repeated twice—and goes on quite a long time. But they are tired. They have, in fact, been sitting down in the roadway. They remind me of children who keep insisting they are not sleepy when in reality they are virtually asleep on the carpet. This seems to me the end. Unlikely that they will press on for the release of their *camarades*.

MAY 10

Walked from Île Saint-Louis to top of Boul' Mich'. Light evening. The bridges are guarded by C.R.S. (Compagnies Republicaines de Sécurité)—riot police, under the Ministry of the Interior. Self-conscious as one walks by (they, not I). Middle-aged men, professionals. "*Laissez passer la dame*," etc. They must know they are hated now. They may wonder why. One fastening the other's helmet chin strap, as if going to a party. I mistake their grenade-throwers for guns, and I think: If they have these guns, they must intend to use them. Place Saint-Michel. I am part of a stupid, respectable-looking small crowd staring—just dumbly staring—at the spectacle of massed power on the bridge. Up the Boul' Mich'. Crowds, feeling of tension. Street dirtier than usual, and it is never very clean. Still has that feeling of a Cairo bazaar. Side streets leading to Sorbonne and Latin Quarter blocked by more police, and I have that feeling of helpless anger I had earlier today. The Sorbonne is empty, and it is kept empty by a lot of ignorant gumshoes. The last stand of the illiterate. Difference between now and early afternoon is that the students are back from their mass meeting in Denfert-Rochereau and—shifting, excited, sullen, angry, determined—they want to get by those large, armed men and back to *their* Latin Quarter. Electric, uneasy, but oddly gay. Yes, it is like a holiday in a village, with the whole town out on the square.

Home, turn on news. Suddenly wonder about Barbara, who was at Denfert-Rochereau. She turned up at her family's apartment between ten and eleven tonight with some hairy youth and said, "*Maman, je voudrais la permission de passer la nuit au Quartier Latin—il y a des barricades.*" She is seventeen. Nice kid, came all the way home, knew they'd be worried. Parents handled it beautifully—said they hadn't eaten, took both kids to a restaurant. Barbara, *pure et dure*, said, "How can I eat in a restaurant while my *camarades* are out there, etc.?" Call their apartment and am told that parents have persuaded boy to spend night at their place, and, without actually forbidding anything, have kept both kids out of it. Z. tells me this in low voice. Boy is sleeping in living room. Both kids worn out, upset.

MAY 11

Listened to nightmare news half the night. Around two o'clock, when the C.R.S. were "regrouped and ordered to charge," I said to no one, "Oh no! No!" I've never seen barricades "charged," but once you have seen any kind of police charge in Paris you never forget it. They charge on the double—they seem invincible. How brave these kids are now! Until now I'd never seen them do anything but run. Finally fell asleep, thought I had dreamed it, but on the eight-o'clock news (Europe I) the speaker said, "Have you slept well? Because this is what went on in your city last night," and told.

The ripped streets around the Luxembourg Station. People who live around here seem dazed. Stand there looking dazed. Paving torn up. The Rue Royer-Collard, where I used to live, looks bombed. Burned cars—ugly, grey-black. These are small cars, the kind you can lift and push around easily. Not the cars of the rich. It's said that even the car owners haven't complained, because they had watched the police charge from their windows. Armed men, and unarmed children. I used to think that the young in France were all little aged men. Oh! We all feel sick. Rumor of two deaths, one a student, one a C.R.S. Rumor that a student had his throat cut "against a window at 24 Rue Gay-Lussac"—so a tract (already!) informs. They say it was the police incendiary grenades, and not the students, that set the cars on fire, but it was probably both. A friend of H.'s who lost his car found tracts still stuffed in it, half charred, used as kindling. Rumor that police beat the wounded with clubs, that people hid them (the students) and looked after them, and that police went into private homes. When the police threw the first tear-gas bombs, everyone in the houses nearby threw out basins of water to keep the gas close to the ground.

Shopkeeper saying, "I sold nothing all day. I gave water away, without charge. That's all the business I did." Feeling of slight, unpleasant pressure. I don't like it. Shopkeepers "encouraged" (by whom?) to proclaim, with signs, publicly, their "solidarity" with the students. Well, they did have their shops wrecked, and shopkeepers have no solidarity with anyone. Anyway, I don't like it. Too much like post-Occupation.

Am told that a Belgian tourist bus stopped, a father and son descended, son stood on remains of barricade with a stone in each hand while father took his picture. Then they got back in the bus. Didn't see this, but saw plenty of people taking pictures. Last thing I'd want to photograph. Curious tendency—men and boys pick up these paving stones, weigh them, make as if to throw them. See themselves as heroes. Am embarrassed by elderly professors suddenly on the side of students. If they thought these reforms were essential, why the hell didn't they do something about it before the kids were driven to use paving stones? Maurice Duverger, professor of political science—grey crewcut on TV, romanticism of barricades. Wanted to say, "Come off it, *vieux père*."

Voice of the people: Wife of a Garde Mobile (paramilitary police, the Gardes Mobiles belong to the Army) lives in my *quartier*. Much surrounded. Very simple, plain creature. Says, "When my husband came in this morning, he told me that the barricades were manned by North Africans aged forty and fifty. That was why the police had to be so rough." This is *believed*. Indignant housewives. "Send them back to North Africa!" I have a queer feeling this is going to be blamed on foreigners—I mean the new proles, the Spanish and Portuguese. And, of course, the North Africans are good for everything.

Evening. The Boul' Mich' still smells of tear gas. Last night like a year ago. One's eyes sting and smart under the lids, the inner corners swell. Aimless youths wander up and down under the trees and street lights. No cars. It is a pleasant evening, and this aimless walking up and down (curious onlookers on the sidewalks, young people in the roadway) is like a *corso* in a Mediterranean town.

Gardes Mobiles and the C.R.S. here now are big, tough middle-aged men. Their black cars and their armored grey cars have brought them from Marseille and from Bordeaux—we recognize the license plates. Stout, oddly relaxed, they stand around and about the intersection of the Boul' Mich' and the Boulevard Saint-Germain, both of which are thronged with a holiday sort of sightseeing crowd. I can't believe these young people are students. I think the students were last night, on the barricades. These boys simply don't resemble the kids I saw last night. They look like suburban working-class boys on any Saturday night—like the boys we called *blousons noirs* in the nineteen-fifties. H. T. says I am mistaken. Anyway, they form an untidy knot, spread out, begin to walk up the Boulevard Saint-Germain. The police stand still, and those kids going up and down the road, restless, moving, more and more of them, remind me of waves on a rock. The police just in themselves seem to be a sort of provocation, and for the life of me I can't see why the police aren't taken right out of the Latin Quarter at once. Finally, a compact crowd crosses the Boulevard Saint-Germain singing the "Marseillaise" and giving the cops the Nazi salute. The police laugh. These are obviously a fresh lot. If they had been around last night, they wouldn't be laughing.

The police: The police involved in last night's debacle had been brought in from Brittany, where Breton nationalists had been staging a strike. They travelled all night. From the morning, when they arrived—from their breakfast time, say—they were given no more food. They stood from noon until two o'clock in the morning without one scrap of food—they stood, they didn't sit down—and they watched the barricades going up, knowing they were going to have to demolish them and the kids behind them. At around two in the morning, they were given the order to charge. They had been given clubs to hit with and gas bombs to throw. What were they supposed to do? Boy who lives in my building tells me a story that sounds like a dream. How the people who lived on those streets showered the students with *saucissons* and chocolate and brought them coffee (not the police!). How some of the students actually began to talk to the police. Not arguing—discussing. Talking (he says seriously) about their problems and, dear God, the structure of society. The C.R.S. were just people, and not all of them middle-aged, some of them only boys. At around two, their order came: Regroup, get back in your lines, put on your helmets, and charge. He says it was unreal, dreamlike—the tear gas, the armed men with those great round shields, the beatings, but they were the same men.

Talk with young Barbara. "The German students are being deported," she tells me. "But we need them here—they are organized, they can tell us what to do. *Oui, nous avons besoin des allemands.*" Her mother, who spent the war years in a concentration camp, says nothing. I feel as if I were watching two screens simultaneously.

De Gaulle still invisible. Says nothing.

MAY 13

On the Boulevard du Montparnasse, not a traffic policeman in sight. Students (I suppose they are) direct traffic. From about the Rue de Montparnasse on, considerable crowd collected on pavements. Reach intersection Saint-Michel-Montparnasse a little after five: Marchers pouring by, red flags, black flags. On a pole near me are a poster sign for the Gothic exhibition at the Louvre and a French flag. Demonstrator, young man, shinnies up, rips off the flag, lets it drop. I burst out, "*Ce n'est pas élégant!*" Am given some funny looks, but no one answers. Man in crowd picks flag up off the pavement, hangs it over the poster. In the middle of the road, small island for pedestrians. Make my way over to traffic island between a wave of Anarchists and a ripple of North Vietnam supporters. Stand on step of traffic island, which means standing with one foot in front of the other, heel to toe, and hang on to *borne* with arm straight back from the shoulder. Remain in this position, with only minor shifts, until a quarter to nine. I can see straight down the Boulevard Saint-Michel. Nothing but people, a river running uphill. Red flags, black flags, flag of old Spanish Republic, flags I can't identify. Mixture of students and workers. O.R.T.F. (Office de Radiodiffusion-Télévision Française, the state-owned radio-TV organization), led by the critic Max-Pol Fouchet, who gets a hand. Hospital personnel, lawyers (small group), film stars—recognize Jean-Pierre Cassel, Michel Piccoli. Recognize film directors—all the New Wave, except for those still in Cannes. Helicopter overhead, the same helicopter that hovers over all demonstrations, making a count. I am joined by a nurse from Pitié Hospital. Tells me she is on night duty but wanted to see this anyway. Confirms rumor that one student had a hand amputated, denies rumor about "secret" deaths (i.e., student deaths kept secret under police pressure)—says impossible to camouflage a death in a hospital. Tells me one or two things about police. Confirms what I'd heard, but she is a calm girl and does not add imaginary trimmings. Truth quite enough. Yes, they continued to beat the wounded who were lying on stretchers. True that they would not let anyone be taken to hospital until they had checked that person's identity, no matter how serious the injury. We are joined by a *lycée* professor, woman of about forty, who has marched as far as Denfert-Rochereau and come back as a spectator. She holds a sign on a stick—"À BAS LA RÉPRESSION POLICIÈRE," in rather wobbly capitals. Holds stick upside down and leans on it. Says she had been a Gaullist all her life until last Friday. Are joined by young man with a beard; young girl whose political vocabulary is C.P. but ordinary vocabulary just rather slangy (could be a salesgirl in a small store); boy who dropped out of Anarchist group; another boy, who stands for about three hours repeating "*Camarades, hôpital*," so that they won't sing or chant slogans, because we are in a hospital zone. From about half past five until a quarter to nine, waves of people flood up the boulevard. The Anarchist has a small radio; we learn that as the head of the cortege is dispersing at the Place Denfert-Rochereau, thousands of marchers still are waiting at the Place de la République. The students have had a longer walk—they started from the Gare de l'Est. The tone of the demonstration is one of great dignity. The union people are used to marching— one can see that. I loathe slogans; I hate shouting; I am most suspicious of a man wearing a raincoat who walks with his hands in his pockets and who whispers slogans out of the corner of his mouth to a brigade of students; but it is impossible not to understand that this is very serious. A whole factory marches by, men in dark suits at the head, workers straggling along, large sign: "NOS PATRONS SONT AVEC NOUS." Also read "BON ANNIVERSAIRE"— this for de Gaulle. The thirteenth of May was the day he took over ten years ago. He isn't mentioned much. The police come in for it, which is to be expected. That is what the demonstration is probably about. The helicopter has relayed news to the radio, and now we are told something staggering: the count is about three million. The population of Greater Paris is about eight and a half million, so common sense tells one this is lunatic. Nevertheless, we— the little group standing on the traffic island—are caught in a collective fantasy. It is as if everyone in the world had been marching up the boulevard and parting at the traffic island, which is to say at our feet. We hear the roar of slogans and the "Internationale," but because of the young man and his tireless "*Camarades, hôpital*" we are here on our little island in a silent sea. We are up, they are down; we are noisy, they are quiet. Why couldn't three million people surge up the hill? The bearded boy turns to me and says, "We are seeing something historic, aren't we?" He looks dazed. The girl with the impressive vocabulary begins telling everyone, "*Vous êtes trois millions!*" The marchers seem to think it quite natural. It can't be. I touch one of them on the arm, and say, "The radio says you are three million." "It's a ridiculous figure," he answers. "What's the population of the city?" *Merci, Monsieur.* I see familiar faces, and the sight adds to the slightly feverish quality of the afternoon. Julie B., surrounded by what must be the best-looking boys in the School of Medicine, rushes up and kisses me. She is looking for her sister, who is marching with the film technicians. Barbara marching behind the banner of Lycée Saint-Louis. Lovely girl. I recognize all the children, but where are the parents? A parents' association seems to have no more than about fifty behind its banner. They are all home listening to the radio and worrying. Wouldn't they worry less if they were here? Perhaps it's none of their business, as a great deal of it is none of mine? But I'm not French and these aren't my children. The small group with me begin to quarrel. Two of the boys say they were on the barricades last Friday. They are, already, Old Veterans. All they need is the beret. One says, "What a glorious sight it is to see the paving stones pulled out of the road!" "That is simply folklore," says the little Communist girl severely. "What is important is . . ." And she tells them. The Party disapproves of barricades and Cuban confusion. Wages, shorter hours of work . . . This bores the two boys. The lycée professor joins in. She is about to tell her entire political history, which began only last Friday but can be stretched, when the boy with the radio says, "The police have fired on students on the Boulevard Raspail!" He steps into the sea, still flowing on either side of our island, and I hear him telling people that two students, he thinks, have been wounded or killed. I beg the bearded one to make him stop; finally, backed by the professor, I say something sharp about spreading rumors, and tell him that if he turns this into a riot they will lose everything they have achieved, etc., which works. Curious movement of a crowd when a rumor moves through it. Something quick, like a boxer feinting. Mendès France goes by, looking exhausted, pale grey, as if he could scarcely imagine the next few feet of road. They say he is ill. Curious business with the radio: We, on our island, are convinced we are seeing some sort of spontaneous generation, a mixture of people who have never marched together before. But the radio tells us that at Denfert-Rochereau, the destination, they are already quarrelling among themselves—the unions and the students. And while that is going on, part of the cortege is still waiting in the Place de la République to begin the march. The end of it, just before nine, is a chain of students, about forty across, holding hands. I am convinced I have seen something remarkable.

D. C., medical student who lives in my building, tells me that when the students came to the houses of people (on the Boulevard Saint-Michel) who had taken them indoors on Friday, given them something to eat, or simply protected them from the police, the cortege called in cadence "*Mer-ci! Mer-ci!*" and that the people watching on their balconies were in tears. Didn't see this. Where I was, two little girls stood on a third-floor balcony piping, "*Vive les étudiants! À bas les C.R.S.!*" This got a laugh and a hand. The little monkeys were careful about their timing. They'd wait about ten mintues before starting again.

H. T. saw the cortege taking off from the Place de la République. He wants to know why there was no delegation of people whose cars were burned last Friday night. "Instead of a banner or a flag, they could have carried a piece of burned metal." Not a bad idea. I imagine a banner reading, "ET NOUS AUTRES?"

MAY 14

Yesterday, at the big *manif*, the woman professor kept looking at me coyly, with her head to one side, and speaking to me as if I were a plucky child recovering from brain fever in a Russian novel. Turned out she thought I was an Algerian, and that was her way of showing she wasn't racist. Brief flash of what it must be like on the receiving end of liberal kindness. The awful sugar. Lesson and warning. TV apparently gave a very low figure—a hundred and seventy thousand or so. Weren't they there? E. annoyed and irritated when I said the *manif* had the same chemical makeup as the Resistance—workers, intellectuals, the left, and the young. She kept saying, "This isn't a war." Everyone enjoyed the general strike so much that no one has gone back to work, from the sound of it.

MAY 15

Decided to put the car in a garage somewhere and forget about it. All garages full—I suppose a lot of other people want their cars off the streets. I finally put it in Rue de Vaugirard for a wash, and simply don't go back.

Rumors: First there were two dead, then three. A doctor came and spoke to the students at the Lycée Saint-Louis and told them that there had been two dead among the students but that the bodies had been smuggled out of the hospital by the police. Who is this doctor? Was he a doctor? I find this story impossible to believe. You would need the complicity of the students' families, for one thing, and why would they co-operate? Someone from the students' union, in an interview over Europe I, spoke of six deaths. The reporter, quite rightly, said, in effect, " I am a newsman and until you give me the names of the dead there are none." The student leader said, "Police pressure on families."

MAY 16

Catherine, E.'s elder daughter, says the story now is that there were seven dead. Their bodies are supposed to have been thrown in the Seine by the police. Only to rise again a few miles downstream? For the kind of complicity this requires among police, doctors, and even parents you would need a truly Fascist state that had been in power a long, long time. Until I know the names, I shan't believe it. The one death that was mentioned of a C.R.S. was never referred to again. We never learned his name. He was hit with a paving stone dropped from a roof. Cohn-Bendit on TV. Intelligent, cunning, devious, has the memory of everything he has ever read; impertinent; good, rapid speaker; wraps up his opponents (a trio of middle-aged newsmen). He has the ruthlessness of someone unable to put himself in another's place. Pompidou then speaks for what seems no more than two minutes. We look at each other and say, "Is that all?"

MAY 17

Dinner with C. R. and Z. and H. T. and young Barbara.
C. R. says, "I want only one thing—*la paix dans le pays que
j'habite.*" Z. tells me that last night Barbara went to her
room saying, "I haven't the least desire to discuss the student situation with your friends." I gather they were fairly
gloom-and-doom. We all wish de G. had not gone to Rumania (his Rumanian trip is virtually all that the TV news
gives us; it is as if nothing were taking place in Paris, in a
sense), and we wish he would come back. Only one of us—
C. R.—expects much. The expression for de G. for years
has been "*qui-vous-savez.*" We lift glasses, H. T. says, "*À qui-
vous-pensez.*" Even anti-Gaullists are hoping for something.
Funny—even among close friends, we don't say it. Ask Barbara what goes on at the Faculté des Sciences, where she
attends meeting after meeting. She says, "We vote and vote
and vote." Students don't know if there will be exams, what
form they will take, if they will be put off this year or forever.
Watching Barbara, I suddenly wonder if she has read her
mother's books, if her mother's youth (concentration camp)
can possibly have any meaning for her, and if she knows
that her father was really quite remarkable in the last war.

MAY 18

Morning news nothing but a list of strikes. It is like
watching a brick wall fall down.

A. J. scathing about the students' trying to "help" the
workers. Tells me the student leader, the one aptly named

Castro, said something like "Poor workers, begin every morning at eight." Had never heard of the 6 A.M. shift. A. J. walked to the Sorbonne every day when a student, didn't drive a car. But nobody did then—anyway, not here. Class walls virtually impossible for me to understand. When workers are asked, in interviews, what they think of the students, they invariably refer to them as "our future bosses," and say they hope this experience will make better *chefs* of them than their fathers have been. French Revolution all for nothing?

Last night, when the cortege of students walked from the Latin Quarter to Boulogne-Billancourt to bring aid and comfort to striking Renault workers, it was first funny, then sad. How could one not laugh at that presumptuous banner about the handing over of the torch of resistance—"DES MAINS FRAGILES DES ÉTUDIANTS"? This to a working class in battle for thirty years. Thought of the Seizième, and kids straggling through behind a red flag. Wonder if people fainted, or went on rushing away for the weekend and saw the cortege as a mild traffic jam? But then how could one not feel their disappointment when the C.P., anxious to keep its children from playing with nasty children who use foul language, locked them out? Daughter's purity was protected and the rejected suitor walked once around the block singing the "Internationale."

The occupied Sorbonne is "Paris by Night"—something to visit after dinner. *Quartier* crowded, cars triple-parked. Outside the École des Chartes, an arrow points: "*Sorbonne par là.*" Afraid of being invaded. Bright, cold night.

This autumn coldness (the heat has been turned on in my apartment) adds to the unreality. Squeeze into the court-yard with difficulty—steady flow of people in and out. In the vast forecourt, a long table piled with Mao's red book, selling at one franc twenty. Cheap banners with Mao, Le-nin, and so on, and Stalin. So shocked to see Stalin that H. T., Z., and I stare. Girl behind the counter not French, could be Mexican. We ask, "Why Stalin?" She hesitates, has been asked this before, says in a parrot's voice, "We are prepared to admit his errors, but he was a revolution-ary, too." Then so was Hitler. H. T. steers Z. and me away before polemic develops. China-tendency paraphernalia trashy, tawdry, cheap, and I remember, as so often, A. S. saying, "It is the ugliness that attracts them." Z. is up-set because of Stalin, trembling. Walls plastered with Pe-king-style papers and posters, including quotations from *Harpo* Marx. Throngs of every kind of person you might see in any Paris restaurant, just wandering. Sandwiches. Someone sleeping on a bench in a dark corridor with his face to the wall. Hairy discussion groups sitting on the floor. In the large amphitheatre, packed to the very ceiling, the light (dim, brownish, as in East Berlin, for instance, but this must be the normal Sorbonne level) produces Goya faces—little blobs of paint in dimness. A "worker from Renault" has the microphone. Seems to be telling his life story. Key words bring boos or applause. I am re-minded of meetings to promote the Second Front in the last war—meetings that consisted of phrases repeated and repeated until they produced an automatic reaction, but lost all meaning for N. and me. Intent young faces, tense, listening. Near me, a middle-aged man answers, says something difficult to understand, and there is an ugly movement of hatred: "*Tu veux qu'on te cogne sur la gueule?*" This bothers me as Stalin bothers Z., and I push my way out. Have the feeling that people are releasing emotions, and not saying what they think. That idiot cheering at key words—no, it is not good enough. But this is only the scum on the pond. Upstairs, notices on closed doors read, "Tourists Keep Out," and I can only hope something other than "*Je te cogne sur la gueule*" is being said.

Everything tatty, a folklore now—China, Cuba, Godard's films. Our tatty era. I see Jean-Pierre, Jacques H.'s friend, looking pleased and superior, as if this were the aim of the revolution. As if this were all he wanted. I remember the luncheon I had with him, and his suddenly saying, "Too many foreigners in France—they should all be helping construct Socialism in their own countries, if they happen to be Polish, for instance," and my suddenly thinking: Why, you are just a mean little bourgeois after all!

In the milling courtyard at midnight, from a lighted window, someone calls, "*Camarades!* The *camarades* from Turin need ten thousand francs [about twenty dollars; nobody speaks in new francs] to get home with. Bring the money to Room No. X." "Watch the stampede," says H. T. He is disturbed at the filth of the place. "They have been given their university now to do as they like with, and this is all they can do—*parler et pisser.*" Drive to Montparnasse. Just behind the Odéon, we see Jean-Louis Barrault on the pavement with a couple of young friends. Z., particularly enraged by his behavior, rolls the window down, leans out, and says, "*Êtes-vous un homme, Jean-Louis Barrault? Non!*" Is revenged for Stalin. She minds because he jumped on the train after it left the station.

MAY 19

Rain and cold. Can't sleep, get dressed—loden, boots, umbrella—walk as far as the end of the street. Sleeping houses. Rain reminds me of Menton and the drenched garden in midwinter. It is cold. I realize that we are in a dream condition here, in France, and that I am frightened for these children who would be angry at being called children. It is the dream feeling of the weekend when President Kennedy was killed. Not a sound anywhere. De Gaulle back from Rumania last night. Even I hope for something from him. This is the second time since *les événements* began that I have had this claustrophobic feeling in the middle of the night and had to go out—though the first time it was to see what the shouting was about at Rennes-Raspail. . . .

In daylight, the above seems absurd. Still cool, with a cold wind. From the Rotonde, before lunch, see thirteen armored police cars creeping by. Three young men at the next table lift beer glasses in ironic salute. One of the unfortunate police actually waves back. Probably the first friendly gesture they've seen since May 3rd. *Journal du Dimanche* is out; vast post-Mass First Communion crowd takes newsstand by storm. Everyone nervous, expectant, waiting for de G. to speak. M. L. says she has seen a kind of Sunday-morning shopping that seems to her unusual, and thinks it must be the beginning of hoarding.

Rumors: Paris is surrounded by tanks. Bruno Coquatrix has closed the Olympia Music Hall and put it "at the service of the movement." Rumor that banner in front of Opéra reads, "AT THE SERVICE OF THE PEOPLE." Rumor of definite connection between Cohn-Bendit and C.I.A.

As soon as the news of de G.'s only remark on the situation ("*La réforme, oui; la chienlit, non*") comes over the radio, the phone starts ringing. Nobody knows what it means. Look it up in Larousse, find it means "carnival mask." But if read as pronounced it is very ugly. Suzanne B. rings up, says that her brother says it is a filthy expression. On my way out, at eight o'clock, find *Journal du Dimanche* out with a new front page, with the word very large. Look it up in E.'s Littré, and find it is, indeed, three words, exactly as it sounds.

MAY 20

The big *manifestation* a week ago today seems like an hour ago. Every day a Sunday now. Today a new Sunday—no mail, no papers, no trains, no Métro, garbage not collected. Banks to vote a strike. H. T. very kindly turns up with a hundred dollars in case of bank strikes. No one but H. would think of this. Find that everyone is shocked and upset over the "*chienlit*" bit. Notice in conversations a deep feeling of resentment: "We have been waiting for him to speak, and he dismisses us with this." Wonder why my street so silent. Turns out the hotel training school across the street is on strike. Usually the kids' power bikes roar down the street early every morning. Today, phone rings all morning. Even friends who live within walking distance compare news. Have you got any money? Have you been to a bank? New popular term for money: "*du liquide.*" Morning news almost entirely taken up with "*chienlit.*" Announcers read definition out of dictionary and give page number of dictionary. Everyone sounds outraged.

Today's rumors: Red flags on naval ships in Marseille. Cohn-Bendit secretly engaged to daughter of one of de Gaulle's ministers. Cohn-Bendit getting revenge on society because both parents gassed in camps. (Utter rubbish. He is only twenty-three, has a ten-year-old sister! It is true that his parents have died, but since 1958.) Cohn-Bendit "protected" by someone "close to de G." His police residence permit is delivered to his door by special messenger. Someone I know knows someone "high up" on the special committee that discusses the case of unwanted foreigners. When C.-B.'s name came up, this committee was told C.-B. was not to be touched—and so on and on. A red-hot-Gaullist friend harps on C.-B.'s being "foreign," says, "How would you, a Canadian, feel if some foreigner went to Canada and tried to interfere?" I say, "Some foreigner did." Point missed, so I say, "It was some Mexican or other, I think."

Live with the transistor, carry it from room to room. News not so much a list of strikes as a list of things still functioning: gas, electricity, water. Bitterly cold day. The concierge has turned the heat on "for as long as the oil lasts." Why should there be an oil shortage? De G. meets with heads of Army, security, police. Dockers on strike. This time, I do hear on the morning news, "Red flags on naval ships." Not followed up. Noise of traffic jams reaches down the quiet street and into the flat. Concierge's husband, a striking postman, who once told me he thought strikes never went far enough, pads about pretending to dust door handles.

Walking up the Rue de Rennes, I saw what seemed to be a fleeing population. They had packed whatever could be stuffed into a few cases and sacks. The half-destroyed old Montparnasse railway station looks bombed, and they seemed to be turning their backs on some catastrophe no one could stop to describe. Suitcases, push-carts, cardboard boxes full of—yes, it is food. Monday is closing day for most shops, but the Monoprix is always open, and so is its basement supermarket, and the shops along the Rue Littré have Monday opening. So that is the catastrophe. The Monoprix has gone on strike—the ground floor is empty, in darkness. Downstairs, the *directeur* and *directrice* are alone with hoarders. These are a solid lava stream, unmoving, or barely, stretching back up the broad stairs and out into the street and around the corner. From another door, left open for them, they come out, one at a time, with sugar, rice, noodles, flour, oil, cornflakes (!), and those great drums of detergent. Potatoes. No conversation in the lava stream. Have never observed a crowd so silent. Young man distributing anti-student tracts: "Unite, unite, and save the country." I dare him to hand tracts into that crowd. He wanders off. A few doors later, a similar queue at the bank, not as long, mostly men. Won't join it—they all make me sick now. Down Rue Littré. In front of greengrocer's, see an American sight—a woman loading a car with groceries. Out of the ordinary here, where virtually no one has a deep freeze, the refrigerator is really not all that common, and it is the custom to shop for each meal, everything fresh, small quantities. She has a crate of oranges, another of potatoes, a case of about twelve bottles of oil, and I hear her saying to her little boy, "I told Mémé [Granny] to get some, too."

During the Suez crisis, everyone bought candles and salt. Candles for power failures, and salt because of an extraordinary rumor that it protects one from radioactivity. You were supposed to fill the tub with salt and water and pop the whole family in the tub and be saved. Not more preposterous than what I am seeing today. It is now about half past ten; the greengrocer's seems just about cleaned out. At the baker's, there is plenty of ordinary bread, but no one is buying that. Rush on the wrapped stuff, which keeps, on *biscottes*, and on pastry flour. Girl tells me they've sold one week's supply of wrapped bread in three hours. Don't buy anything, and decide I shall never eat again. Hate all Parisians until five minutes later, when the laundress who does the sheets offers to lend me money should I run short. Final stop for a newspaper. No hope: delivery strike. Only paper in sight is a gossip sheet with headline "QUEEN ELIZABETH HUMILIATES MICHÈLE MORGAN." Pictures of both ladies, and then, boxed: "Why Did the Queen Do It?" Shop owner turns out to be a revolutionary. Has pictures of police and students from last week's *Paris-Match* pinned up: "People must be made to see."

Discover most of my friends feel as I do—don't want to buy anything, don't want to eat, can't spend, don't care. Everyone compares notes on loss of appetite, disgust with hoarders, etc. No one gives two pins for the Vietnam peace conference—it might just as well be taking place in Sydney, Australia. Yet until May 3rd Vietnam was all we talked about.

When you aren't able to do anything (no transport, no money), you have no problems. You discover nothing was important after all. Very peaceful. You think, out of habit, I must do something about this or that, find you can't, and forget it. Live with the radio. Carry it everywhere in the flat. Bitterly cold. G. F. says, "We seem to be in a tunnel wondering what is at the other end."

MAY 22

Le Monde reports on a ripple of the Cultural Revolution: YOUNG JEWS OCCUPY THE ISRAELITE CONSISTORY. "Several dozens of young Jews" are in occupation and holding "a permanent general assembly." Their aim is to "contest the archaic and undemocratic structure of the present community.... They appeal to Jewish youth to join them." The item ends with this: "The telephone switchboard is in their hands. No incident has been reported." Professional football players now occupying *their* headquarters. Not quite sure what they are demanding.

Phone conversation with J. de T., who is "like a tiger in a cage." Can't get to the hospital in the morning and his patients can't get to him in the afternoon.

Grey, cold. Hear on all sides, "No sugar, no flour, no potatoes." Feel the change in people in the shops: those buying enormous quantities of anything sense the disapproval. Bank strike. How simple life becomes without mail, without money! Z. (ever the anxious one) says solemnly, of mail, "*Mais il y a des gens malades de qui on voudrait avoir des nouvelles.*"

The tyrant grandfather who made the whole house tremble is suddenly in a wheelchair. The grandchildren are edging the wheelchair toward the staircase, and the grandfather's favored children, who owe him something, or once said they did, are not lifting a finger. The rest of the family are in the parlor making conversation and waiting for the crash, and wondering what to do.

Sartre, speaking to students in the Sorbonne, says de G. destroyed the Resistance as a structure when he returned to power. A student says, "You are a good artist, M. Sartre, but a lousy politician."

Schools on strike. Anne-Marie does not know what to do with her little boy. She can't take him to work with her, and so she locks him up in the flat. Says, "He knows about never answering the door." Bitterly cold, with a cold wind. See a collection of fascinating old cookbooks, including an original Ali Baba (Curnonsky), but the shop is shut and looks barricaded. Hairdresser's empty. Something squalid, uneasy about a food shop closed because of hoarding. Primistère near the Boulevard du Montparnasse shut for lack of provisions. The customers broke into the shop storeroom and helped themselves, and finally the manager just shut the place altogether.

Cohn-Bendit inspires (in my friends) apprehension among the Jews, who are afraid he is attracting too much attention, and jealousy among the old Marxists: "*C'est de la blague! Il n'a aucune idéologie!*" There is also, though not among the young, "*Qu'est-ce que c'est que cet étranger?*" When I answer, "Régis Debray," I am told, "That was different."

No papers, no magazines, no plays, no good music. (France-Musique plays pop and syrup all day; all three FM stations have the same program now, like the music you hear in a cocktail lounge in a hotel in America.) No telegrams, no mail, no *biscottes*, no sugar. I chase nothing except newspapers, and the only strike I dread is electricity: It is like the blood stopping. They will save that until the end.

Occident has wrecked the Conservatoire, Rue Madrid. Now, why that particular place?

TV wavy, like a window blind rippling. Receive explanation of which I don't understand a word. Something about factories' not using all the power they are supposed to. "*Les secteurs sont disjoints.*" Turn my mind off, snap back in time to say, "Thank you *very* much. Now I understand." Debate on the motion of censure. Blah-blah-blah. Like something out of the Fourth Republic. Feeling of something new fading in debates, rhetoric, talk of referendum. "Thank God the Communist Party has taken this movement over!" This from A. J.—meaning they are sensible men who like a quiet Sunday. Taxi strike. In the well-to-do suburbs, the lawn-and-private-school belt, they are stealing gas from each other's cars.

Barbara is strike picket at her *lycée*. Her mother says nothing. "At her age, I would have been the same." But she worries. The evening Barbara went to that big demonstration at Denfert-Rochereau, I saw her father's face: "Donc, *elle est là? Elie est là aussi?*" I can imagine what he was thinking: She will lose an eye, she will be trampled, she will be beaten by the police. But they have brought her up to think for herself (best parents I know), and if they seemed inconsistent now she would never respect them again.

"*Les copains ont fait une gaffe,*" a student said. They have indeed. When they were renaming all the amphitheatres in the Sorbonne, one of the first they changed was Jean Cavaillès. Resistance hero, shot at forty-one. Never heard of him, I guess. It must seem so far away! A nineteen-year-old doesn't know de G. was voted (and how overwhelmingly) into power in 1958. Thinks he took over with some kind of Army march on Paris. I say, "Ask your mother and father. They probably voted him in." Mother, there, says nothing.

H. T. says Stalin's picture gone from the Sorbonne.

G.'s Russian friend at the Sorbonne every day, wild with enthusiasm. Is reminded of Petrograd when friend was on the barricades, at the age of seventeen. "Now we know the age of my friend," says G. Rich with my five hundred francs, offer money to G., who offers even more back to me. Tiny, red-haired wife of *marchand de couleurs* (hardware) on Rue du Cherche-Midi says if I run out I am to come to her, and Jacqueline, who has plenty of responsibilities of her own, calls up to see if I am all right. As in a city under siege.

Grey, rain, cold. Think of people walking miles and miles to work and wondering what is going to happen next. Radio says, "Still milk, bread, electricity, gas, water." That is what adds to the unreality. Suppose that in any city—in Montreal, say—everyone heard on the morning news, "You still have gas, light, and so forth," wouldn't everyone panic? Rush out and buy sugar because the man forgot to say "You still have sugar"? You would think it was the siege of Leningrad and we were all eating rats.

Everyone disgusted with the way the movement has taken a political turn, and with the debate. In every conversation: "When will it end?" (Meaning the strikes.) F. W. tells me that a C.G.T. (Confédération Générale du Travail, the Communist-led labor union) official told the U.N.E.F. (Union Nationale des Étudiants de France, the students' union) that the unions could hold out four months. Still no vote in the Chamber, but the power is so clearly in the hands of the unions you wonder why the bother. Nobody cares.

Touching appeal on radio to the younger *lycée* students a few days ago. Some are eleven, twelve, thirteen. Tactful man from a parents' association. Said please don't parade around in the streets; the most useful thing you can do is go home at once and explain to your parents the meaning of the movement.

Cold drizzle. Walk to Right Bank with M. L., who has to get to her bank. Less traffic than usual—the depart-

ment stores on strike, for one thing. And yesterday's traffic jams (three hours to cross the Concorde; some drivers
simply abandoned their cars) may have kept people at
home. Probably faster to walk. Every second shop closed.
It is like Monday closing. In front of the Chamber, little
queue under umbrellas. Think of utter misery of people
walking home tonight in this cold and wet. M. L.'s bank
the Royal Bank of Canada, on the Rue Scribe. Manager
worried about "image" of Royal Bank and "bad publicity,"
because the bank mentioned by name in the *Daily Express*.
Accused of not making any payments over two hundred
dollars (something like that). Tell him that all the banks
in Paris have limited payments and some not paying anything at all. Say to M. L., "Who cares about the Royal
Bank and its image?" M. L. chides me, "You don't know
what it is to have a head office." Look into Morgan Guar-
anty, on the Place Vendôme. Entirely empty. No queue.
They say that Monday was frantic. Cash check with no
trouble, so as to repay H. T. Every employee has an opinion—all very lively. Food shops probably have their normal quota of food, but to us they look overstuffed. Some
kind of collective hallucination must be at work. We are
already so installed in the abnormal, have so quickly settled into it, that anything usual seems suspect, peculiar.
Delivery trucks all over the streets, replacing stocks after
the hoarding rush.

The D.s are revolutionary! My most conservative
friends! Gilles is "reforming" his engineering school
"night and day," Hugues is all for the students, and his
mother is furious because his father's ministry is not tak-

ing advantage of the situation to go on strike. "Not that we want the Communists," she says, "but de G. must go." She sounds as if she had just stepped off a barricade. In the last election, they voted so far to the right that I lost sight of them—they slipped over the horizon. Husband not only won't strike but walks to his *ministère* every day. Tells me that steel industry will take longer to pick up than we think, that even after they agree to go back to work there will be a gap of about fourteen days before things roll. Wife interrupts: "Who cares about boring old steel production?" *Vive la révolution!* Says she doesn't mind walking—walked all the way to the Hôtel Druout for sale of antique furniture.

G. P. and A. J. have both let their books go. Feel it is futile. A. J. says that book doesn't fit into new world, that everything will be changed. How to tell? I live between typewriter and transistor, TV news (everything else seems trivial), telephone (rings like a machine gone mad).

The recording that tells the time over the telephone is on strike. No watch or clock owned by me has ever worked. Didn't realize how much I depended on *l'horloge parlante*. The concierges are on strike! Their instructions are to look after the garbage, "in the interests of salubrity," but "not to answer questions or give any more information." Our concierge probably can't read. Works harder than ever, polishing mirrors and the glass doors, Gauloise hanging on lower lip, and gives information of all kinds. Her cat, M. Pussy (pronounced "poosy"), neglected. Spends his time having doors opened for him. No one can be bothered now. Victim of *les événements*.

A few days ago—whenever the last sunny day was, Sunday perhaps—two tall girls looking like New Zealanders (longish skirts, rolled woolen socks, gym shoes, and enormous packsacks) but with Irish accents asked the way to the Eiffel Tower. I said, "It's a long way to walk, and they may not let you up." "Why not?" "It's guarded by police." "Why?" I said, "You do sense there is something going on in Paris, don't you?" "Oh, yes. No buses." Off they went anyway, with two hundred pounds of worldly goods strapped to their shoulders.

Suddenly found it difficult to buy stockings. Everything shut or on strike. Magasins Réunis on Rue de Rennes open, across from striking Gaz de France and from striking Monoprix. It is like a dream—I am the only customer. After a few moments, other customers wander in to the cosmetics counter, but the place resembles a hangar.

Say that the student movement is not French, that it started in America. Receive skeptical smiles. Everyone knows U.S. students eat ice cream all day. (The same smiles that Anthony S. found so discouraging when he was teaching at the British Institute here. He would say that Samuel Johnson was important, for example. But everyone knew that only Charles Morgan and Lawrence Durrell were important.) Press on, explain about Columbia. No one has ever heard of Columbia. Give up.

J. de T. walks to hospital and back each day. About an hour and a half each way, I should imagine. Afternoons and evenings, some patients get to him. Says that the young—the disturbed young, that is, his patients—are *"traumatisés"* by the events, that the young move out of

reality all too easily at the best of times. Bad phone connection; can't hear more. A psychiatrist friend of A. J.'s
goes to the Odéon every day taking notes. Collective
hysteria.

Bought weekly lottery tickets, discovered drawing
put off "indefinitely." Pari-mutuel betting, the sacrosanct
P.M.U., also out. There is talk of Mother's Day being put
off, perhaps made a joint holiday with Father's Day in
June. Astonished to discover the French do not know this
is a commercial holiday. It is thought of as ancient and
immutable, like Christmas. Florists protesting—all their
potted plants are ready. Parents upset: "How can we explain it to our children?" Like the truth about Santa Claus.
Bank on the Rue Littré closed. Frail young girl stands
with her arm across the door. You can put money in, but
you can't take any out. Radio Luxembourg partly replaces
mail and breakdown of telephone. (Only kind of phone
working is *l'automatique*.) Radio explains it will relay only
important messages, between half past nine and midnight,
every ten minutes, and that it is "not substituting for public services"; i.e., not interfering with strikers.

Schools on strike. Teachers out, students in—they are
occupying. No provision was made for the boarding students at the *lycées*. Those who live outside Paris and who
can't get home because of the transport strike are on their
own. What if they have no money? The parents, who can't
send them anything, must be frantic. The R.s have taken
in a boy, a classmate of their daughter. Moody boy, sits
and broods. Won't help around the place. Says at home he
is paid if he helps.

Snake queues outside the banks. Empty grocery shelves (canned goods gone, mostly). No mineral water— very hard on mothers who need it for *biberons*. They can always boil the tap water, of course. The fruit merchant puts down his iron shutter early—too much sold. Gas pumps now have a sign, "*Panne Sèche*" meaning dry as dry. It is what you say if your car runs out—"*J'ai une panne sèche.*" Gas shortage caused by nothing but panic.

Weather cold, bitter. Motion of censure to be voted to-day. E. so opposed to hoarding she won't even buy a candle in case there is a power strike. All my smoker friends dread cigarette shortage. (Hasn't happened, but there is a run on *tabac-brun* cigarettes, such as Gauloises and Gitanes.) Revolutionary *élan*, the Barcelona feeling, fades in votes, debates, rumors of a referendum. Forty-eight-hour strike at Les Halles. Theatres on strike. No TV except for the news. Department stores closed. Friend with small children at home (schools out), husband going mad (can't get to work), no *liquide* (didn't get to a bank), says, "I keep going, make the same daily gestures."

Suddenly remember G. is coming to dinner and we are supposed to go to Censier (Sorbonne annex) for medical-psychiatric-all-out-discussion, which G. assures me is worth the walk. Forty-five-minute break between Pompidou's speech and the voting, rush out to shop for food. *Stupéfaction*: I am the only customer. The hoarders have spent all their money! Buy everything I need—strawberries, cream, etc. Buy roses. Florist upset over threat of change in Mother's Day. At the *charcutier's*, ask girl to hurry, want to see result of vote on TV. Large, stupid eyes. She says, "I heard something on the radio." Ask if she knows what is going on. She hesitates, and says, "Something sad? Bizarre?" Then says, "We did good business on Monday."

Dream image (but real) of middle-aged men shuffling up in alphabetical order to vote. Phone call from London. I watch the screen, I reassure. The London papers must be showing the streets here running with blood. Phone call from one of G.'s patients, or husband of one: G. will be late or perhaps not get here at all. Caught in traffic, still visiting patients in 18th, 19th Arrondissements. Brave G., in that *Deux-chevaux*, as ill as the patients, if they only knew. Call from New York. Tell B. M. I am probably going to medical thing at Censier, shall not go to demonstration tonight. He says, "I trust your common sense," hear his voice fade with "Take care." After I hang up, I hear the demonstration not far away, pull on boots, coat, leave note on door (though don't really expect G. now). Drizzly night. Carry umbrella. On Rue de Rennes, they sweep by, the young: really students—no *"éléments,"* as they are called. At first, I don't know what I am hearing, it is so strange. Then it becomes clear; it is like rubbing frost away from a window. I hear them chanting, *"Nous sommes tous des juifs allemands."* It is because of Cohn-Bendit, because that is how he is dismissed. They are answering their parents. This is France, they are French, I am not dreaming. *Nous sommes tous des juifs allemands.* It is really so unlucky to be either one here—imagine what it means to say one is both! It is the most important event, I think, since the beginning of this fantastic month of May, because it means a mutation in the French character: a generosity. For the first time, I hear a French voice go outside the boundaries of being French. I walk along beside them, on the pavement. Two boys from *Action Française*, a rightwing group, silently hold up banner reading, "NO RED FLAGS OVER THE SORBONNE." That is brave of them. They are only two. They simply stand there. But this crowd glances, just like that, and the slogan changes to "*On s'en fout des frontières.*" Of course, there are only a few thousand of them, and they are excited, with that black flag and that red flag—perhaps they would say anything. They are still answering their parents—I feel that. We all sweep down the Boulevard Raspail. A woman shakes a red flag out of a window; the kids applaud. I am on the *terre-plein* with trees, in the middle of the boulevard, where the market is held twice a week; the kids are on the roadway. New slogans: "*De Gaulle en Suisse*" and "*De Gaulle chienlit*" (he asked for that one). Suddenly they begin that "hop-hop-hop" cry and start to run. It is a Korean (I think) *pas gymnastique*, stepping along fast with your knees very high. When it is done properly, it gives the walker great mobility; you can move a mass of people sharp left or right quite quickly, fluidly. It was with this step that about thirty thousand students swept over the Pont de la Concorde on May 7th; the C.R.S. were simply taken by surprise. They must have thought they were dreaming—imagine thousands of people suddenly saying "hop-hop-hop" and quite literally hopping over a bridge! But tonight the marchers don't know the *pas*; they simply run and scatter suddenly, up on the *terre-plein*, where I seem to be the only observer.

People are watching the marchers, but on the left-hand pavement, separated from them by the southbound half of the Boulevard Raspail. I find this running frightening, always—the sound of it behind one. I stand behind a plane tree, and they scatter by on either side. Cross to left-hand pavement when all clear. Wonder about their parents (because this is a monologue, about being *juifs allemands*), and on the corner of the Rue de Sèvres am answered: A nice-looking couple, well dressed, don't look stuffy, just puzzled. "If *that's* what they want," the man says. He doesn't sound angry, just stunned, almost hurt: "*Si c'est ça qu'ils veulent—d'être des juifs allemands!*"

Unreal—lamplight, indigo sky, small bright leaves all over the trees, "*On s'en fout des frontières!*" Only a few thousand. Two? Three? I can't judge. But what a turning upside down and inside out of the French character! It seems to me more important than today's vote, of which I don't yet know the result. No one in my generation said it, and God knows *il y avait de quoi*. I am convinced this lot are better than we were. For one thing, they have never been frightened. Frightened in theory but not in fact. Cohn-Bendit born a refugee, but after the war. He doesn't *know*. He can imagine, as I could have imagined the 1914 war. Something else.

A man says to me, "Where are they going?" In fact, he says, "*Où vont ces troupes?*" Tell him not to get close unless he is involved with the movement—could be dangerous. "What movement?" Too long to explain, and his French isn't good. We walk along together. Can't share my umbrella with him—he is miles tall. "Why are you going if it is dangerous?" I understand him to say. Tells me he has a passport. When we come to the first cordon of police up a side street (cordon of students holding hands in front of the police, to prevent other students from doing something stupid), I point to the police, and, when we are a little past them, make the gesture of being hit over the head, using my umbrella, implore him to leave—it would be foolish for him to be involved, understanding nothing. Understands, nods, does an about-face. I have finally realized we are going to the Palais Bourbon.

Kids don't look at police, sweep by them. "Hop-hop-hop" under the trees. Umbrellas. A few tourists. Grown man (American, from his hair) gives clenched-fist salute. Being funny? Only a month ago, I was still saying, "The young in France? Senile. Little old men." They have written on the walls of the Sorbonne, "*L'imagination prend le pouvoir.*" People find this irritating—pretentious. Why? It seems to me more important than their not having swept out the courtyard.

Girl rushes from side street to catch up, singing, out of breath, out of tune, the "Internationale." Long hair floating. Well dressed, good shoes, clothes too fragile for the night. That seems to be it. I go home. Radio says they've dispersed.

MAY 23

Now about nine million out. No strike pay in France. How long can they go on? C.G.T. now openly breaks with students. Fear that strikers will have some idea beyond and outside material demands, I suppose. The Communist Party seems like *Papa-Maman*, and the student movement like an interfering social worker. *Papa-Maman* explain to the children, "Think with your stomachs. We are the brains."

There were about five thousand kids last night—more than I'd imagined. The *heurts avec la police* took place in the Place Maubert and at several other points. *No* radio reporter mentions what I saw and heard—they merely say the students "expressed their contempt for Parliament." I have three different versions of what went on in the Place Maubert. E. tells me her daughter woke her up in the middle of the night, said the demonstrators were all toughs from the suburbs, setting fire to cars. H. T. says that it was a mixture of students and toughs, that they set fire to the garbage now all over the streets.

Mme. L. says, "Oh, I see you have stocked up on matches." Always have several boxes in the kitchen, and, anyway, these are taper matches someone brought me from Germany. Can see she is nervous about matches, so I give her a box. There is *no shortage of matches*. Everyone mad, afraid of something imaginary.

E. comes around. Her bank won't give her a *rond*. She won't accept more than a hundred new francs, though it won't go far with the hordes of young she seems to be feeding twice a day now. Says she dreads a cigarette shortage more than anything. "In my internment camp, I traded everything they gave me to eat for cigarettes." Tell her that in her place I would stock up—she has a choice of feeling guilty and sane or civic-minded and bonkers.

What she wanted to hear. Give her an opaque shopping bag so no one will know, and off she goes.

Look at appointment book. Everything cancelled. What a relief! I needn't go anywhere.

Red-haired German in the Select is mistaken for Cohn-Bendit and escorted (in car with German plates) by motorcycle cops to nearest police station. Is photographed from all angles. Comes back a hero.

H. T. describes non-stop discussion at Faculté des Sciences. Each laboratory to be on its own, a private soviet. "But where is the money to come from? They are dividing up a cake they haven't got." Discuss Cohn-Bendit's having said in Berlin that there were eleven dead. "He has signed his expulsion papers with that remark," says H. T. "He will never be allowed back." We both think statement irresponsible. I am more and more suspicious of C.-B. What is all this publicity? It smells.

Taxi strike still on. Today like a Sunday. *Femme de ménage* says that the parties and receptions where she does work as cook and *serveuse*—is much in demand—are not cancelled; people come on foot. She informs me that Cohn-Bendit is financed "by Cuba and by the Americans." What Americans? "The F.B.I.," she says. Haven't heard about F.B.I. in such a long time that they almost sound like stodgy old relations.

E. tells me about the Musée de l'Homme ethnologists trying to occupy the apartment of the Minister of the Interior. They climbed over a trellis onto the Fouchet balcony. E.: "All they had to do was ring the bell at the front door and walk in." Then they cut the phone wires, but they cut the wrong wires, being intellectuals all the way, and Mme. Fouchet was on the phone to the police while they were still sawing away at the wrong thing. Police came and took them off to jail. All they succeeded in doing was frightening one of the Fouchet children into hysterics. I have the feeling that even in jail they were all saying to each other, "I haven't felt as young as this in thirty years."

The flight of the *beau monde*. The *gens du monde* have fled to Switzerland, to the Midi, to Germany, to Italy. With what gasoline? The J. D.s went without even waiting for de G. to speak.

Walked to Petit Palais in downpour. Hadn't realized *all* museums on strike. Wanted to see the Dead Sea Scrolls. Wonder if they are still there or if they have been taken back to Israel.

Around seven, meet D. M. in the Rotonde. Streets thick with police cars—reminds me of Algerian war. D. looking pretty, freshly washed golden hair. Waiter tells neighbor that Coca-Cola stocks will be gone in two days. Man says he doesn't care, but what about Pernod? Waiter says beer and bottled water will go next, upon which man looks grave. Garbage trucks go by manned by soldiers.

At home, turn on radio—riots on Boul' Mich', fires, "uncontrollable elements," student leaders trying to get them back to the Sorbonne. Turn it off, dash off to États-Généraux of the Photography School, around the corner on Rue de Vaugirard, to which G. F. has invited me. A state School of Photography and Cinematography. I've never been inside, but I know some of the students by sight from the café that is across the street from it and just

up the street from me. The students are on strike and occupying the school—sleeping in—and they feel it is now
or never if they are to reorganize the school from top to
bottom. Their chance. They've invited the top photographers, technicians, photo editors, etc., in Paris, and about
fifty have turned up, which is astonishing—no transport,
after all. The school is desolate, filthy. A row of latrines in
the courtyard. Go into what would be furnace and store-
rooms in, say, a small Protestant church in America, or in
a very poor country school, and into the *salle de projection*.
Church-basement feeling reinforced: filthy, splintered
board floor; collection of hard little chairs that look as
if fished out of a junkyard. Everything tacky, wretched,
except for the lighting, which is modern but very ugly
indeed. Meeting presided over by a pale boy who looks
about fifteen. No more than eighteen or twenty students (this is photography only, not film, which has a
larger student body), mostly sitting around walls and not
saying much. Nothing abstract about the meeting; they
want advice from the professionals. The professors sit at
the back looking surly. One of them—large, in tweeds,
looks like a boxer—takes the microphone and says something about the teaching profession's being dragged in
the mud. Only one of the teachers sits with the students
and the professionals. He stands up and tells us something I can hardly believe: There isn't a single photograph
in the whole school. Not one. Not only is there no film
library, there is nothing at all. When he wants to show
his pupils the work of celebrated photographers ("some
of you here right now"), he says, he has to "drag his class

here and there across Paris to exhibitions"—when there are exhibitions. Until two years ago (I believe it has been a state school only two years; it was private before), there wasn't a book in the place. "I have managed to obtain a few books—very few," he says. So much for the school. No library, no pix. The professionals are unbelievable. Their one terror seems to be that these kids will grow up and become photographers. It reminds me of the Odéon (occupied by so-called Anarchists), where everyone gets up and tells his life story in a kind of permanent psychodrama. One after another, the professionals describe how (a) they went to school and learned nothing, or (b) they never went to school at all. One white-haired gent, who is in analysis, if one can judge by his vocabulary, stands up and implores these serious, exhausted, and extremely sympathetic kids to "explore their conscious and unconscious motivations—to see what subconscious needs and desires have impelled them to choose this profession" (where there is no room for them, he implies). Nice kid takes the microphone, says politely that they haven't time just now for self-analysis—that what they really want is help in turning a school everyone seems to agree is second-rate into something better. Picture editor of fashion magazine complains that when young people bring her their work they can't answer the question "Why do you want to be a photographer?" Kids look glum, don't reply. Another professional accuses them of all wanting to be "*des virtuoses*," tells them that they all want fast cars and four-star hotels, that they see themselves as stars. Here follows a flurry of testimonials, all from virtuosos: Why don't you become technicians? You can be just as happy in a laboratory. Kids completely crushed, it seems to me. Some want to be technicians, some don't, but they murmur this to each other. Only one student tries to explain: "We are in an inadequate school. You, the professionals, say we don't learn anything here—tell us what is wrong. Here is our program—look at it. Tell us what you think." What they encounter is the secret hostility and jealousy of the entrenched. They can expect very little. Around midnight, committees are formed. Man stands up and says, "It isn't up to us to help you. It's up to the young to supply their own cultural revolution." I hear a couple of kids calling him Frankenstein among themselves. I ask one of the kids why so few of them are here tonight. He is all beard and pipe; I know him by sight, as he seems to know me. "Some are on the Boul' Mich'," he says. "Some who live in the provinces left Paris just before the railway strike. They had to go home, as their parents weren't able to send them any money." He adds, "*Nous dépendons de nos parents*," which seems very touching—a paradox. "We get one or two hours' sleep a night," he adds. Only two of the professionals say anything concrete. One describes exactly how these schools function in Germany and Belgium, and speaks of the old Bauhaus, which in this locale is something like evoking Versailles to Eskimos. Another gives an account of the famous school at Vevey. Kids listen. They seem bewildered, disappointed. I don't wonder. They will have to act *in spite* of their elders. Unfortunately, these are the elders they will depend on for jobs. Leave meeting just after midnight. The students at this school have forgotten one problem—money. I would guess that after the strikes are settled there will be very little left over for film libraries, that the sullen-looking teachers will be back where they started. Hope, enthusiasm. Suddenly wish students at American colleges could see this place. Occupying a place like Columbia would seem like living in what that dumb photographer called a four-star hotel.

Group on pavement with transistor. My street deserted, lovely night. Perhaps spring arriving after all. *Le joli mai.* Windows open, lights, everyone listening to Radio Luxembourg or Europe I, the non-government stations. I recognize the voices now. Tell of fighting, fires, grenades, all only ten minutes' walk away. Not a sound here but radios. Want to go there, but my presence would be entirely useless. It could be Asia, from immediate evidence, but it isn't Asia—it is ten minutes' walk. All I would want to say is "Please stop." Listen to the radio much of the night. Around two, I realize I have forgotten to eat any dinner.

MAY 24

This morning, I had trouble remembering whether the news was real or I'd dreamed it. Last thing I heard (or dreamed) was "Small groups setting fire to trash in Les Halles." Shall never know, because the newsstands now on strike until Monday. Europe I gives two versions of last night's fighting: the official one and its own. *Manifestations* all over France today—farmers, tonight the students again. The announcer says, "Today is going to be a long day."

Friend calls, says, "*Ce soir il y aura peut-être des morts. Quelque chose se prépare.*" I am offered a window in Boul' Mich' to see the fight. Turn it down. Talk with Jacques—ask him if National School of Oriental Languages had ever attempted any sort of reform before the students went into action. "*Vous me posez une question sérieuse?*" he says. Yes, they had, but the Ministry of Education never so much as acknowledged their letter. When they asked for more teachers, they were told that as they had asked for too much, they wouldn't be given anything. He was "out" last night—thinks that as his students are out fighting he ought to be with them. Tells me about material difficulties in his school. Like School of Photography and Cinematography, but more and worse.

Am astonished to see carpenters working outside barbershop on Rue du Cherche-Midi. Butcher's dark, gloomy, everyone nervous, curious atmosphere in the sense that everyone seemed to be trying to be nice to the butcher, in case of a shortage, and he, usually so pleasant, was being a little dictator, sneering. Yet there is no shortage of meat! They were all acting in an imaginary situation!

Femme de menage comes in calling, "*Il y a de tout!*" Has found oil, potatoes, etc., in the market this morning. Says stocking still heavy—nothing left in the market by noon. No racing, no lottery, no papers, no garbage collection, Rue de l'Abbé-Grégoire like a city dump (shops). My street (no shops) perfectly clean. Garbage indoors. Astonish man in shoe shop by buying shoes. I'm almost the first customer they've seen since May 11th. After telling about strikes, shortages, last night's fighting, and future prospects, radio breaks into "Bye Bye Blues."

H. T. dined with friends in the Latin Quarter last night, came out to a wall of flame. Girl with their party had to get home ("My mother will be frantic"), no phone. H. ties a handkerchief over the girl's face (tear gas) and they walk across Rue des Écoles between a burning barricade and the lined-up police. Leaves her at her door, walks back. Tells this as he might say, "I walked along the Seine." Have never seen him frightened at any time, but he does have an odd tendency (a European tendency, I'd say) to be aggressive with the police, and that could have been the only danger.

From Odéon Métro station onward, the Boulevard Saint-Germain has something desolate, ruined about it, as if swept by a very old war, a long time ago. Or like a poor and shabby street no one has time or money to keep clean. Grilles up from around the trees, stop signs and one-way signs lying in the gutter, traffic lights smashed. This odd look of seeming as if it had always been like that. Shops closed, or striking. Outside Hachette, a cardboard streamer hanging from the sixth floor to ground level with one word: "OCCUPATION." I knew that trees had been cut down and that it would shock me, but I had not expected to feel true grief. A lovely tree. They tried to burn it—the leaves are singed. Some of the leaves on the standing trees singed, too. We waited all winter for the leaves, and now they have tried to kill them. Great sections of Rue des Écoles torn up. Agitation around the Sorbonne. Don't go in. H. T., who loathes destruction, suddenly bursts out, "*Ils n'ont jamais connu la misère!*" He was a brilliant scholarship boy from a poorish family, has a reverence for universities, for learning, for the very stones of an old school. School was miraculous. As for the war . . . I daren't answer (because it would be impertinent) that their not having known *la misère* and *la guerre* is the source of their nerve. Think of Canadians marked by the Depression, really affected by it. It made them ambitious but not daring, and certainly not strong. Can't say any of this. Remains of a barricade on Rue Saint-Jacques. These stones are larger, not paving stones, and, anyway, the street isn't torn up. H. T. interested, does rapid tour of immediate neighborhood. I stay there, watch as people pick up stones (several men do this; it seems to be irresistible), make as if to fling, imagine themselves on barricades. All say too heavy to throw. H. T. comes back, says these stones from a building site, obviously brought here by truck. That means the barricade was not, could not have been, "spontaneously" built by students. You need the time, the plan, the gas, the stones, and the truck. *Bon.* Place Maubert like one of those dumps that smolder all the time, with a low fire that you can smell for miles. Blackened garbage, singed trees, a burned car. Don't want to see more. Walk down the Seine. Keep turning my ankles—so many holes in the ground, and so many stray wood, stone, and iron *things*. Nothing has a shape or a name. Along the quai, walking grimly, with a purpose, five young men. Not students, not working-class boys. Helmets, long leather gauntlets, black windbreakers, long, greasy hair under the helmets, faces that look like those faces the police assemble from descriptions given by several witnesses—the lumpy faces you see in a newspaper over "The killer looks like this." Walk with their shoulders hunched forward. One has a *nerf-de-boeuf*—one of those thin, licoricelike blackjacks—at his waist. You can kill with it if you know how. What used to be called *les blousons noirs* during the nineteen-fifties, and then they just disappeared, and I used to tell strangers, "There is little or no juvenile delinquency in France." They seem to be about thirty. The same boys grown up?

The Place Saint-Michel still full of tear gas. Crossing to the fountain, start to sneeze, eyelids smart, tears form. The fountain is like the Cour des Miracles. A man of thirty or so, sandy hair, sandy face, small, one of those one-color men (could be albino but happens to be sand), stands beating with a stick on the metal covering over the lights that light the fountain at night. He beats the three-plus-two rhythm that used to mean "*Al-gé-rie fran-çaise*" but now stands for "*C-R-S S-S.*" He beats and beats, he can't stop, he grins, he can't, can't stop, he stares at the bridge across the Place (cars and police), he is without any doubt a poor, sick rag of a man. You can't mistake the grin, the repeated action (he could just as easily be sitting rocking), and eyes that look *toward* but not *at*. On the rim of the fountain, sitting, waiting, grinning, men like him. They wear the rather shabby, nondescript suits you see on men in institutions, and for a moment I have the unreal idea that they were being taken from observation to a mental hospital and that their doctor had to leave them there. One of them squawks over and over, "Speech-

speech-speech-speech." H. T. pulls me away: "Stop staring at them! Can't you see?" "But they're mad!" "Yes. They're attracted by the violence, the blood. They're waiting for tonight, for something more to happen."

Cohn-Bendit at frontier, met by *sous-prefet*, escorted back to Germany. If he is paranoid (as someone who knows him swears), he must be in heaven. But paranoia is an easy rumor, too. At eight o'clock, de G. speaks. Stare at the screen after he has stopped. Feel again it is like the Kennedy weekend. De G. looks old; nagging childhood memory finally comes up as George Arliss, the actor. He looks like Arliss playing someone distraught, not attending. Is that all? Nothing more? Phone rings: "Did you ever?" "No, never." Only A. J. says, "Well, what else could he say?" Am confused by news—fighting in Lyon (the city) and at the Gare de Lyon. As the announcer predicted this morning, it has been a long day; it merges into another night of radio.

MAY 25

Cloudy, mild, oppressive. Can't remember which day today is. Listened to the radio until about 3 A.M., when the Minister of the Interior spoke of "*la pègre*" (gangsters) in the same breath as "*les anarchistes*." Inaccurate, unreal, unfair. Fell asleep and went on dreaming the news.

Ex-Army men astonished at the professional skill of barricade-builders, how quickly they get the barricades up, their choice of materials. Whose idea was it to cut down the beautiful trees everywhere, Right Bank and Left? *Students*? Is it normal for students to carry power saws?

Seem to be about an inch from civil war, ripples spreading. I think of the education of French children: *Il faut que tu sois raisonnable.* But no one is reasonable. The students who set the Bourse on fire knew without hesitation where everything was kept, even ladders to enable them to get up on the roof. They threatened to burn the concierge's daughter alive. Students, who had never been inside a stock exchange in their lives before.

Law students active last night for the first time. Most conservative of *facultés*, they would have nothing to do with the *contestation*. Suddenly have become more than active—positively virulent. They were distinguished yesterday by their dress (they dress for a demonstration as if going somewhere for lunch—anyway, ties), by their rather snobby way of speaking, which they cultivate in order to annoy the plebs, and by their miniskirted girls. In action last night, among the most *enragés*.

Walk in morning rain to Luxembourg Gardens, on an impulse I cannot define. To see uninjured trees? Gates are shut, chained, and padlocked. Behind them the silent trees. Walk all the way around, past the Senate, past the occupied Odéon—its curb a hedge of spilled garbage. This is the fringe of the battleground: more and more spilled *ordures*, a blackened car still running, another car looking as if it had been kicked and punched. Something dreamlike about the locked secret garden: green on green, chestnut petals all over the filthy pavement; behind the iron-spike fence a Sisley in the rain, a Corot with the sun gone. A fountain jet still playing. The final unreality—three workmen and a small bright-orange jeeplike thing for transporting rakes and shovels. I believe—I do believe—they were about to sweep the paths and rake the gravel. Anyway, they were in working blues. A man shaking their hands through the grille fence. Traffic lights working. Turn away from the park, walk into broken glass, garbage, upturned road signs. Only one café open—curious brown light over the bar, men reading newspapers as if it were any Saturday. Pons patisserie closed, the café next to it smashed, I think—I look away. This is tear-gas country; the rain keeps the gas close to the ground, and there is no wind. In the middle of the Place, a hole like a bomb crater. People stand silently around it. Woman says to her mother (I think), "*Moi, je suis malade pour les arbres.*" Enormous truck on its side. Charred cars pushed half on each other, like the dead after an accident; the cars look like the *people* you see lying beside the highway after a smash, half sprawled over each other. Something indecent. Partly, not entirely, burned. Like lips drawn back from the teeth of the dead. It reminds me of that. One, a Gordini, stuffed with bags of garbage—to make it burn faster, I suppose. The garbage intact. I sneeze, cry, am blinded, stumble across the street and into the branches of a murdered tree lying across the pavement. I actually stumble into the leaves. Very strange, for it is not a place for grown people; you swing up into leaves as a child. Wreck of Dupont's (the café). Just wrecked. There are perhaps fifty of us, ten with cameras. We all stand weeping, red-eyed; we seem to be mourning the death of the square. Stunned, grieved. How quickly a street becomes mud and garbage! I cannot identify this new ground I am walking on. A

pavement of mud, papers, tracts, clay, iron sheeting, piles
of stones, bombs (they look like little tuna-fish tins), yet
nothing is as definite as that. Weeping, remembering not
to rub the eyes (a sort of prickly itching under the lids
makes one want to scratch, but the most unpleasant feeling to me is the painful irritation at the inner corner of
the eye, that little pink bit), turn down Rue Monsieur le
Prince. This end of the street all steps and terraces. Part
of the iron railings torn up. Barricade of paving stones.
In rain, mud, we seem to be skirting a minor precipice.
Only steps. I remember A. S., the first time he came out
of Warsaw, saying, "You think you will win because you
have prettier teacups, but the new young crave ugliness.
It is the very ugliness, the material ugliness, that attracts
them. You will see." Walking back along Rue de Vaugirard,
see slogan on a wall: "LA CULTURE EST L'INVERSION
DE LA VIE." Nuts.

Radio, after news of two deaths, one in Lyon, gives
us "Douce France." Police cars as far as the eye can see
crawl along Boulevard du Montparnasse. Apart from that,
Paris as always, in a Sunday-Monday way. Day suddenly
goes dark. At eleven-thirty, I turn all the lights on. Phone
rings and rings—the tone of the day is disappointment
over last night's speech. People were hoping for (1) a cur-
few to calm everyone down, and (2) garbage collection.
This last seems to bother them most. They aren't used
to dirty streets, as we are in English-speaking countries.
The condition of Paris is sad but not startling to a North
American. Concierges have been asked to put everything
in large, stout bags distributed by the *mairies* and to keep

it in the basements, not outside. Ours is stacked along the wall in the courtyard and looks for all the world like sacks of mail or potatoes or flour. Neat, battened down. Some streets are bad—streets with shops. One realizes now how well the streets are usually kept here—washed and sluiced and swept.

Lunch with A. J. Chez Josephine. First time I have been in a restaurant since the start of "the events." Only four tables besides our own—place usually so packed at lunchtime you need to book. Feel it is wartime and we are all black-marketeers. Man beside me looks like one, he really does, drinking very good Beaujolais with ice up to the top of the glass, fussing over his cheese. "*Menu de la révolution*," A.J. says sardonically. *Saucisson, pain, beurre, veau aux morilles, fraises au sucre*, etc. Mme. D., the owner's wife, "offers" two whacking glasses of *poire*. A. J. has brought two tins of Kitekat, picked up on the way. Cat is having a "*crise de désespoir*" and is tearing out all its own fur. Mme. D. takes this to heart, says Kitekat "too strong"—too many vitamins. I think this cat is some sort of refugee. Talk at next table really is black-market—how to get gas for your car at a pump marked by a red cross and reserved for people like G. You drive your car *in* the garage; you pretend you are having something repaired, looked at; the garage man (properly tipped) gives you the petrol in a jerry can, strictly illegal, this without being seen by the the C.G.T. inspector who is there to watch that fair is fair. At another table, "the events" are discussed rather as Françoise Sagan is discussed in normal times. M. D. thinking of closing the restaurant. Can't get deliveries; no customers; no laundry, even—these are the last clean tablecloths. Lipp Brasserie using paper, plastic. A. J. very bitter about Cohn-Bendit. Sighs, says, "*Quel dommage, ce juif.*" "What?" "*Ce juif qui parle allemand.*" I tease, "And you a Catholic!" Yes, but Jewish all the same. I describe the students saying "*Nous sommes tous des juifs allemands.*" A. J. says, "If you had been here in the war, during the Occupation, and if you had been Jewish, and if you had been a Resistant, you would be less *exaltée* about the French." A. J. can't forgive Cohn-Bendit's father, because he chose to go back to Germany. "He wasn't *rancunier.* Well, I am." Think A. J.'s feeling not a matter of being Jewish but a matter of generations. Jews of that generation wish Cohn-Bendit weren't making himself so damned conspicuous; non-Jews of that generation say, "*Qu'est-ce que c'est que ce petit juif* [or *allemand*]?" But to the kids it simply has no meaning, and that is why I continue to be *exaltée* (in silence). Voices float out: "*Donc ils font l'amour à trois?*" "*Parfaitement. Et avant avec encore une autre. Elle en avail marre, elle s'est suicidée.*" All sounds normal.

Flooded with offers of *liquide.* M. D., Chez Josephine, says he will cash a check "whenever I like," and my *femme de ménage* says that I am to come to her at once if I run short—that her husband keeps the equivalent of about two hundred dollars in cash at all times. As she insists, I say I shall weep. She seems scandalized.

Theme of conversation, over and over: "Would you leave Paris if you could?" "No." Hard for me to realize that, save for the gas shortage, hundreds of thousands of people are not really touched. Think of embassy wife saying,

"I'm just not interested." Everyone I know is so involved, so concerned. One of my most conservative friends: "If only the C.P. would take over! *Nous aurions la tranquillité.*" Meaning a very tough law and order, I guess. Read confusing article about something called "talky-walkies," in abandoned newspaper on bench. Have no shame about scavenging papers. They say no magazines will appear next week. Schools still on strike, and today Anne-Marie's little boy finally refused to be locked up. She can't take him to work, so he was passed from hand to hand. I volunteered to take him for a walk as I searched for *Le Monde.* He trotted along, in his teal-blue corduroy velvet *costume Mao* and his soft Chelsea boots—very elegant. Blond Norman child, a bit small for seven. Dark eyes. Plays with a tape measure. I offer conversation about the weather (cool). In front of a toy display, he comes to a halt. His approach is "I suppose I have enough cars." "Which one are you looking at?" A red jeep with a yellow driver, all plastic, in a plastic bag. "What if I got it for you?" "*Je veux bien.*" My mind labels it thirty-five cents, but it is about a dollar-thirty, and trashy. He says, "I use these cars for catching *bêtes.*" I think he means insects, have vision of cockroaches, beetles. But no. "Lions, camels," he says. A mini-safari. As we part, he says, with a French shrug, "*Merci quand-même, eh?*" That is how he will talk to women when he is thirty.

When you see a knot of people on the street now, you know that newspapers are being sold—piled on the ground, sometimes even on a chair. Search for *Le Monde.* Stop a number of people walking along reading it, but each person always says, "It was the last copy." Find a pile of papers and a boy selling them near the Bon Marché, which has that strange Monday aspect of being shut up.

Lay in modest hoard—two one-half pounds of coffee, and extra batteries for the transistor, which is very hard-worked. I can understand now why people panic over food. Mme. D., the wife of the owner of Chez Josephine, said of the hoarders, "My husband and I laughed at them, but now we begin to wonder if they weren't the intelligent ones." Shopping in the Primistère chain store across the street from Josephine, I see that the shelves of canned goods are empty again—only the prices are left. Third time since Monday the stock has been cleaned out. Nobody buys anything fresh—tomatoes, lettuces untouched. The yogurt and cottage-cheese people on strike—last lot there, in the cold counter. I discover the first impulse to stock—to take countless yogurts, just in case. In case what? Idiotic. Later, I learned that the Basque restaurant along the street will close next week if the strike hasn't ended. The wife of the man in the shoe shop (she carrying what seems to be a ton of bread) says that they may close, too, that de G. has let them down, that she hopes I haven't worn my new shoes in the rain.

Fouchet's statement in the middle of the night last night: "In spite of our sympathy with the students ..." M. L.'s comment: "Giving sympathy with a bulldozer!"

Pharmacy in the Latin Quarter. Man and two women (owners of the place?) sit huddled on three chairs. I ask for eye lotion, because I am bothered by the gas in the streets. Remembering a warning I've read, I say, "Something neutral, not dangerous with tear gas." All three stare at me with *fear* and *hostility*. It is an animal expression. I suddenly realize they think I have been setting fire to cars. I want to say to them, "Why don't you speak up? Why don't you say you hate all this, if you do hate it?" No, they are like dark little animals.

No theatres, no TV, except for the news, and newsmen will probably strike tomorrow; movies may strike next. People driven to reading books (no magazines, either). Driven to reading. God, what a fate! Women more patient, I notice. But inactivity is driving all the men I know off their rockers. E. walked through tear gas and felled trees to buy a Bach record for me at Gibert's. The shop had looked wrecked to me. They must still be doing business inside. Z. down to reading nothing but *Le Monde* and anything she can find about the Commune. Feel claustrophobic; queer cravings—for, for instance, Offenbach (another France?), for Italian poetry (because of claustrophobia, and Italy not France?). Discover I can no longer read it without a dictionary. Gone.

Sit down with pencil and try to make sense of the organized groups called "commandos." Who are trained in armed combat and street fighting? Parachutists. Who know about Molotov cocktails? The O.A.S. did. What clandestine training camps have we heard about in France? The mercenaries'. Matching ingredients, to me. Take my theories down the street to Jacqueline's bookshop. She says her friends have come to same conclusions: extreme right but not intellectuals—no, the bullies, the toughs. The nothing-at-all boys who like being paid (or promised) and like hitting people. Floods of book-buying customers. During the first week of the *contestation*, people came in asking for "something to explain the situation." After that, detective novels. A woman comes in and says, "Something with sun it it—*j'ai besoin de soleil*." I sit there reading a translation of Painter's *Gide*, and finally am so deep in it I buy it. Jacqueline gives me hilarious account of how the Writers' Union (new) invaded and occupied the Hôtel de Massa and established a "permanent discussion"—as if they needed special quarters for that! She and G. P. and some bewildered students crept out while they (the writers) were still analyzing "from the point of view of various perspectives" every phrase they intended to put in their *déclaration*. Some were Catholics, some Communists, some Marxist-Leninists, some nothing much. She says they must still be talking.

H. T. calls from the Select, comes round, tells me about last night. In Les Halles, the new *manifestants* overturning crates of food, fruit, smashing, spilling. Truck drivers who had brought the food in, trying to maneuver among broken crates, vegetables, "students," finally threaten to run them over. Describes scene out of purgatory: *manifestants*, helmeted, wading in cherries out of crates they've overturned, picking up handfuls, pressing the fruit to their mouths, juice running; stained, spitting; and they are joined by the whores of the quarter, who had lately been driven underground by the police. "Students?" he says. "Impossible. Workers? I saw the real workers in Les Halles." When a tree was cut down on the Right Bank, everyone clapped and cheered. He saw bystanders who laughed and thought it was funny. Parisians don't deserve their beautiful city, he said. Let them all go and live in Roubaix and Lille. Perhaps its beauty was imposed on them. Etc.

Latin Quarter quiet now. Students have a good *service d'ordre*; they are sending away all the tourists and sightseers, holding hands, forming chains, blocking off the side streets, so that the Army can clean up the mess, and so that unnecessary elements won't hang about.

From the children's nursery in the Sorbonne comes a dramatic call for milk and bread. There is plenty of milk and bread in Paris, though their quarter may have run out. You feel they (the parents) are inventing a false siege, imagining they are in the siege of Leningrad. First they create the psychosis, then they create the physical conditions, as if it were part of something needed. I rang up F. W., who is a step from the Sorbonne, who is a granddaughter of a former Rector and whose mother was actually born in the Sorbonne, and who has two babies of her own. Plenty of bread and milk in the quarter. Confirms my theory of siege psychosis. Apart from that, her whole family on the side of the students, against the present Rector; some of them marched May 13th, including her father, a sick man. Her husband night and day at O.R.T.F., on the Reorganization Committee, striking. She part of the teachers' strike. No complaints. Says she has been so nauseated since the hoarding began that her husband thought she was pregnant.

Europe I uses as a signal a recording—American, I imagine—of "Where the Rainbow Ends," someone whistling. A nostalgic, persistent kind of tune. It accompanies, in my mind, burning rubbish in the streets and sad fallen trees.

Find I am asking all my friends: Can you (1) eat, (2) read, (3) work, (4) listen to music? No, no, no, and no, in most cases. In music, I can't stand anything but the pop between news bulletins. Gilbert Bécaud singing "Les cerisiers sont blancs," or the Sinatras we are suddenly flooded with. When I was sixteen, a rather pompous writer said to me, "When bombs fall on New York, I will listen to Mozart." It infuriated me then. Remembering it now, I'd like to say, "I doubt if you could. I just doubt it."

Everyone sick about the trees. The wife of my *marchand de couleurs* in tears.

The Events in May:
A Paris Notebook—II

MAY 26

Conversation with D. C., my medical-student neighbor. Tells me he was on duty in the Faculté de Médecine until yesterday. Came home and slept twelve hours. Med students, in order to be allowed to operate a safe infirmary in the Faculté, had to be neutral—anyway, noncombatant. Tried to keep two streets open so ambulances could get through—formed cordons. He says that he and others stood linking arms to keep the street clear. That when police would charge past, sticks raised, roaring that awful roar of theirs, like a great animal, it was too much for some of the med students—they wanted to attack them, or at least shout back. The calmer ones had all the trouble in the world. When he and some others put out a fire, the students who had started the fire nearly attacked *them*. So much rubbish in the streets one can start fires easily now. Says that on Friday night he saw the same toughs I had seen in the afternoon. Each of them arrived dragging his *grille d'arbre*, which they must have brought from another *quartier*—none left in the Latin Quarter now. Tells me about fake Red Cross vans used for carrying iron bars and the like. Finally, doctors took to painting blue crosses on their cars. Each of these improvised ambulances had an interne or an externe. All volunteer. Police very rough on them—considered them suspect. "Gladiators" is his word for the toughs. Seems embarrassed when he talks about them, so I don't insist. He doesn't want to criticize the student movement in any way. Ask about the dead. Looks unhappy, says none official, yet says there must have been some. Tells me some story I can't follow about police taking away a list of names. Interrupted by telephone, forgot to ask end of story.

Journal du Dimanche mentions (as a rumor) that Cohn-Bendit in pay of C.I.A., a common story now. Also (as a rumor) that there is a direct line to Peking in the Sorbonne basement. According to A. J., who had some wartime connection, C.-B. inherited money from his late parents. Father was a lawyer. Never occurs to anyone one can act on conviction, without payment. Also, anyone with a clean shirt is automatically in pay of Americans.

Yesterday, at seven-thirty in the evening, crowd by the Volontaires Métro station. Turned out to be waiting for a truck, which presently arrived bearing bicycles. Bicycles rushed into nearby shop, where queue formed for rapid sales.

Still puzzled about who set fire to the Stock Exchange. E. tells me Jacques (professor) told her that he was there, that it was all professors and students, that it is nonsense to say one needed to know the place in order to get in—all you had to do was get the keys. ("Get the keys" must mean when they threatened to burn the concierge's daughter alive.) I say that if that *is* the truth Jacques should be ashamed, that I would prefer to have gone on thinking it was the work of delinquents, that it is like a child's breaking her own dolls when she actually wants to throw the dining-room table at Mother. Did they really think they could destroy capitalism by setting the Bourse on fire? E. indignant: "We have no right to judge Jacques." Why not? I don't think it was wicked—I think it was asinine. It could just as easily have been the Louvre. If someone had cried "*Au Louvre!*" instead of "*À la Bourse!*" they'd have swarmed there.

Don't know if Mother's Day was put off—don't see much in the way of *fleurs* or *chocolats* on the streets. At the Deux Magots, it seems like any Sunday—perhaps fewer people. Crowds (they say) on the Boulevard Saint-Michel inspecting the damage. Have seen enough of that.

Marie-Élise calls from Toulon, wanting news of her sister. Reassure her. Asks if I will call her brother and check, but as her sister isn't speaking to him at the moment . . . (I wonder where the myth grew up about the "closed" character of French families. On the contrary. All the stranger has to remember is who is speaking to whom, never to repeat anything, even if it sounds innocuous, and not to take sides. You also have to remember who inherited the grandfather clock and how the others felt about it.) Tell her I am dead certain the brother did not join the teachers' strike, is probably in every day lecturing to an empty classroom. Laughter from the Mediterranean. Marie-Élise has a job in a detention home for delinquent and disturbed girls. Says the strikes and *mouvements divers* are having an effect. A number of the girls are Algerians, and won't accept the authority of other women even at the best of times. They feel the slackening of the staff, the confusion, the semi-strike state. "It is like living in boiling soup," she says. As for her fiancé, the ultra-conservative banker, he "refuses to see or hear what is going on," she says. "Pretends it doesn't touch him. But I am *in* it, and it means we are in different worlds. *Il aime son petit confort bourgeois*"—she having only just noticed. One of the rippling effects of the *contestation* may be to keep a bright and charming girl from marrying a dolt.

Say to H. T., "Nothing shows. This could be any Paris street, any Sunday. Nothing looks different. But in here . . ."—meaning the knot in the stomach.

Late last night, heard something on the radio about "grenades" and "*faculté*." Began to feel sick, but it was in Bordeaux. (Reminds me of wartime joke—"The Germans are raping all the Paris women!" "*Vraiment? Moi, je suis de Marseille*"—because my first reaction was relief that it wasn't here.) How normal, how gentle the news seemed at seven o'clock this morning! A heart transplant in Virginia. President Johnson something-something. Sweden. Strike-settlement talks. (Insane idea that everything will be settled by Tuesday.) "Not a drop of gas in Paris except for doctors and food-supply trucks."

TV newsmen, the last to remain working, finally on strike. They decided to go out because of some flagrant distortion in last night's eight-o'clock "Journal Télévisé," apparently. Announce, "The eight-o'clock journal will continue, but we cannot guarantee its impartiality." Did they ever?

D. C. says the medical students have been called back to the Faculté "*en permanence*" for tomorrow. He had been there steadily, came home at dawn yesterday, slept hours and hours. He is worried about tomorrow and the new demonstration, says, "*Il faut si peu*"—to turn it into a riot. Tells me that the students are very bitter now. They think they have been forgotten. They say: We were the first to go out and face the police and be beaten up; the unions came along later; very few workers actually fought along with us until two days ago, and now the heads of the unions are being received by M. Pompidou; they will get everything they ask for, and we shall be forgotten. D. C. says, "If the basic wage rate for workers has been raised, it is thanks to the students." He repeats, as if afraid I am not paying attention, "*We* went out, *we* received the blows, the workers caught the train after it left the station, *they* are being received by M. Pompidou, *we* are forgotten. *Les étudiants sont furieux—nous, on s'est fait taper sur la figure. Ils sont reçus par M. Pompidou—grâce aux étudiants ils ont ce qu'ils veulent.*" Tells me about Friday's and yesterday's guerrilla fighting. The police use three kinds of grenades. There's one that the students call "*offensive*," because of the noise it makes, and because, on direct contact, it can start fires. This is always followed by tear-gas grenades. The third kind he calls "*phosphore*"—if you are close when it explodes, you need "*soins urgents*" and have to be revived with oxygen. D. C. has a tidy mind; he puts everything into one-two-three categories—even the kind and nature of the injuries he has seen and helped doctor. One, the head bashed in by *matraques*; fractures of the wrist and forearm, the arm having been raised to protect the head; fractures of the ankle after a fall (running), the pursuer having smashed down on whatever he could reach. (This last thing I saw here in Paris during the Algerian crisis ten years ago this month. As D. describes it, I see it— the kid tripped, down, the grown man . . .) Two, *les gazés*, some knocked out cold, some with eye injuries. Three, the results of a grenade explosion—the debris, that is: eyes, fingers torn off. He saw someone's calf muscle torn out of the leg, and he describes, coolly, a "frequent" injury— the smashed ankle when a grenade has exploded at one's feet. The two medical faculties—the "old" school, on the Boulevard Saint-Germain, and the "new" one, on the Rue des Saints-Pères—were turned into emergency hospitals. Not yet a doctor, he is so proud of the "solidarity" of the medical profession—all the doctors and nurses and the specialists who worked with them—and of the people who live in the neighborhood, in the Latin Quarter, who walked through the fighting, past the police, with sheets and blankets and whatever medicines they had.

Julie's friend Jean tells E. of a "nightmare" conversation on the barricades. Two or three grown men, ordinary workingmen. One says, "The best way to kill is with a knife." The others don't know how; the man takes out a knife and shows them how to use it and where. They seem interested, not excited. Jean suddenly realizes what he is hearing, tells them to stop. Jean, Julie, and someone else E. knows, a professor, are firm: There were "only students"; there were only "ordinary working people"; they did not see any of the "*éléments*" the police describe. I tell E. what I saw. What H. T. saw. My medical-student neighbor is just as firm: After half past ten, the fighting was in the hands of "gladiators." He describes exactly what I saw on the quais on Friday afternoon—the helmets, the gloves. Student who belongs to central committee of the students' union, the U.N.E.F., says, "We were overrun by the boys from the suburbs. All we can try to do now is *calmer la folie*." Jean and Julie say that the stones I saw on the Rue Saint-Jacques were brought from outside Paris by car—by students only, not by "*éléments*." But in that case what happened last Thursday night was not spontaneous. They can't have it both ways.

Dream: Am having long conversation about "the events" with two men I have never seen in my life (in life) but whom I would recognize if I were to meet them today on the street. Faces distinct, like the faces of strangers close to one in a demonstration. In a strange city upset by strikes. Talkative man says he knows a restaurant still open. He says that if the *idea* of revolution fails (as distinct from revolution itself) he will not feel able to continue his life—that is, a serious life. In dream, had thought he was the more intelligent of the two men. (Now think that if your whole life depends on an abstract idea you aren't much.) Along comes E. F., of all people, saying he is backing the revolution. Carries, as he would in life, papers, books, magazines to support his point of view. Say, as I would in life, "*Comment! Toi, un revolutionnaire?*" E. F. furious (lifelike). I remember (in dream) how impressed he was with China in 1957 (in life). Don't trust him as a revolutionary, or at all, but would much rather hear what he has to say—ex-intelligent man really not very interesting. E. F. says, as in life, "Get rid of them." Third man calm type, waiting to see what the outcome of all this conversation will be, as so often in life. Absolutely logical conversation, but the city unknown to me.

Dream: City besieged, strikebound. Rivers of people in the streets. Have to meet someone (who?), and walk *à contre-courant*. Faces all strange to me, but distinct. Everyone very polite. City not Paris.

Dream: Someone asks in dream question that increasingly irritates me in life (because there is no answer): "These kids want to tear everything down, but they don't know what they want to put up instead. What do they want?"

Add to list of stupid questions: "What do these people want? After all, they all have cars."

The Writers' Union is sinister. Incredible that anyone should want it, with the writers' trials in Russia still fresh in everyone's mind. Whenever a new society seems imminent, everyone wants to be Minister of Culture. Uneasy feeling that old scores are being settled. Z. called on her editor and found the publishing house on strike. Com-

mittees formed and everyone talking. All book production halted. Her editor, usually something of a windbag,
now anxious and silent. Worried by the new Union, what
it will mean. The future is imaginary, but everyone is living
in it as if it had happened. It is a collective hallucination.

Mija, strongly against "the events," says nonetheless
that without them she would never have known that only
eight per cent of the country's university students are
working-class. Thinks this should change. Tell her figures
had been published over and over. She says, "Well, I suppose I never had time." Everyone has discovered something. I have discovered a population of rootless, drifting
teen-agers, who seem to have no homes, or else homes
they don't care about. Z. has had up to six teen-agers at a
time—had to take them to the country finally, because no
room in Paris. She said to one, "Shouldn't you ring your
mother and say where you are?" He replied, "Don't want
to give my family bad habits. They will go on expecting to
hear from me." Z. upset because they formed a clan, hostile, never helping or taking part in the life of the house.
Her daughter, who has always got on so well with her
parents until now, torn—would come to kiss her mother
secretly. No conversation at meals. Z says, "I felt they had
never been encouraged to talk at mealtime." One of them
said to her, coldly, "We would like to *participer aux frais*"
and offered her money—a collection they had taken up. Z.
hurt—they were her guests. She says they had an astonishing amount of pocket money; it seemed to be no problem
whatever. Though they talked (among themselves) about
worker power, they offended Z.'s farmer neighbor by tip-

ping when they used the telephone. Had no idea that a simple person might be offended. My women friends are struck by how dirty they are (the kids), and how insolent. A friend of J. de T.'s who is living with a horde of students—mattresses all over the floors—finally gave up making suggestions, thought she would see how far it could go, found that they would leave dirty water standing in the tub for her to deal with. Slaves at home? The servant-mother? Mystifying. Say to Z., "Who is sleeping in the living room tonight—the Marxist-Leninist?" "*Mon Dieu*, I hope not, but if so he will have to take a bath. And wash the tub. *J'aime la révolution, mais qu'ils lavent la baignoire!*" Fascinating conversation with J. de T. about French family life. He says my ideas out of date by four or five years (i.e., that there is less juvenile delinquency than elsewhere, because of strong family structure, everyone home for the evening meal, etc.). "*La table familiale n'existe plus*," he says. I knew Christmas no longer existed (children sent to the mountains in groups for skiing now while parents dine in a restaurant somewhere). Says the fathers have "abdicated" and the mothers "*ne sont plus à la hauteur*" Surely he means only in Paris? Am certain family structures exist as they always did, starting thirty miles outside Paris limits.

Parents and children again: Mme. C. tells me that of her three sons the youngest (seventeen and a half) is *un peu fascisant*, very right; the middle one is actively engaged; the eldest goes to the barricades "just to see." Says family meals now difficult *pour une mère de famille*. Says her husband ("*toujours à l'avant-garde*," she says proudly)

pushes the boys to action—he crossed the Spanish frontier at eighteen to join the Free French. But the middle
son, D. C., had quite a different angle—seemed to feel his
father was hostile to the movement until May 7th, when
father went out at midnight to see the demonstration on
the Rue de Rennes, was impressed by how orderly they
were, and how determined. D. C., speaking of parents and
Cohn-Bendit, says "*Pour eux, c'est l'allemand.*" Says med
students kept out of it at the beginning, joined movement
only as a reaction against the police. Tells me that *sec-
ouristes* were beaten up. That it wasn't safe for a doctor to
help the wounded unless the doctor was wearing a helmet.
He saw wounded on stretchers beaten in a kind of frenzy.

In Latin Quarter now, faces bruised, Mercuro-
chrome-stained. Casts and bandages for what would seem
to be ski accidents in another season, but these are fresh.
Tendency of boys to behave like Old Soldiers: "I was on
the barricades," like "I was in the Resistance."

Why do they keep on about Marcuse? Except for Z.'s
dentist friend, no one even knows who he is. The last thing
they would read now is someone writing from America.
No one has mentioned Régis Debray—not a student, not
a journalist, no one. I now discover no one has really read
him. No one seems to know that the C.P. was opposed
to Castro at the beginning. Romantic Che Guevara—but
does anyone know anything he wrote or said? Philippe A.
said he looked like Christ. My reaction to that was what
my mother used to call "a swift pain." Seems to me the
reality of the revolution is in people's minds. (That is, the
revolution they are imagining—nothing has taken place.)

Debray, not Marcuse. Funny Debray should be so quickly forgotten, in his own city.

After the fighting, the hippies emerge. Pale, sick copies of American photos seen in *Paris-Match*. When you hear them, they are not often speaking French—usually Dutch, English. They don't try to stop the fighting; they merely vanish, then reappear on the ruined streets. *Zéro de conduite.*

How can you talk about the Spanish Civil War to people who don't even know what happened in 1958, or 1961, or what the O.A.S. was about? E.'s daughter had never heard of Bastien-Thiry. When her mother said it was the injustice for which she would never forgive de G., her nineteen-year-old daughter didn't know what she was talking about. What one has to remember is they have known nothing but de G. They don't distinguish between veterans of 1944 and the paratroopers of Indochina and Algiers, whom they consider Fascists.

France in throes of *la parlote*. Tried to find, in *Oblomov*, the bit that goes something like "'That's exactly what I don't like,' said Oblomov. 'Everyone talking.'" Because of transport problem, Z., H. T., and I meet at the Cluny, which is midway for all three. K. Mansfield's café, now much done over. Sunny day. Boulevards filthy, papers blowing everywhere; *grilles* missing from around the trees leave areas of mud strewn with crumpled tracts, cigarette wrappers, etc. Power strike, but some traffic lights smashed anyway. New hazard: the four or five inches of metal sticking out of the pavement where one-way signs and the like have been ripped away. Policemen arresting a

North African are followed by a silent crowd. No one can be arrested for anything now without bystanders' following along, suspicious. Second floor of café sunny, bright, leaves at the windows, sounds (now normal) of ambulances and police cars. We discuss Mendès France, who seems to be quietly ripening in the shade, and the remarkable amount of talk going on everywhere. Just as we say this, we look at the clock on the wall and see we have been talking three and a half hours, non-stop. Z. has brought me a packet of coffee in case coffee runs out. Z. says that she has discovered the violence in the streets is exciting to her homosexual friends—that someone told her he had never seen anything so "beautiful" as young boys pushing over a bus. Don't know about that, but I know I have never seen so many sexually *détraqués* wandering about and pestering. It is like London and those dreary men in raincoats. Z. confirms what I feel about growing xenophobia since the beginning of "the events." I say, "Yes, but the young . . ." She says that except for supporting Cohn-Bendit they are worse than ever. I think we must be more nervous than we pretend to be. They tease me about wearing a red suit. H. T. convinced that one of the roots of the revolution is nothing but boredom, and that a number of people are anxious to suppress the exams because they couldn't pass them anyway. "*Révolution de cancres,*" he says. He is fed up with not working. Curious atmosphere: One expects to be told, "No coffee, no sugar," etc., but there is plenty of everything; the sugar bowl, heaped, sits on the table. Students come in looking as if they had come straight off the barricades, but I *know* that except for the look of the streets, and the whine of the ambulances, the city is quiet. We are all living in a future, in something that has not taken place.

Some of my friends now going in for orgies of house-cleaning—"something constructive."

Tell Suzanne B.: Thank God no guns in France—so far, not a shot. She says that there are guns—that the arms distributed by the police in 1961, when we expected that paratroop invasion, were never collected. My notebooks have it that men sat all night outside the commissariats waiting for arms, and that the police hesitated, knowing they would never get them back; that people went bravely out to Orly (as M. Debré had requested) unarmed, the mayors of the working-class suburbs wearing their red-white-and-blue sashes and their service medals, their only defense at that point. When I saw these same people in the demonstration May 13th, I was close to tears, remembering 1961.

Don't know when, if ever, I shall have a train for the south. No one seems to know if liquidated trains are replaced or if a reservation gives one any priority. Tried to call M. S., and also G.'s great-aunt, in the Alpes-Maritimes, but the *indicatif* just a faint buzz on the line. Finally got the C.s. Spoke to Antoinette. She says the customs are on strike at the Italian border and cars lined up right around the bay. For Italian gasoline? Yes, she says, but also for washing machines, refrigerators, radios, all much cheaper than in France. Some people have hired taxis to transport the loot; shops all the way to San Remo cleaned out of *frigos* and washing machines. The Italians are burning "large candles to the Madonna" and praying the French crisis will go on forever, but now they are starting to refuse French money, which will mean an end to the rush. Her mother-in-law, eighty-three, says the working-man isn't what he used to be.

MAY 27

Cold, rain. Listen to "*négociations*" during the night over the radio but don't always take in what I'm hearing.

Change in attitude toward students now that everyone thinks things are "getting back to normal." Irritates me. I stop answering the phone. The more thoughtful among the young, the more intelligent, and the bravest are in for a lesson now: how affairs are managed. One famous political commentator, who had *slavishly* backed the movement, did a complete about-face on this morning's news. Sounded like a doleful Sunday-school teacher, but sure of his influence. I wonder if the parents, *qui s'étaient faits tout petits*, will be life-size again; I wonder if the kids will again become what they always seemed to me—little old men. I hear "*On s'en fout des frontières!*" *Bon*. But when they started to run I hid behind a tree.

Pound off through the rain to a morning meeting at the Société de Géographie, Boulevard Saint-Germain. Chinese section of the National School of Oriental Languages meeting to discuss reform of degree they are given, and possible merger with Chinese section of Sorbonne. Louis Hémon went to the Langues Orientales. He is still my favorite Frenchman, because of his life, but scarcely

anyone has ever heard of him here. Always have to identify him by a book I don't much like—*Maria Chapdelaine*.
Can't remember if I had any dinner at all last night. Meet
vague writer neighbor with large shopping bag. Ask if atmosphere interfering with work, say I can do nothing. Am
told that writer neighbor has lavish interior life, which
always sounds to me like stomach lined with Moroccan
leatherwork. March on. Rich interior life produces forgotten marching verse: "No bloody sports/ No bloody
games/ No bloody fun/ With bloody dames/ Won't even
tell/ Their bloody names/ Oh bloody bloody bloody." This
gets me to Société de Géographic: totally dark; nothing
about except a note for the postman (do they still exist?)
on which someone has scratched out "*Monsieur le Facteur*"
replacing it with "*Camarade.*" Buy morning papers and
sit outside the Flore to wait. Only customer. Find in coat
pocket a slip of paper with "Aglaë Bonaventure" and the
words "The Goal" boxed with a red pencil. It is my writing,
and I think, for one of those dizzy seconds, I have gone
mad. Remember, at last, that Aglaë is a filly and Bonaventure her trainer, and The Goal an outsider. This for yesterday's race at Longchamp, had there been a race—all called
off. Bright-colored filth and garbage piled up in front of
Lipp, across the street. Not much traffic; it is like a holiday,
with everyone out of town. People trudging to work in the
rain glance at café. All the terraces empty. Tables arranged
as if for a normal morning—hard-boiled eggs, plastic
fruitcake. Smell of bitter black coffee, smell of dark cigarettes; even the rain, which is like winter, entirely nostalgic.
Reminds me of arriving in provincial cities in France early

in the morning, drinking, in steamy, Gauloise-smelling cafés, the same coffee, with its aftertaste of iodine. Overwhelmed with feelings for France, Paris, etc. Plunge into *Combat*. All *Combat* editorialists (on that paper even the sports reporter is an editorialist) feel, as I do, that students have been betrayed. Mention "betrayal" and the more subtle word "*malentendu.*" The "Cultural Revolution" is ending in "sordid negotiations about salary percentages." Another editorial, by Maurice Clavel, who used to be a Gaullist, urges everyone to boycott the referendum. This interests me, because the D.s, my most right-wing friends, are boycotting it, too: "Reforms must come, but not from *him.*" Wonder if this will be widespread. Notice Mendès France's name more and more. When he marched past me May 13th, in that big demonstration, I was the only person to recognize him (where I was, anyway). Now, two weeks later, if he were to sit down outside the Flore, he would probably be mobbed by new-found friends. Marie-Élise, ringing up from Toulon, said her hairdresser had confided that "France would be saved in its present crisis by the Martians." Marie-Élise said she, the hairdresser, meant it—really thought that up there on Mars they were keeping an eye on France. (Logical followup of God saving France through Joan of Arc? Same principle.)

Several people in Société de Géographie. Man named Boris, shirt-sleeves, nice face, distributes four brooms (the place is, in fact, a pigsty; must be used for meetings all the time now)—distributes them to girls only. Girl sweeping says, "*C'est aux femmes de balayer*" like the wife in the dream in *8½*. J. P., professor of Chinese at Oriental Languages, arrives. I tell him Cultural Revolution has a long way to go. Meeting gets under way; everyone takes notes. J. P. says, "Here come the Sorbonne troublemakers." Sorbonne troublemakers make a point of slamming out after about fifteen minutes. "*Les troupes de choc nous quittent,*" someone remarks. Sign, "DÉFENSE DE FUMER," but on blackboard someone has written, "*Ne Fumez Pas Trop.*" I discover that it takes as long to get a degree in Chinese as in medicine, that the two Chinese schools are not co-ordinated, that they want to join up "geographically," as they put it, and then decide if they wish to join (they say with straight faces) "*organiquement.*" The blithe talk of moving faculties, changing the system of obtaining degrees, moving whole libraries around the city makes me giddy. I write "Who's paying for it?" on a slip of paper and pass it to J. P. No answer. They are short of space, like all the schools and faculties. J. P. takes the microphone. He wears the brown corduroy suit that is the only thing I've ever seen on him. Has probably been wearing it day and night now. One of his students, behind me, says irreverently, "*Allez, Pimpim!*" "We are short of space," he says, "and we need a building. I suggest that we choose some large building that serves no purpose whatever, and that we storm it with a team of commandos. I suggest for this the Musée de la Chasse et de la Pêche à la Ligne." Applause and laughter, but next to me someone says, "Does he mean it, or is it a joke?" No one knows.

Power strike. It is the one strike I find depressing. It is as if the circulation of the blood had stopped. The traffic lights stop working, and since there are no traffic police about at all (as if they had said, "You don't like us? Do without us"), and since no motorist will give way, it is impossible for pedestrians to get across any large avenue except by forming a squad. It seems to me that a tree is missing in front of the Deux Magots. My *femme de ménage* says to me, "Now we know who has been responsible for all the troubles here. *Des commandos d'étrangers et d'apatrides.* They have been sent in by car." "Who says so?" "Everyone," she says. Well, now we know. Foreigners and stateless ones.

L'Express appeared today in its old form, like a tabloid newspaper. This is the way it looked during the Algerian war, when it was meat and drink. Even the sight of it on the newsstand adds to this feeling I have that we have somehow come full circle back to 1958. Cover: "LA RÉVOLUTION DE MAI." Reading it, one concludes that Father will leave, but only if he can leave a tidy house, and that a revolution really *has* taken place. That everything is new, changed, different. I also discover that, thanks to their common sense and their instinct for happiness, the French have collectively rejected the consumer society. That this could have happened only in France. (Delighted to have something to laugh over this rainy, cold, grey day.) Is it so astonishing that this movement—which is a movement in favor of happiness—has begun here? In the French character, "Eros triumphs over Thanatos." And so on. Strong desire to hurl paper on café floor and walk all over it, but instead take it home to add to the pile.

"*Aux français, on pardonne tout,*" a journalist friend once said to me. As usual, they are going to have it both ways:

the foreigners did it; only the French could have done it.

Discover that the American Diaper Service has never stopped delivering and collecting. Sometimes the delivery was late, but it never failed. So mother of infant tells me. The plant is out in Saint-Cloud. Not on strike? Had private reserve of gas for cars? Sail through traffic jams? Mystery. God bless the American Diaper Service.

In the midst of chaos, Con and M. L. decided to have their bedroom painted and move to hotel. No trouble finding paint, apparently, though shops are said to have run out. (Men at home and bored take to painting the kitchen.) In the midst of bedroom painting, two strangers turn up and say they have come to sweep the chimneys. Fireplace flue in bedroom. Who are these sweeps, and why aren't *they* on strike?

Noticed this morning that Jacques, who goes out "on the streets" with the Anarchists, is addressed as "*Monsieur*" by his students, and not "*Camarade*" Decorum stronger than chaos, apparently.

The unions haven't accepted the agreements. That is, the unions would have accepted but the strikers refused. Z., who had been listening to the radio out in the country over the weekend, returned with food for her starving friends: eggs, fresh butter, milk. She can't give any of it away—there is plenty of everything here. On our street, the garbage was collected this afternoon by two Algerians in an open truck. Nearly everyone had used those enormous paper bags the *mairies* have been distributing; the truck might have been piled with sacks of shavings or meal. A minute after it vanished, three concierges were

out in the road with push brooms. Again this unreality:
The radio speaks of shortages, of garbage and the dangers
of an epidemic. We are told to pour Javel water in garbage
pails to stun the microbes.

This morning, at the meeting at the Société de Géographie, J. P. gets up and explains to the students of Chinese "what the system is at the university in Peking." It
consists of a major and a minor subject—Chinese and
Russian, Chinese and ethnology, or what have you. Students enthusiastic, applaud. When he sits down, I say,
"But that is the *American* university system." He replies, "I
know, but I couldn't possibly say that. They would never
have accepted it. It had to be from Peking." Similarly, seventeen-year-old Barbara's friends don't like her to sing
English or American songs. They don't mind the tunes,
but the words must be in French. Z.'s dentist friend "has
read the first and the last page of Marcuse" and explained
to Z. what Marcuse is about: "If we don't eat as well as
we used to in France, and if we don't make love as often
as we used to, it is because of the Americans." Simple as
that. At the meeting this morning, I said, "What if I asked
for two minutes of microphone time and used them to
say that Americans helped defeat Fascism between 1941
and 1945?" I was told, "You would be lynched," and it was
a serious answer, not a *boutade*. Cohn-Bendit, asking for
political freedom in the universities—freedom to recruit,
and to state a political position, that is—said (and was
never challenged), "But we would never allow free speech
to any defender of the Americans. It would be like allow-
ing a Nazi to praise the killing of millions of Jews." My

young med-student neighbor D. C. says, "Cohn-Bendit is frightening to our parents because he is *l'allemand*. Not to us. My best foreign *camarades* are Germans. But the *English*!" He makes a face.

Echoes of the hospital strikes: G. unable to have patients picked up by ambulance now. J. de T. tells me that the pickets outside his hospital (who are not doctors or nurses) have the power to decide what is an emergency case and what isn't, and which of his patients he is allowed to see. His patients all nervous cases—attempted suicides and that sort of thing. How can the pickets judge? Pickets in the X-ray rooms also decide who needs an X-ray—whether or not it is an emergency. Young externes all voting in committees over hospital reform; meanwhile, the *grand patron* of the hospital goes around taking blood pressures. J. de T. furious not so much over the strikes as over this interference. He tells me there have been fewer suicides since the beginning of the events.

H. T. gets up during meeting where everyone is discussing committees and subcommittees and how each laboratory will shift for itself (with what funds?). He says, "*Et pendant ce temps-là, qui fera de la physique?*"—and walks out. Outside, meets professor who has been keeping out of the way, not taking sides. Professor says, "*Très rigolo*, all this. Reminds me of the Popular Front. Doesn't it remind you of Hitler addressing little groups in little auditoriums?" H. T. says, "When I was old enough to know about Hitler, he was already out of the little auditoriums." H. T. doesn't say much. Wants to get back to work. Is suspicious of movements that begin "on the streets," and he loathes destruction. On the other hand, was utterly and absolutely opposed to the police having gone inside the Sorbonne. *Alors?*

New version of How the Americans Are Responsible: "If they had not created the Vietnam situation, de G. would not have been obliged to oppose it. If he had not been obliged to oppose it, the students would never have begun thinking in terms of opposition. It's all the Americans' fault." Not eating much these days, so couldn't even throw up.

Listened to accounts of the student-worker meeting at Charléty Stadium. Kept turning from one station to another, sick with worry. Nothing happened. It sounded more like a political meeting than anything else. I can't help wondering: If a simple *mot d'ordre* from the student leadership was enough to keep things quiet, why wasn't the *mot* given on Thursday and Friday nights?

Last Friday, when it seemed pretty certain there would be a new explosion in the evening, the concierge of a house on the Boulevard Saint-Michel went to each of the tenants and said, "This time, no one is to help the students. I don't want anyone throwing water out of the windows, or letting any of the wounded inside their flats. I am going to lock the outside door, and that is that." Only *one person*, the man who told the story, disobeyed the concierge. Why were they so frightened of her? Dirty old woman in felt shoes, just literate enough to hold one's mail up to the light. Because of the connection of the concierges with the police, he says. From the time of Napoleon.

Suzanne B. reads me over the telephone some predictions she found in *Horoscope*, a thing that comes out every month. Everything predicted, including the barricades. As soon as the printing strike is over, I am going to buy it every month and stop having to guess.

MAY 28

Normal Paris sounds: Concierge sweeping pavement. Sparrows. Man says, "*Tu as bien dormi?*" Broom stops. "*Oui—enfin!*" The Tuesday market on the Boulevard Raspail overflows. Fruit, meat, vegetables, fish, even the potatoes, the *pâtes* (macaroni, etc.) that are supposed to have been wiped off the map. My Tunisian greengrocer has a sign on the same white calico that people bring to demonstrations: prices *down* on fresh vegetables and fruit. Nobody wants them. Still stocking things like dried kidney beans and refusing cheap, delicious asparagus, lettuces, all the spring vegetables, strawberries. The first wild strawberries are on display. Only three customers in the place. Next door, woman ahead of me in the queue, corduroy trouser suit, ponytail, asks for sugar. Two salesgirls. To divert me, one says, "*Vous, par ici, s'il vous plaît,*" and moves me up to the other end of the counter. The sugar lives under the counter in a brown paper bag. I see it slipped into ponytail's shopping basket. "Where is it?" She panics. "There, in the basket." The girl grimaces and points. They are like children. I find it funny, but the little blond florist from the Rue Saint-Placide is outraged. "*Elles jouent à la guerre,*" she says. Yes, they are playing. Z. calls. The first thing she says is "*Ul y a de tout.*" In her *quartier*, there is so much food, and so much food garbage all over the streets (she lives in the Marais), that she is nauseated and never wants to eat again. The obsession with food revolts her. She spent four years in a concentration camp. "*La France est prise d'un grand vomissement,*" she says. "Stuffing food and vomiting rubbish."

New problem: Clothes accepted at the cleaner's, but when will they come back? No one knows. Get out *Household Encyclopedia*; don't understand a word about "Stains and Spots," cling to Maurice Thorez's famous remark "*Il faut savoir terminer une grève*" and deposit it all at cleaner's anyway. Folies-Bergère on strike. I wish I understood about the football affair. "*Le football aux footballeurs,*" it seems, is their slogan now. But who had taken over *le football* in the past? The Old Soldiers?

Florists, Rue du Cherche-Midi. Two sisters. One was five when her father died in the 1914 war, the other was born four months later. The elder, little, round, grey, gives herself a strange mouth with pale-orange lipstick. The younger wears her hair in an Alice B. Toklas bob and is nearly deaf. Both standing in doorway as I go by. They have been to the Sorbonne, are horribly upset. Probably first time they ever set foot there. "No matter how one feels about de Gaulle—and God knows he did nothing for shopkeepers, he never cared about us—But no matter how one felt one would never have written those insults on a wall." They are upset about Cohn-Bendit. I am surprised they speak so openly. Two sturdy sisters from the Haute-Savoie. Say what they feel. What they say is "He is a German Jew. His parents survived the war because they were hidden in France. What right has he to spit on our dead?" Here follow accounts of Jews saved in the Haute-Savoie and conducted to Switzerland. I have never been able to find out exactly what the Anarchist students did to the tomb of the Unknown Soldier on May 7th. I wasn't there, and the newspapers weren't specific. Some people say they spat, G. says they placed a red flag over the tomb, and now the two florists say they urinated. Feel acutely unhappy over all this and wish C.-B. would just vanish forever. Suzanne B. has told me that people are again beginning to say "Boche" because of him. I have heard that he was in the pay of the Cubans, of the Chinese, and of the C.I.A., and now the florists tell me it is the Jews. What Jews? The Israelis. It is a form of revenge because of de G.'s stand last year during the Six-Day War—backing the Arabs. I say, "Do you really believe this?" They say, "No, not really, but it is what everyone else is saying now."

Everyone reports strange dreams and nightmares. H. T. dreamed his rooms were broken into and everything destroyed—books all over the floor, furniture burned, etc. In dream, was astonished—who could possibly have it in for him this way? Suddenly (in dream) thought: Of course, it was the Anarchists. Nothing personal.

The professional footballers have "ceased their occupation" of whatever they were occupying. Never was able to figure that one out. Railway strikers firm, so there will probably be no trains on Friday, when I was supposed to be leaving for the south. Made my reservation in April, before Easter, to be absolutely certain. The *auto-couchette* trains (which you put your car on—the car travels in one wagon and you in another) are booked months in advance. Now even the train has vanished. People keep asking me what I mean to do, as if I knew, and as if it even mattered. No importance. If there is a train, I'll be on it. Mystery: Saw every kind of food in the market this morning, but housewives in my neighborhood keep saying, "No coffee, no flour, no salt." True about the salt. One woman in my building bought five kilos of salt. It would last me a lifetime. Now there is only what they call "*sel de luxe,*" and the shopkeeper says, "We stood in line over an hour for it." So *they* are queueing, too!

Young girl calmly describes to her mother and me how she and a friend accidentally became caught between police and students last Friday night. Several times, police made her show her hands—dirty hands meant one had been building a barricade. The awful feeling as he stands there, nonchalantly swinging his club, saying, "Show your hands." This told so calmly that it seems true. Girl's mother is speechless. Parents aren't saying much these days. But then the girl begins the rumors. Isn't the truth ever bad enough? Says that a girl was raped four times in a police van on way to station, that van was full of students watching. Not only unlikely—ludicrous. Think of design of van, complication of entire proceeding. There just isn't room. Ask if she saw this. No. Why always rape in these stories, and why always four times? Isn't it bad enough to be beaten up and called "*putain*"? Also tells us that in police van one of the C.R.S. (Compagnies Républicaines de Sécurité) dropped a tear-gas bomb inside someone's trousers "and so he was castrated." Just like that, neat. She says, "When I am forty, I shall always remember this contact I had with the workers," on which I explode. Tell her that police have been beating people up for years, without the romanticism of barricades, and that if the Night of the Barricades had taken place in a working-class suburb like Saint-Denis we would have known no more about it.

Mija, who is the wife of a Paris lawyer, says that the bourgeoisie haven't said much but are fed up—that they will also go out to the street and fight if they have to, and that they will vote for de Gaulle in the referendum, or for "his successor."

One fear I haven't mentioned to anyone: What if any of us is taken ill—say, in the night? Hospitals on strike, phones working badly. No time for a bad appendix. Z. said casually that she was to have an operation but that her doctor won't put her in hospital now. Power strikes, uncertainty about staffs, medicines. He prescribes some sort of sedative to keep her going (she has never once mentioned that she was in any sort of pain), but all the pharmacies have run out. D. C. tells me there is even a shortage of penicillin now. So quickly? He also describes to me how an unfortunate woman unlucky enough to be on the point of giving birth in the Latin Quarter, where she lives, was got out and to a hospital in one of the cars they were using to evacuate the gassed-and-fractured wounded.

Now they say the referendum is illegal—at least, in the terms suggested by de G. Don't know if it is illegal, but certainly dishonest: Are you still beating your wife, yes or no? Radio keeps repeating bits of Mitterrand's press conference. Shy white violet, offers himself to the nation. A new de G. but not so imposing. It is as if de G. were dead. Mendès France like an actor pretending to be overwhelmed as he comes out for one more curtain. Begin to feel sorry for de G. What do they mean by "interim government"? Is this all that May 13th was about? Are elections what everyone wanted, then?

Kids parade around the streets close to the Odéon wearing costumes stolen from the wardrobes. Girl dressed as a gypsy dances (badly) in a café for stony-faced audience. Everyone silent as she and friends show off, eat sandwiches, sweep out without paying. *Patron* doesn't say a word. Gypsy says endearingly, "I shall pay next time—it is a promise." Someone says to the *patron*, "Why don't you call the police?" Which sounds terribly funny now. Call the *police*? Everyone either revolutionary or frightened. Bright, sunny day.

MAY 29

Cool, grey morning. London sky. Up very early to beat ' possible early-morning power strike. Can't see to run a bath without light. Out early, no sign of concierge, cat looking rejected on the stairs. Walk all over Saint-Germain-des-Prés, leave letter with a Belgian journalist who is getting out of Paris and is taking along letters to be posted. Have to leave French money for postage, which they are not accepting now in Belgium. Mountains of garbage all over the streets—sometimes have to step off the curb. On the Rue Saint-Benoît, stickers all over the walls:

"MAMAN J'AI PEUR." Left over from ancient time, before May 3rd, when slogans were still supposed to be funny. Wall newspaper outside elementary school. Everyone has an opinion about education, has added a comment. Shops still shut, people walking to work. Go to the Café Flore. Staff still dusting and polishing. World's most delicious *croissant*. Am glad I'm not at home and answering telephone.

Power strike. Impulse to walk all over Paris, as if the city were about to disappear. The occupied Beaux-Arts (has another name now) solid wall of posters; one shows Cohn-Bendit as he was in the picture in *Paris-Match*, excited little fox taunting a policeman, with the legend *"Nous Sommes Tous Indesirables."* Hope they will remember they once said this. Tuileries filthy; Concorde looks covered with oil. Pickets outside the Printemps. Opéra shut, great streamer asking for "OUR RIGHTS." Right Bank looks unwanted. Cafés deserted. Place Vendôme, cars all over the pavements now. Drift into E. Arden. Place in darkness—power strike. About three customers in the place, someone says. Staff looks anxious, glum. Lights come on. I say I want my hair cut short for the Revolution. This makes them glummer than ever. Some of them walk as much as two hours each way, morning and night. Describe garbage at the *portes de Paris*. Am told about revolutionary coiffeur who all at once said *"Mais j'ai tout à perdre, moi!"* and at once changed his mind. Conversation zero—people who live on tips pick up the attitudes of the tippers. Am told about poor Mme. So-and-So who doesn't dare take her Rolls out of the garage because it might make her seem bourgeois. Stories of people leaving the country with suitcases full of money. Only attitude I sense is that they would have done the same if they'd had the money to put in the suitcase. Sun comes out. *France-Soir* has scare headline about de G. going to Colombey, presumably to draft his resignation. Sun well out, so lunch at a kiosk in the Tuileries. Lawns and flower beds covered with papers, tracts, beer bottles. In *France-Soir*, picture of the now suspect (to me) Cohn-Bendit at the Sorbonne, with his hair dyed black. Doesn't suit him. Appeal to help the aged, but no one says *how*. Salvation Army will feed them if they can prove they are pensioners. Nine-line item says six hundred persons "disappeared" last Thursday and Friday nights. Must be a mistake. If true, why is the item buried at the bottom of an inside page? Power strike, evidently on again, makes it virtually impossible to cross streets. No more police to cope with traffic. Gone.

Book sales are up forty per cent. No TV—on strike.

I am reading *Le Siège de Paris*, by Francisque Sarcey. Book I picked up ages ago on the quais. All spotted, as if pages were freckled. Read, "*Il faut connaître Paris pour comprendre à quels excés peut se porter une idée fixe, chez cette population bouillante, où tous les sentiments sont en quelque sorte surchauffés. . . .*" Z. is reading a book about the Commune. Ask H. T. what he is reading: "Marx's notes on the Commune." H. T. says, out of context of a conversation, "Marx, Hegel, Feuerbach, *toute la racaille*." He is being driven mad by pop music. Isn't used to it. All we can get on radio now. Has a particular hatred for song called "Qu'est-ce que tu as fait avec l'enfant que je t'ai fait?" I can't get "Alouette, Alouette" out of my head. Theme of these days. "*L'amour et l'été,/ Comme les ciga-rettes,/ S'en vont en fumée,/ Alouette, Alouette.*" Couldn't be trashier, or more haunting.

On Rue de Rennes, two gas pumps still working. One serves a line of cars backed up round the block; the other has a large Red Cross banner, meaning it is reserved for doctors and nurses. G. furious about doctors' wives using priorities. Today an attendant was beaten up by five driv-ers, after he told them he'd run out of gas. He is in hos-pital with head injuries, "in serious condition." Nobody got the drivers' names. They just left him there. A driver was shot at by men who wanted to siphon gas out of his tank. This in daylight, near the Place Dauphine. Drivers of tanker-trucks being attacked. Gas stealing rampant. In Marseille all service stations ordered closed: it was too dangerous for the attendants.

Garbage piled on curb of Rue de Sèvres. Cluster of pedestrians staring at something. Five plastic bags, each holding a kilo of peeled new potatoes rotting in the sun. Hoarder evidently didn't know that peeled potatoes in plastic bags rot quickly, have to be used almost the day you buy them. Five kilos!

Papers have been talking about old people. The aged, often feeble and ill, can't stand in line to stock food. Of-ten they virtually live on *nouilles* and macaroni, all they can afford, which are hard to find now (though I've seen packets in the Boulevard Raspail market). Post office on strike means their old-age pensions are held up, and even if they weren't held up the old people wouldn't be able to cash them. Salvation Army will feed old-age pensioners who can prove they *are* pensioners. But how do they get to these Salvation Army centers? Who takes them there? No transport, no gas. Harrowing articles do not tell what one can *do*. Begin by ringing up paper where I read original article. Hopeless runaround, and line goes dead. Try ringing *mairie* of my *arrondissement*. No one seems to understand what I want. Furious. Hate all French. Stamp around to Jacqueline, who says she will take it up at the Revolutionary Committee meeting tonight in the Beaux-Arts. Fat chance of anyone's doing anything. Not spectacular enough. Someone says Boy Scouts are swinging into action to help the old. Remember things G. has told me about cancer patients alone in slum bedrooms. Must be even worse now. What can you do? Stand out in the street and shout?

At twenty to six in the afternoon, concert of motor horns. Turn on radio, discover that de G. is "*introuvable*." Everyone thinks he will resign. Instant feeling is pity. Tragedy, the flaw of pride. When he dies, they will line up for hours to look at his grave.

C.G.T. (Confédération Générale du Travail) demonstration today, a sort of answer to the worker-student thing at Charléty. As if to show that the Communist Party has the workers firmly in hand. Z. saw it. "Like a picnic. They came with the children." H. T. saw it, too. Same feeling of "picnic"—says they waved extremely dirty handkerchiefs and sang, "*Adieu, Charlot, adieu.*" Says there were students, too, but not representing the students—on their own. Carried signs saying this: "I Am on My Own."

Says the students were enormously applauded by working-class population on sidewalks. All *populo*, good-natured, broke up without fuss. Communist Party obviously making every effort to prevent Cuba-youthful enthusiasm and Cultural Revolution. They seem really quite stodgy—nothing is so conservative as the working classes, as British liberals were dismayed to find out. What does the C.P. care about the university? C.P.'s battles have always been in the factories. Hard for students to understand. Kid in my building almost weeping with rage.

H. T. turns up, takes me to see *La Mariée Était en Noir*—"*pour se changer les idées.*" Doesn't change any of mine; silliest film imaginable. Lovely night, shadows on pavement of the Rue Littré. H. T. tells me episode in life of Schiller that illustrates present situation. I keep thinking of Pompidou, though would much rather not. Stupefied to see harmless little pastry shop on the Rue de Rennes now unveiled all red with large white polka dots, balloon size, and the name "LE CRÊPE SHOW" spelled out in light bulbs. Don't they know there's a revolution on? Wondered if the kids are still occupying School of Photography and Cinematography. They seem to have been forgotten. Red flag still over the door. My feeling for de G. nothing but pity now. Proud, ruthless—I suppose one diluted the other, and that was the flaw. We talk of him as if he were dead. H. T. says the C.G.T. demonstration had a definitely political turn, which he didn't feel was spontaneous. They were all good-natured union members who had been told to say "Off with his head!" and said it and then dispersed to cafés for a glass of beer. Says he saw what seemed to be whole hospital staffs with reassuring signs reading, "LE SERVICE EST ASSURÉ," though from what J. de T. tells me it is just barely.

Students so puzzled when strikers asked for higher wages. Seemed to think everyone fighting for less. C.P. seems gross, new-rich.

From *Le Monde*: "RATS IN THE STREETS OF PARIS." The Ville de Paris and the Army are trying to get garbage off the streets, but "rats have made their appearance. Interrogated on the danger that these undesirable visitors represent, M. Caldaguès, President of the Council of Paris, indicated that the only solution resided in the removal of garbage." But the trucks are sabotaged, and those drivers who are not on strike are afraid of "incidents."

MAY 30

Grey, cold. Horrible day. Waiting for de G. to speak. Phone call early in the morning: "*Mas où est Malraux?*" As if it would make any difference. The voice was desperate. Really snatching at straws. Claustrophobic. Go out, stand dumbly at greengrocer's (could have been anywhere). Piles of everything—luxury. Why do we keep imagining we are pinched? I am the only customer, and I don't want anything in particular. Wake up and say I am sick of eating strawberries without sugar, just for something to say. Greengrocer says "*Mais qu'à cela ne tienne!*" and sends a *commis* to the shop across the street, after telling him "Say you want two kilos of sugar for *me*." Kilo of sugar one franc sixty, nothing in it for him—just a favor. Greengrocer keeps a kilo for himself, after asking if I'm sure I don't want it. If I were to tell him a kilo lasts me about six months, I know he wouldn't believe me. Nice man—says he will cash a check if I want *du liquide*. But how funny about the sugar.

Telephones never work well in Paris—it is often easier to get London. Today they seem particularly dead. Occasionally, one has to dial a number four times. Either it doesn't ring or a recording comes on saying the number doesn't exist or one hears hundreds of ghost voices in a tunnel. Pity for de G. is what we seem to feel. I have always felt sorry for lions whose teeth had been pulled. Friend calls and says a Maoist we know has packed up his family and left Paris "*au petit matin!*" Where did he get the gas? Someone else explains why everyone is hoarding: It isn't a question of having food to eat so much as of having goods to exchange when the banks run out of money. Polish student here on a scholarship laughs and says this is small beer—we haven't seen anything. *Bon.*

Conversation with Mme. C. She tells me of the change in her sons. Only one of the three (the medical student) had been concerned in the student movement. Now the two others "are becoming Socialist." Even the future accountant? Especially the future accountant. Their father says, "*C'est facile avec l'argent de Papa.*" D. C. (the active one of the three, the med student) is "revolted" at the way the movement has become "political." Mme. C. looks about twenty.

Z. says to me, "The students are losing on all fronts." I agree.

We are quite literally waiting to see if there will be a civil war. De G. has vanished. There could not have been an accident with the helicopter—someone would know. Rumor that he has been to see his son-in-law with the Army in Mulhouse. Checking on what would happen if he quit? If he stayed? Rumor of troop movements and of tanks around Paris. Talk of a *gouvernement de transition*. Again, I think of 1958. This is a true *déjà vu*. I have the feeling that everything will be settled before the Whitsun weekend, one way or another. I want to know where everyone is. Where is G.? Where is H. T.?

Headache down the back of the neck. Can't read, can't work, can't swallow, can't listen to music. Phone rings. I hear, "Can't read, can't concentrate, can't eat," etc., and, "How cruel to make us wait!"

Noon. This hideous wait. The grey, the cold are all of a piece with the waiting. Have the French really used him up? Look up *The Golden Bough*, can't make sense of anything. No matter how horrible tomorrow may be, I wish the waiting were over and it were tomorrow.

Mme. L., *femme de ménage*, arrives carrying her portable radio. I say, "You can't possibly feel like working, so forget it." She says no, she feels better doing something; working seems normal. She and her husband admire de G., but they think for the sake of the country he should go. And then what? They don't know. That is what is frightening them. "Anyone but Mitterrand," she says. She calls him "*l'affreux Jo-Jo*," as if he were an ill-behaved little boy. Says that they don't want the Communists but that Waldeck Rochet "at least is honest" and "we know where we are." Anything, anything but a civil war. I tell her the word I have been hearing all day is "anguished." "What else can one feel?" she says. "The only word is '*angoissé*.'" I say, "But you all seem so calm. No one weeping in the streets." "*À quoi bon?*"

Phone rings. B. D. says rather calmly they are all going away for the weekend. In her *arrondissement* (the 16th), people are rallying around de G. The D.s, righter than right, have never forgiven him for Algeria, and have gone full circle and joined the revolution. Joined it? They are going to the country without waiting to see. Are they driving? How? Oh, easily: "My mother-in-law's private nurse lent us her professional card, and we were able to fill up at a tank reserved for the medical profession." One of those gas stations with a big red cross over it. Think of poor G. trying to get enough petrol to visit patients. This is said to me very calmly, as if it were normal.

Mme. L. and I sit at the kitchen table. We make strong coffee and turn *both* our radios on at once to Radio Luxembourg. At five minutes to four, we hear on two radios someone singing "I Like the Likes of You." Mme. L., who is always self-contained, little and round and very sweet-tempered, makes a gesture as if grasping someone by the shoulders and cries, "Oh, why don't they tell us something *now*?" We learn that banks in Italy and in Belgium are not buying francs. "My Blue Heaven." The ministers are out; we are given an interpretation of the way they look, what their expressions mean. Edgar Faure is supposed to have said, "I am optimistic by nature." We know now that de G. saw the Army, that there *are* tanks *around* Paris. It begins to seem like a carefully planned scenario: letting the country get out of hand, then leaving Paris, then disappearing, now the Resurrection. The press seems solidly in favor of his going; we can't imagine an alternative now. But what will happen then? I remind Mme. L. that tanks were actually in Paris in 1958 and in 1961, but she had forgotten. "I can't wait this way," she says, and begins to fiddle with a carpet sweeper. I think she should go home. "What I am afraid of," she says, "is *la dictature en plein.*" We seem to feel we shall never see each other again; we embrace. She is carrying her radio. I say, "Well, all we need now is the Comte de Paris." She says seriously, "If he became king, my husband would be a baronet. *Mais moi, je préfère la tranquillité à tous ces trucs-là.*" Radio gives "Restes-là, ne ten vas pas." Disc jockey with a sense of history? Between four and half past four, I trim all the primulas of their dead leaves, then take them off the windowsill, wash the windowsill, start to dust the bookshelves.

Ça y est. Firm, clear, angry, the old soldier, perhaps a little mad. Walk up and down. Sun on the carpet. The "Marseillaise."

Walked off to see the demonstration for de Gaulle on the Champs-Élysées. Lovely afternoon. Stopped in at Jacqueline's bookshop. Shop is in darkness. She and a group of friends—I recognize her mother—sit around a radio listening to the first commentaries on the declaration. They say nothing, stare at the radio. The streets seem normal. I begin to wonder if I dreamed the day. Rue de Sèvres filthy, the sort of scruffy, messy pavement you see in New York. Everything looks trashy, unloved. Power strike.

Traffic lights dead. Walk miles out of my way, just to walk. Down the Boulevard des Invalides, Rue de Grenelle, Boulevard de La Tour-Maubourg, along the Quai d'Orsay a short distance, the Pont Alexandre III. People, not a crowd, hurrying over the bridge. About every third person is listening to a radio. Tracts all over the pavements, in the gutters. The first thing I see is a fleet of tricolor flags moving toward the Arc de Triomphe. Slogans. The first I can understand, as I draw nearer, is *"La France aux français."* I have walked into an incident: I am between two students and a civilian with a tricolor card half out of his vest pocket who is with a paratrooper in combat uniform. I don't know what took place—what was taking place before I became aware. The para stands in the middle of the Champs-Élysées, knees bent, hands tense, and cries, "Let me at them! Give me four, five of them, so I can smash their faces!" He says this to the contingent of marchers just in front of me, who say "No, no," and calm him down, rather as one calms a child. They move on slowly—the whole incident is only a few seconds long. The civilian, a man of about thirty, curly fair hair, remains there, cries, *"Vous faites la loi à la Sorbonne, mais pas ici!"* I am exactly between them. I turn to the boys and say, "Don't answer— *ne vous laissez pas provoquer."* I needn't have said anything; they are perfectly calm. The taller boy says placidly, *"Je n'ai rien dit."* I would guess from the look of them, from their clothes and manner, that they might be law students. I then see that behind me there are two or three more, but they don't speak to one another, they don't exchange looks; they are evidently not sympathetic to what we are seeing, and are being extremely careful. Groups pour up the Champs-Élysées. These are people who aren't used to marching or to parading around in the streets. Their *service d'ordre* is improvised, and I have the feeling that until an hour beforehand they didn't know if they would be here at all. We are pushed back; I accidentally step on the feet of an elderly man, who punches me in the back, so that I am flung forward, against the line of *service d'ordre*. (He really hit out; it still hurts.) I have a feeling of panic, for the first time since the beginning of this month, in any crowd. No one has shoved or hit at *this kind* of demonstration. I am acutely unhappy at the slogans I am hearing: "*La France aux français,*" "*La police avec nous.*" I find this ugly. When I heard the students last week shouting "*Nous sommes tous des juifs allemands!*" I thought they were speaking to their parents. Today the parents answer: "*La France aux français.*" This is a much older crowd, better dressed. Yes, these are the parents. They sing the "Marseillaise," which would move a stone, but for the first time I feel a foreigner; I don't join in. I didn't sing the "Internationale" with the students. It is a song that is none of my business. But I liked those kids. They were generous, and they were very brave. And when they shouted a slogan they were always asking for some sort of justice, usually for someone else. What is generous about "*La police avec nous*"? When an *agent de police* crosses to the opposite pavement, he is almost hysterically cheered. I hear "*De Gaulle, nous sommes là,*" which I expect—that is what they have turned out to say. But by now I am feeling ungenerous, too, and I wonder why they didn't turn out and say this a week ago. Why did they wait until the tanks were around Paris, and Father had given them the all-clear? I see working-class people, students—not many, and the students near me nudge each other as they go by. At the cry "Liberate the Sorbonne!" one of the boys next to me says, under his breath, "I thought we had."

There is a much uglier cry, "*Vidangez la Sorbonne!*" (*vidanger* is to clean out a cesspool), but Suzanne B. heard the demonstrators on Red Friday crying "*Vidangez l'Élysée!*" so they are all one down for vulgarity. I am astonished at how often I hear Cohn-Bendit's name—at least as often as de Gaulle's. They send him to Peking, back to Germany. The mass of this demonstration is made up of *le petit peuple*. Not the girl who works in a factory but the waitress from the bistro, the girl who washes your hair. They are fed up with losing time, being tired, losing their pay, and they want to get back to work. "*Nous voulons travailler!*" "You see, they want to work," someone says. I can't help repeating "*They*," which gets a quick, amused look from the students. There is one sign I particularly like: "LES SILENCIEUX EN ONT MARRE"—"The Silent Ones Are Fed Up." I laugh, and when I look again the students have gone. Probably a coincidence?

Turning to leave, I bump into a man I know. I can't remember his name—I used to see him at his wife's aunt's parties. This aunt held soirées that I liked because there was something provincial about them. She would collect the people I can imagine at an evening in, say, Aix-en-Provence before the 1914 war; there would be the journalist, the distinguished Army officer, the painter, the man who owns all the vineyards, and so forth. All I can remember about this man is that he once showed me a poem of his and told me something about his personal life. I said, "*C'est du Mauriac*," and he was pleased, and said how true. We walk back over the bridge together. He isn't entirely delighted about the *défilé*—I'm not sure why, and I ask nothing whatever—but he is glad they turned out anyway. It was time. He says that he predicted this all along. That in 1962 he said, "*Si on ne fait pas du social*, there will be trouble." I love "*faire du social*"—it takes in housing, hospitals, schools, feeding people, child welfare, the lot. "*Du social.*" He admires the scenario: the uncertainty, the disappearance of the helicopter, the reappearance of the savior. "I have never liked him," he says. No name is given for "him." "*Mais ça force l'admiration.*" He knows (how?) that the helicopter was in Germany. I say I had heard Mulhouse. His wife is such a passionate Gaullist that not only has she not hoarded food but she has refused to buy anything at all. "*Ce n'est pas prudent.* We have four children." Suddenly remember his wife—she is an authentic and highly decorated *Résistante.* The real thing. Nice woman. He says, "You were once kind enough to read one of my poems." I say I remember "*le petit renard du matin*"—some such thing. "No, it was '*Je vois le renard qui s'enfuit à l'aube.*'" This is a conversation in a dream. We are walking up the Boulevard de La Tour-Maubourg. I say, "Do you think there will be a civil war?" "It is possible," he says politely. I then tell him what I have been telling others (and myself) for three days now: There is no such thing as a *coup d'état* without an army—your own or someone else's. Element of farce: I see three large Army vehicles and say, "Troop movements in Paris?" He says, always polite, "*C'est ça que vous appelez des mouvements de troupes?*" Look again, and see they are the improvised buses the Army is using to get people to work and back. In front of the Church of St. Francis Xavier, where we are to separate, he produces a sheaf of manuscript poems from a pocket and reads me one. It is called "Tu m'as nommée." (From the Bible, he says, explaining the title.) Cars are going by, and bicycles, and any number of people walking. He reads with expression. He reads, "*Un mur troué d'oiseaux* ... "*Ça, c'est joli,*" I say, shaking with tiredness; at least, I feel that I am trembling, and that everyone can see. He puts the poems away and says his wife will be giving a cocktail party. *Now?* Oh, no. When it is possible.

After the Champs-Élysées demonstration, the revolutionary posters along the Boulevard Montparnasse look used up—finished. Con, M., and I eat an enormous dinner, with floods of wine, in the Coupole. We have spells of *fou-rire* that remind me of the time Con, M. Black, and I were stuck in an elevator and were in such fits of laughter that I later realized we must have been frightened. Coupole lights go off at one-fifteen—earliest ever. From something Con says, I realize it was yesterday that de G. vanished (to see the generals), and not today. All run together in my mind. Tell Con I am more afraid of trouble now than before de G.'s speech. He quiet and sensible, as always. Earlier in evening, saw new moon, had vague wish that everything would end well. What a horrible day.

MAY 31

Talk to F. and M. B., tell them I feel rotten, like a minority, and hate it. F. says "You are not a minority; many
of us feel the same way." No *explosion de joie*, as papers
suddenly have it—just depressed feeling, as after an illness.
Uneasy atmosphere; a lot of horse trading going on. F. was
revolted by Champs-Élysées late at night, the expensive
cars trailing large flags whipping round and round the
Étoile honking "*Al-gé-rie fran-çaise*" while police smiled
paternally. He calls them "the *blousons noirs* of the Right
Bank." Both B.s shocked at the weekend exodus already
beginning.

Z. and I, early in the morning, talk about Maupassant
story about the old grandmother who wakes up on her
deathbed, sees that the inheritors have already moved her
favorite clock, comes back to life, and changes her will
(something like that). Tell Z. what I saw yesterday. She
says sadly, "One can't always choose one's allies."

Agnès: From a long line of generals and aristos. Used
to see her wearing her father's combat-leopard-Algerian
things, miles too large. Country neighbors of the D.s.
Never liked them—all the spontaneity trained out. If they
were horses, I wouldn't back them. She turned up at the
Société de Géographie the other day with a commando
of débutantes; slim, long hair. Gave the impression of
slumming on the Left Bank—I made some sharp remark,
which she didn't answer. Too thoroughly trained. Nothing to do with manners—they aren't really polite. Remembered her this morning with some remorse, rang up,

said that, like everyone, I was slightly on edge these days, that I had no right to take it out on someone else. Like talking to a china teacup. Said something sharp all over again—something like "If you don't know how to accept an apology, you will never be a person." End of china teacup. Had extraordinary conversation. Her voice came alive. Told me she was not as silly as I seemed to think, had been in the movement from the beginning, along with her sister. Told me how "the police watch, single out, certain students, then, when they charge, four or five police will attack that one person." Said that she had never thrown anything—"*J'ai beaucoup trop peur*"—but had seen enough, and that the next time there were barricades she would join them. This romantic, but when she said she had been to Charléty it sounded serious. Did not say "my parents" (whose image danced before my eyes as I listened to her) but "my entourage": "You can imagine the difficulty with my entourage. And my brother is a Fascist with Occident." Yes, I can imagine. She talked non-stop several minutes before becoming a china teacup again. That awful training. Such a crime with a bright mind—tight-minded parents, snob schools. Like packing up a parachute. Was astonished at how much she understood about the union negotiations. The daughters of the general. *Où allons-nous?*

In the Faculté de Médecine: pictures of students taken during debates, posted up, which they can buy. Something to show the children. "You see, Papa *was* a revolutionary!"

Suzanne B. hates the students, I think. She says that, after all, they are the sons of the men who behaved so badly in 1940. I think (but don't say) that if the police had fought the Germans as they now fight these children, there might not have been a 1940.

Suzanne's aged father thinks de G. was acting from the beginning—pretending to be the worn-out old man and then pretending he might step down, and now being the firm old soldier. S. says, "*Il en est bien capable.*" But I think the family will vote for him anyway. I remember that in the last election but one they voted Communist, in opposition to de G.! But now it has been too close for games.

All I can think of is the phrase of de Gaulle's, the famous phrase "*Les français sont des veaux.*" I am absolutely certain he is saying it to himself this minute, and knows exactly who his allies are. Change in speakers on radio stupefying. All sniffing the air and wheeling round. Noon news exactly as if yesterday had never happened; as if no one had been worried; as if everyone had known all along it was only a game. The month of May wiped out of time. Enraged to think I ever felt pity for de G. Furious at having been taken in. What an actor! Call up Jacqueline and ask her if the French are serious people, to be taken seriously. She says she supposes they are as serious as anyone else. I say, "*Les français sont des veaux.*" Jacqueline brings a total stranger to the telephone. Stranger says, reasonably, French no worse than anyone else. Poor Jacqueline—am so awful to her (why her, of all people?) that I go around to see her later in the day. Jacqueline laughs, says only, "*J'aime la spontanéité*"—a lot nicer than anything I'd have said in her place.

Everyone going to the country. Police using tear-gas grenades to rout strike pickets—not a ripple of protest.

This in less than twenty-four hours. J. de T. says I was too optimistic all along. E. simply says, "I hate them all," which gets us nowhere—she hated the whole movement from the beginning. Says disturbance disturbs her and makes her feel lonely. Blond *antiquaire* on the Rue du Cherche-Midi says anti-Semitic inscriptions appeared on walls in the Sixteenth Arrondissement (where she lives), as if by magic, during the night. She is both anti-Communist and anti-de G., and sounds fed up and bitter.

At noon, the Sorbonne is empty. Not a soul in the large amphitheatre where the "permanent discussion" has been taking place. A few men talk to students out on the pavement, tell them it is time to get back to work. About two hundred people in the Odéon talking about the coming elections. The grassy square on the Rue des Écoles, opposite the Sorbonne, is a pigsty. They have burned the little kiosk. Students lie all over the grass—why shouldn't they? It is a bright, sunny day. Reminds me of London. But as I draw near I see that the square is full of bread crusts, empty Camembert boxes, greasy papers, bits of cold sausage—that the fountain looks like a cold-water tap in a slum courtyard. Students lying in and on garbage. Mother and little girl enter the square. Mother looks bewildered—no place for a child. By evening, a fire has broken out under the roof of the Sorbonne. Hoses, ladders, trucks, water on the pavements. Kids walk over hoses in the wet. I then walk to the Odéon again, where there are long queues, and outside the Odéon see posters saying that evidence of police brutality is being taken by the students' union. Seems years ago. Waiting lines outside cinemas. Restaurants nearly filled. Red and black flags still up outside the Sorbonne. Seems like an old movie set.

Suddenly plenty of gas for cars. Where did it come from? Man I know who owns garages, and who had put up signs saying "PANNE SÈCHE" on the pumps, meaning they'd run out, has to get rid of the evidence in a hurry. The *camions-citernes* are going to be round any minute, and the gas-oil people might be rather astonished to see that a few thousand litres are still in his reservoirs. By magic, sugar appears in every shop in my neighborhood. No sudden deliveries—it was in the back of the store all along. A sudden buying mania, but not of food. Dress shop on the Rue de Rennes suddenly in business. Normal instinct after having been frightened, but does it mean everyone had *du liquide* all along? I see rather a lot of it.

The papers don't describe the rally I saw. No one speaks of "*La police avec nous,*" which I hated. Begin to think I no longer see clearly, until phone call from G., who saw exactly what I saw and whose reaction was like mine. G.'s father used to read *Mein Kampf* in French to his children during the Occupation. G. gives me a rapid roundup of collaborator family connections now chanting "*De Gaulle n'est pas seul.*" Am astonished to hear from the wife of a foreign diplomat that her reaction was like G.'s and like mine. Can't tell anyone in her circle, or even her husband, "because we don't agree on the father image." I discover today that my most anti-Gaullist friends (though not the D.s) also turned out. But also Philippe and his brother, and Mija's elder son. Just people who like law and order. I say to Suzanne B., "But the Communist bogey is nonsense." She says, "It doesn't matter. De G. had to bring it up. There was no other way."

Suzanne B. opposed in every possible way to student movement: the disorder, the violence, the mud stirred up from the very bottom. I tell her that the core of it is *pur*, that they are bewildered at how political parties have taken over, and disgusted that it turned into an interminable wrangle about wages and hours. That they were innocent enough to want a change without realizing what "change" means or the forms it takes. That this sordid *cuisine* is not what they fought for. Suzanne says bitterly, "Do you think that those who died in the Resistance died for the life we have had since 1944?"

Until about two in the morning, kids in open sports cars rush all over the city sounding the old notes of "*Al-gé-rie fran-çaise*." Paradox that this should be in support of de Gaulle. Tonight, the enormous tricolor is hung from the top of the Arc de Triomphe—flag usually kept for July 14th and important state occasions. Wind picks it up, sweeps it under the arch. Red-white-blue colored searchlights up to the top of the sky. Suzanne B. for de Gaulle but disapproving of this—"Who has ordered this?" Answers herself: "*Le gouvernement.*" City split in two more than ever by the river. Gaullists on Champs-Élysées, students in Latin Quarter.

Telephone conversation late at night: "*Mavis, qu'est-ce que nous avions voulu, exactement?*" What people will be asking themselves for a long time. Something marvellous such as never has taken place? A change that had nothing to do with politics? A revolution with nothing broken and no one hurt? Tone of conversations is relief, bewilderment, disappointment, fatigue. It is like the feeling after a miscarriage—instant thanksgiving that the pain has ceased, plus the feeling of zero because it was all for nothing. Jacques says *"J'ai l'impression que nous sommes passés à côté de quelque chose."* But what? When Z. and I talk on the telephone, we sound about sixteen. As we talk, young Barbara and her friends have put the whole thing behind them, are in another room talking about the Whitsun weekend. They are leaving for the country. There are still pickets outside the Lycée Saint-Louis, expecting to be attacked. Z. says, "They almost want it."

I discover that I know people who were in the demonstration May 13th *and* in the one yesterday on the Champs-Élysées. Demonstrated *against* the police and then *for* de G. But if they then shouted *"La police avec nous,"* what does it mean? Girl who only a few days ago spent an hour telling me about police atrocities now hostile, cold. Change in the wind, or in her? G. says I am seeing the war, the Resistance, the collaboration all in one and all at once.

JUNE 1

G.'s friend says, "We don't hear much about Roche now." I say, "Who is Roche?" Roche was the rector of the Sorbonne, the man who brought the police into the university and started the Month of May. I had forgotten even his name.

"LE MOUVEMENT DE CONTESTATION SE POURSUIT DANS LE FOOTBALL." So that still isn't over. "LES

MONUMENTS HISTORIQUES REJOIGNENT LE MOU-
VEMENT." They have come out on strike *today*.

Talk to Con, tell him about question I was asked very
late at night: "*Qu'est-ce que nous avions voulu?*" Ask him
what he thought they did want, ultimately. He says, "People wanted a change, we thought. Now I'm not so sure. We
thought they wanted more than a face-lift, which is what
they're getting now. This is the opinion of someone fairly
antique, you know, but I think people want a little peace.
We'd like to imagine young people were happy enough
not to kick up a fuss." This depresses me more than ever.
Find a partial answer to the question in today's *Combat*:
People were offered "a marvellous abstraction," and who
can blame them for turning it down?

I read, "ESSENCE CONTRE REVOLUTION," meaning
they opened the gas pumps and drowned the revolution.
Unreality of it: More and more accounts of police going
in to break strikes. Strikers dragged out. No one protests.
Nothing normal about the city yet, except for Magic Petrol and Magic Sugar. Nothing working. During the troubles, saw fewer blacks and North Africans—were keeping
very quiet. Now they emerge, still quiet, sweeping the
streets. Nothing changed.

Hot, sunny day. Wonder if de G. has a direct connection with the Almighty after all—we've had good weather
ever since he made his deal with the Army. I'd love to
know what he promised in exchange. At seven o'clock this
morning, a madwoman made a political speech out on
the street. Clear voice; she was sober. All the phrases we
have been hearing since the beginning of May, all jumbled,

in no particular context: "*la situation actuelle . . . le pouvoir . . . l'ordre établi . . . l'ennemi commun . . . certains secteurs de l'économie . . .*" Wrote down about ten before I gave up.

Someone on the radio finally mentioned "*Les français sont des veaux.*" Heard this morning, "In spite of the present difficulties, the Diners Club continues to make life easier. . . . Government radio still playing nothing but Stockbrokers' Bounce on all three FM stations. Tiddledypom on France-Culture. Tricolors all over the place, red flags still on the Odéon, the Sorbonne, the factories.

Mme. Mercier, a neighbor and friend, returns from the country, where she watched *la révolution* on TV. Someone in a country shop told her, "I am on strike for two hours today," but apart from that there was no sign of trouble. Only two hours from Paris. I expect her to be hostile to the whole business; instead, I find her merely anxious to be informed. I tell her everything I can think of, except what I saw at the de Gaulle rally on Thursday. Virtually everyone she and I know in common was in it—which is to say, her daughter, grandson, son-in-law, and so on. I would never have thought of them as Gaullists. It seems to be hatred of chaos and desire for order. Mme. M., small, blond, fragile, has always reminded me of the way Frenchwomen looked in films twenty years ago. She astonishes me by saying it would be a good thing for the country if de G. were to die now. She lowers her voice, although we are alone in her living room. It is exactly like someone's saying, "Poor grandfather, we love him dearly, but, really, everyone would remember him so fondly if only he were to go now."

Early this morning, as I was talking with the laundress on the Rue Littré—she standing in her doorway—a frail, lame woman came up to us, seemed confused, rushed, said she had been called out to vote at the Monoprix. "Those of us who want to go back to work must vote," she said. "They called me this morning and said I had to come." Laundress says woman had been on sick leave. Later, I had a glimpse of the police pulling the pickets out. The pickets were addressing a totally indifferent crowd of people. I don't know what the result of the vote was—I suppose a majority wanted to get back to work, because their money was running out and there is no strike pay in France. What I can't forget is their incredibly low wage—it was posted on the glass doors during the strike. I didn't stay to watch. I couldn't understand the crowd of bystanders. Why watch people being pulled about? Wish that, like Z., I could curse in four languages.

More about-face: Ask the revolutionary news vender if he has *Combat*. Looks me straight in the face and says, "No, but I have *Minute*." Like saying, "No, but I have the *John Birch Bugle*." Suzanne B. says the atmosphere very like that of the Liberation: the daily rumors, the trucks taking one to work, the strikes, the sudden political switches, and now the flags on the Champs-Élysées. (Says that even at the Liberation there weren't as many flags and people as there were on Thursday.) *France-Soir* has a page-two streamer: "PARIS REMOVES ITS MASK OF FEAR." I don't think they used the word "fear" until today. Anyway, we weren't told anything about a mask of fear. Anxiety, yes. The author of the piece that follows was so pro-movement until today that I asked someone once if he really was a reporter—I thought he might have been a student.

G. to lunch. Hot day—blinds half closed. I translate out of *The Golden Bough* bits about the Priest-King-Magician. G. keeps saying, "But what is left, out of all this? We've been given elections to amuse ourselves with, like a piece of sugar." "What was it you wanted?" "The same as the students. Something different, something clean. Think of the *treize mai*." "They were already quarrelling by the time the cortege broke up." "It doesn't matter," says G. "The extraordinary thing was that it happened at all." We feel deflated, flat.

To the general assembly at the Sorbonne with G. Restructuring of university teaching—specifically, the *sciences de l'homme*: sociology, psychology, psychiatry, psychosociology (what's that?), psychoanalysis, linguistics, ethnology, economy, psychotheraphy, pedagogy, etc. Attempt to regroup in a Université Critique des Sciences de l'Homme. Are given two tracts at entrance to the grand amphitheatre. Read, "*Motifs politiques: dénoncer la participation des sciences humaines à l'oppression adaptatrice—orthopédique—exercée par le capitalisme monopoliste. Motifs épistémologiques: mettre en cause les sciences humaines en tant que sciences 'sous-développées' voire pseudo-sciences dissimulées derrière leur appareil mathématique.*" Am beginning to know the language by heart. Read in second tract, "... *refuse ... conteste ... dénonce ... constate ... affirme.*" Read on: "*Tout étudiant doit être aussi praticien; tout praticien doit être aussi étudiant; tout enseignant et tout chercheur doivent être aussi praticiens.*" Imagine that, reduced to simple language, what they want is fewer barriers between the faculties, groundwork of general knowledge for all, and a sort of interdependence among teachers, students, and professional people. About three thousand present, someone says. Is it possible? No good at judging crowds, and don't know what the amphitheatre holds. Anyway, it is packed. Though I hadn't said so to G., I'd expected to find no one. Pentecost Saturday, cars rushing out of Paris—I thought the students would have given up, too. Blazing heat under the skylight. My hair is soaking wet. Member of each study group (sociology, psychology, linguistics, etc.) reporting back to general assembly. Suggestions for reform. G. whispers each name to me. Some students, some top men in field (*dixit* G.). Psychiatrist from Sainte-Anne's says we all need a stone in one hand and a pen in the other. *Bon*. Mikes not working; I hear about one word in three. Heat all but intolerable. Girl next to me writes, "*Sorbonne: pensée capitalisée*," sees me looking and turns page over. Pale kid, a bit severe. I hear "... opinion, not method ... " Second speaker: "Is philosophy autonomous? Take it away from literature, put it in with *sciences humaines*." Much applauded. Session interrupted: A student representing the *service d'ordre* wants the balconies cleared. It is a safety measure; the balconies have been overworked, people on them night and day, they aren't safe. Ask G. what balconies are for. Am told the *grand amphi* not used all that much. Students in balconies refuse to leave. *Salle* begins to shout, "*Dégagez! Dégagez!*" Third speaker, *sciences économiques*. Someone roars, "*Louder!*" A minute later, same voice roars, "*We're bored!*" Speaker squeaks, ... re-

move competition . . ." All I can hear. Fourth is an ethnologist. Can't hear him at all. Wears an orange shirt. *Service
d'ordre* interrupts again: "I'm sorry, but this assembly cannot continue unless the balconies are cleared." Hard core
of students refuses to leave, on pretext that there is nowhere to sit. We promise to make room, and slide along
on the benches. Fifth speaker says he doesn't understand
the debate. Says, "Marx and Freud—personality cult . . ."
Students still on balconies. Boy from *service d'ordre* says
debate can't go on until they leave: "Last night we had a
fire; we don't want anything else to happen." Only three
students still on balconies. One holds a tall red rose.
Stands up and waves his arms. Finally, all three leave. Sixth
man says that no one knows who wrote one of the tracts
we were given and that "the Liaison Committee wishes to
disengage itself from its text." Next comes elderly party—
distinguished professor, G. says. Is booed. G. says professors haven't a chance, can't open their mouths. Students
climbing back over balcony railings. Professor tries to
make himself heard. Meeting again stopped until balconies cleared. Ask G., "Are balconies dangerous? " G. says
yes. Impossible to understand what professor is saying, or
attitude of kids. Exhibitionist? No, says G. Selfish. During
eighth speech (can't hear), a note is passed urging our at-
tendance at a demonstration at the Gare Montparnasse at
four o'clock. Ninth speaker is famous psychologist. Sound
so bad that I can't tell if he is saying Freud would have
formulated theory of hysteria if he *had* or *hadn't* known
about serial progression in mathematics. Anyway, he gets
a hand, so someone heard. All men so far. One girl gets up.

Slight stir around me—girls don't like other girls to speak. Professor again—is booed before he opens his mouth. Tell G. I didn't know students so exhibitionist. G. makes sound something like "*Oo-là*," which means "You don't know the half of it." Three students climb up. Four. Creep into top balconies. Time presses. I think that they are the sons and daughters of the women who bought all the sugar and of the men who have been coming to blows over gasoline. G. revolted by students in balconies. *Service d'ordre* gives up the battle. Meeting boring, fussing over points. Same student keeps roaring either "*Can't hear!*" or "*We're bored!*" G. asks if I need *du liquide*. Wonder if it's last time I'll hear the word. Speaker suggests system of "*tronc commun*"— literally, common tree trunk, meaning same basic studies for a few years, followed by specialization (tree branches). Tell G. this is the American system—B.A. or B.S., followed by specialization. G. surprised. Wonder what they think American universities are like. Whisper to G., "What if I got up and explained American system?" Such a preposterous idea that G. laughs. Balconies fill more and more. Remember discussion over teaching of Chinese, and how system of major and minor subjects was described to students as the sytem in use at the university in Peking. Professor with lisp gets up and wishes to define "*la personne humaine*" as distinguished from animals. Booed. This is exactly what they want to get away from—this fiddling. Cries of "Sit down!" and "*À la Sorbonne!*" Poor man. Goes on talking. Now they applaud. He still goes on talking. Chairman says something impertinent, and the man sits down. Chairman gets a laugh. Frightening cru-

elty of the young. The young? There are professors in the
audience, too, and some grey heads up on the balconies.
When is a safety measure not a safety measure? Don't admire this. It seems merely stupid. Professor gets up to defend his humiliated friend. Uses word "epistemology" and
is booed. Professor impatient, says it's a term they ought
to know. Cries of "There aren't only students here"—
meaning there are working-class boys, too. Don't see any,
and neither does G. Professor replies, "*Tant pis.*" Gives
dictionary definition of "epistemology." He then makes
the mistake of saying "politico-philosophical," on which
booing and catcalling start all over. Whistles. Doctor gets
up, suggests medical studies should include some groundwork in psychology and sociology. G. applauds this. I say,
"But it seems so evident." G. replies, "Not in France." We
file out early, because of the demonstration at four o'clock.
Hear students saying they may not go. Badly organized.
No one knows what it is for. On wall, see sign mentioning
meeting in Amphithéâtre Cavaillès. Wonder if I was mis-
informed about its having been *rebaptisé*. In courtyard,
voice booms over loudspeaker: "*Camarades!* We need a car
for four days, to fetch provisions from the North of
France." No mistake about this; the message is repeated.
What kind of provisions? Paris is full of food. There is no
shortage of anything whatever except cigarettes. There has
been plenty of gasoline since Friday morning—the day
after de G.'s statement. Provisions of what? Why "four
days"? Long file of people squeeze out through little, narrow door from courtyard to street. G. and I find ourselves
marching out immediately behind red banner (probably

on its way to demonstration). Try to imagine faces of G.'s family or our rightish friends if they were to see us. Cortege forms. We hear "*Le fascisme passera pas.*" On Thursday, I heard "*Le communisme passera pas.*" Like grade-school science experiment—the positive and negative poles and the iron filings.

Today, heard for the first time "*La Guerre Civile Froide.*" The Cold Civil War.

As we were leaving the Sorbonne, G. suddenly said, "Can you imagine *des ouvriers* in there? Because I can't." Utterly taken aback. Thought: That's the aristocrat speaking. But said nothing, because G.'s patients all working class, and even sub. Thanked God, not for the first time, that, owing to North American upbringing, that sort of question would never enter my head. G. goes on to explain how patients were irritated by student interest in their affairs, and now blame them because they can't get their favorite paper, which happens to be *France-Soir*.

To Montparnasse with G. and friend of G.'s, to watch student demonstration. G.'s friend tall young man. A *psycho-sociologue*. Second time I've heard that today. What can it mean? Wonder if this will be the last *manifestation*. An untidy, loose crowd. Hot, dusty afternoon. The red flags look tatty. Bystanders look indignant, outraged—an expression acquired only since half past four last Thursday afternoon. The three of us have the same reaction—that their slogans seem pitiful and lost, and that the "Internationale" sounds merely defiant, doesn't scare the neighbors now. They all look to me like Old Soldiers. They demand a popular government *without* Mendès France (*Tiens!*) and

they chant, "*Le pouvoir aux travailleurs!*" Again this unrequited love. The workers aren't even there to hear them.
Either they're still shut up in their factories or they've
gone away for the long weekend. Demonstrators seemed
to us huddled, unhappy, there in front of Montparnasse
Station, which, half demolished, looks like a ruin in Berlin.
Black flag doesn't seem symbol of death to me but symbol
of absolute despair, which was lacking in this revolution.
The absolute: "*Du travail ou la mort.*" Would like to speak
of Louise Michel and her black petticoat on a broom-
stick, but tall young man's flag all red. Flags should be
either black or white—all the way. G.'s friend says a number of professors haven't turned up, because this is "badly
organized"—no one knows if it is a march or a meeting,
or what. Boulevard du Montparnasse lined with *badauds*,
and all the cafés are open and filled—usually they close
up tight. Nothing to fear now? Not a cop in sight. March
is followed by radio cars belonging to Luxembourg and
Europe I. Reporter inside Europe's car is target of insults—"*Menteur, fumier!*"—because of station's change of
heart all of a sudden. Not the reporter's fault. He sits looking straight ahead. Woman jeers at reporters: "I suppose
you will say it was a small group of about five hundred now!"
Looking back, see whirlwind of white tracts rising from the
now deserted space in front of the station—like seagulls.
Someone selling the horrible *Evening Standard* stands on
the curb. I translate for the others; headlines say de G. gets
loyalty oath from generals, tanks around Paris. The two
laugh. G. wonders, as I do, what de G. had to promise in
exchange. Speculate on conversation between de G. and his

arch-enemy Massu. Transistors say, "About ten to fifteen thousand." We think figure exaggerated, but then we are at the tail end. At home, we learn from radio that demonstrators were led by Cohn-Bendit. G. and friend both think that C.-B. should shut up—that the fears of the Jews are justified, and he has awakened anti-Semitism, which was "*jamais mort!*" Tall friend bitter about the elections. Conversation entirely "What is left? What remains? What was it about?" I feel, in some obsure way, I have been taken in—by the students, by de Gaulle, by the French. Before they go, we listen to the news—exclusively about "*la reprise.*" *Tone* of announcers completely changed. After they've left, I open a paper and read, "LA MORT D'UNE RÉVOLUTION."

H. T. saw the demonstration from someone's apartment over the Bretagne cinema. He says there were easily forty-five thousand people—he could see all the way up the boulevard, and made some sort of numbers-rate-and-distance calculation. Says dryly, "But if I had seen you, I'd have subtracted one."

Why is it that when de G. speaks I always feel like a foreigner? If I had ordinarily felt like a foreigner in France, I would not have stayed here more than a weekend. But whenever he manifests himself, something about the way he thinks, the things he says, and the reactions he arouses in people—even in friends—always leaves me thinking: Thank God I am not a refugee; I can pack up and leave whenever I like.

Can't look at the papers. Feel nausea. This must have been how it was here during and after the war. Only *Combat* and *Le Monde* are consistent.

H. T. astonishes me by remarking, "Elections? There might not be elections." Says that we are down to the hard core now, that anything could still happen. If it were anyone else, I wouldn't listen. Most moderate person I know. Keeps saying, "*Ce n'est pas fini.*"

At 1:30 A.M., heard persistent fire siren nearby, so went out. Fire truck, noisy, parked in front of hotel on the Rue Blaise-Desgoffe. Hotel where K. Mansfield lived when she was having that useless treatment, irradiation of the spleen. Small delivery truck, not much larger than a station wagon, burning outside the Monoprix. Man in dressing gown; a few neighbors, dressed. Man says to me, "*Ils ont foutu le feu.*" Woman says, "*La police a évacué les piquets de grève, de force. Ce sont les conséquences.*" Acutely miserable. Messy, smoldering (rubber-smelling) little truck winds up the month of May. Come in, turn on radio to B.B.C. 2 A.M. news, hear that Helen Keller has died and "The world's walking record has been broken by a man named John Sinclair. He walked a hundred and seventy-six times around an aerodrome." Don't even try to sleep. Try to answer "*Qu'est-ce que nous avions voulu?*" Feel great pity for person who had to ask it. No single answer. *Combat*'s "marvellous abstraction"—all the good without the bad? A change in people? It seemed possible. It was like a wave. So unreal. Keep seeing the crowd down the Boulevard Saint-Michel May 13th. I thought that I was seeing the wave—that they all wanted a life without prisons. Crystalline moment—I'm lucky to have had it once. *Propre et pur*, as people kept saying. All those young faces. I suppose for the young it had to do with that perfect lucidity I remember at seventeen, seeing (as you never do later) exactly what people are like and deciding to have no part of it. But all it came to finally was strikes, wages, and now elections—the favorite French game. "He knew what he was doing," said G.'s tall friend. Hopeless, impossible to describe what took place. Will be classed as "collective folly," "contagious hysteria." Can already imagine all the books and articles I shall most certainly not read. What they wanted at the beginning, at the Sorbonne, was pure delirium, and all sorts of cynical people are already delighted it could not have happened.

Realize that all our phoning meant we were secretly afraid. I wonder how many of my friends walked all over Paris, as I did, or went out in the street in the middle of the night expecting to see I don't know what—people from Mars? All night tonight, heard motor horns. Those open sports cars, as in 1958. They must be leaning on the horn as they rush round and round the city.

Compagnies Républicaines de Sécurité. Gardes (or Gendarmes) Mobiles. Gardiens de la Paix de la Cinquième République. Even I learned to tell them apart.

JUNE 2 —PENTECOST SUNDAY

No one speaks of students now. They are forgotten, except as pests. Talk is of salaries, elections. Day before yesterday a hundred years ago. News is of death on the roads. Sunny day. Flower man outside the Rotonde says revolution was bad for business. Hasn't sold a flower in two weeks, and "they don't keep." His wife is seventy-two, he only sixty-five. No way of knowing if strikes are still on.

On Champs-Élysées, they have finally stopped the unseemly flag-and-tricolor-searchlights display around the Arc de Triomphe, usually reserved for July 14th. Drug-Store des Champs-Élysées seems gross and over-stuffed—seems to have been put there to show what the revolution would have taken away. Kids hanging around are the Right Bank equivalent of the useless hippies. They were in hiding; now they emerge. The Latin Quarter is like a cadaver now; it depresses one. Nonetheless, the lit-tle grubbies holed up in the Sorbonne are infinitely more sympathetic than the languid Right Bank young. At night, the Latin Quarter stuffed with cars and sightseers—a Dis-neyland. Cars creep along slowly; Right Bank faces peep out. Boys and girls sit on the curbs, on the ledges of shop windows. H. T., who from the beginning has believed one of the roots of the revolution was boredom, says, "*Voilà, ils s'emmerdent à nouveau.*" Beautiful weather. Everyone who could leave has gone. All the men I know who are still in Paris are restless and depressed. Nothing settled about transport or work yet.

Everyone keeps asking, "What is left?"

Chez moi.

Tracts: "*Il n'est pas question d'effectuer aujourd'hui une révolution bergsonienne, mais . . .*" Must have been enthrall-ing for the workers at Renault.

Eiffel Tower of newspapers. More important than sugar. So hard to find some days that I couldn't throw them away. Except for *Le Monde* and *Combat*, they have done an about-face, burying de G. only to resurrect him and hope he wouldn't notice he'd been underground. Did they think he couldn't read? From "LA RÉVOLUTION" to "LA FIN D'UNE RÉVOLUTION" without a hair out of place.

Cigarettes of all kinds. Began giving them away yesterday.

Flashlight for power strike.

Address of blood donors, etc.

Motto and moral I lettered and stuck on the wall the night of May 31st: "QUAND LA MORALE TRIOMPHE, IL SE PASSE DES CHOSES TRÈS VILAINES (REMY DE GOURMONT)." Found it in 1958 journal. Still applies. More than ever. I wonder if I shall remember what it is about and why it is there when I see it again in the autumn. Shall leave the whole thing to the moths as soon as trains run again.

Conversation with H. T. Repeat question I was asked late Friday night: "What was it we wanted? "

Like Con, he takes it to mean what is wanted by everyone.

"Peace, work."

"Did you want a revolution? "

"No."

"Did you think there would be one? "

"No."

"Did you approve of the police going into the Sorbonne?"

"No."

"Then what?"

"*Rien. C'est sans issue*. It is like going into a shop and asking for fruit and being told there are only two kinds of vegetables, no fruit at all. In the end, you say, '*Tant pis, je prendrai des carottes.*'"

"And if you burn down the shop there isn't anything. *Bon.* How did you manage to seem so calm?"

"Because I was. *Jusqu'à présent ce n'est que du cinéma.* No shots were fired."

"Well, it's finished."

He isn't so sure.

"How will de Gaulle come out of it?"

"Taller than ever," says H. T. "One, *il ne s'est pas dérangé.* He went to Rumania as planned. Took twenty-four hours off to think, but that's hardly *dérangement.* Two, he didn't fire a single shot. Three, he gave two talks, one lasting seven minutes, one lasting five minutes. Nothing more. He has shown that it's all the same if everyone around him is saying yes-yes-yes or no-no-no. *Qui est le plus grand?*"

JUNE 3

Sunny. Lunch at Rougeot, on terrace. Heard Pompidou's press conference. Speaks of defending the Republic against Communist groups "ready to strike" and financed from the outside. Seems to be addressing a public of concierges. Strikers still striking. H. T. right—this is the hard core.

Mija is the only person I know who spoke out against the revolution before de Gaulle. No wonder the students thought they had the whole world on their side! Everyone was either a revolutionary or silent. Mija said, "We will be perfectly willing to go out in the streets and fight for what we have, if we have to." Said "what we have," not "what we are," but this wouldn't be a *lapsus* coming from her. Tough, honest, outspoken girl.

JUNE 4

Fetch car. No trains, and even when trains start no chance that my train for south (special car-person train) will be *reconstitué*. Everyone will be against my going by car, so I decide to say nothing and do as I like when the time comes. Find car oiled and greased and *vidangé* and with full gas tank, as I left it. (Everyone said I'd find the tank empty.) Congratulate garage owner. He looks nonchalant.

Still no trains, no Métro, no mail, no planes, no schools. Not a cigarette of any kind in my *quartier*. Look over stocks I collected for smoker friends, in case, and see that I was a complete ass—didn't get the only kind I can smoke. Start distribution of cigarettes to frantic friends, promise to keep some for Z. For self, buy small box of mints named Mental (*sic*). "Mental will keep you sane." Gloomy day. Everyone depressed.

This was the day "real life" was supposed to begin. But still no schools, no trains, no transport, no planes, no mail, and now no cigarettes.

A sad thing happened today. I saw the wife of the *marchand de couleurs* standing on the Rue de Vaugirard. She is red-haired, minute, comes about up to my shoulder. Horrible childhood in religious orphanage—probably wasn't fed. She said, "I want to go to the *charcutier* on the Rue Littré, but I'm afraid of those people on the corner." I looked and saw students from the School of Photog-

raphy and Cinematography, just across the street. They
were probably standing around waiting to go in to some
sort of meeting. It was so extraordinary—I see them every
day. Doesn't she? What was sad was the matter of vision:
Where my mind would have registered something like
"Students, intellectuals, readers of *Combat* and *Le Monde*,"
her mind said to her, "Dangerous, brutal, will hurt you." I
took her by the arm and we walked into the group, which,
of course, took no notice of us. She was trembling. She
kept saying, "Are you sure? Will it be safe?" She said, "You
see, it is the red flag. It frightens me and it nauseates me."
There is a red flag over the entrance to the building. (These
flags, even on official buildings, have never seemed to me
more than a kind of folklore.) I told her (thinking to reassure her) that I had been to the School of Photography
for a meeting. It frightened her more than ever. "Did they
let you in? What did they say?" Funny thing is that she
is a brave little person, with a passionate sense of justice.
She says that she dreams about "the events"—that she is
with the Minister of Social Affairs or the Minister of the
Interior, and that they go on and on talking about the
situation, and that *in her dream* it keeps her from sleeping:
"I wake up as if I hadn't slept at all." "Do you tell the Ministers what you think?" "Oh, no. *Je suis beaucoup trop petite.*"

Where are the traffic police? Today's traffic jam is the
worst I have ever seen in any city at any time; it even beats
that day in the spring of 1961 (I think it was) when there
was a power strike, a storm of rain, and a state visit from
the King of Morocco—one could walk across the parvis of
Notre Dame on the hoods of cars, they were so close to-

gether. Today's is the logical end of motor production—a snake biting its tail. Police are busy elsewhere, protecting the Eiffel Tower and government buildings (I discovered only today that the Eiffel Tower is on strike), and are also supposed to be staging an unofficial slow strike of their own. People seem to have forgotten 1958, when the police paraded before the Palais Bourbon in defiance of the government.

For every person who has said to me "What is this going to cost us?" two have said "What trace will it leave on the mind and spirit?" and *"Rien ne sera comme avant,* no matter how it comes out." Man in bank—always, in my mind, "the tall one"—says very quietly, "Our children and our children's children will judge this. *Ils se poseront des questions.* About everything." He is, like me, optimistic. *Bouleversante* conversation with woman in travel agency, Rue de Rennes, where I cancel my *auto-couchette* reservation for last Friday. She begins by asking what I think. We both pussyfoot around the subject, and she then says, "Don't you think that *le social* followed upon something perhaps more lasting and important?" Answer, "Yes, of course." She becomes excited, says that she, for one, will never be the same again—that she will never accept anything again at its face value, that "no one can stop her now" from asking herself questions. She pulls out from under the counter two morning papers, *Le Figaro* and *Combat,* and cries what may be the justification, finally, for the massacre of trees: *"Regardez! Je lis!"* She says, *"Je traîne, je lis, je pense."* Says she goes to the Sorbonne, to the Odéon, to a Catholic discussion group on the Rue Gay-Lussac:

"*J'écoute.*" I say to her, "What did you hope would happen? What did you want?" Seems taken aback, stares at me, says, "*Je ne sais pas. Quelque chose de propre.*" Can't count the number of times I've heard this. Say, "*Une merveilleuse abstraction?*" She shakes her head. Doesn't know.

Immortal Gatito:
The Gabrielle Russier Case

*If she had been a hairdresser,
or if she had slept with a young apprentice,
it would have been different.*
—*The Deputy Public Prosecutor*

To TRANSLATE THE Gabrielle Russier case into American terms you would have to improvise a new society. First, every teacher and professor in the country, from kindergarten on through university, would be a federal employee, like the tax inspector or the postman, with a civil-service career controlled, observed, and directed from Washington. This society would have such a tight cultural unity that in every region and in all walks of life words and expressions would have the same meaning, the same resonance: a doctor in Oregon, an unemployed laborer in Buffalo, a librarian in Los Angeles, and a waitress in New York could respond in much the same way to "the child," "the father," "a teacher," "the family," "a divorced woman," "an educated person," and "authority." Given this background, imagine that somewhere in the South a high-school teacher of thirty-one falls in love with one of her pupils, a boy of sixteen. The boy's parents are both university professors. When they discover the affair, they lodge a complaint in court for corruption of a minor. Suppose that this charge is serious when it is levelled against a woman but not very serious if the accused is a man. The reason for this would be not only a long history of American jurisprudence but a prevailing belief that a Don Juan is simply exercising a normal role in society, whereas women have been troublemakers ever since Genesis. As for the boy in the story, an adolescent who sleeps with a woman older than himself, disobeys his parents, and runs away from home will be considered not only a social delinquent but a mental case, and treated as such. Imagine that habeas corpus does not exist in American law but that preventive detention does: anyone can be put in prison without a trial and kept as long as the judge conducting the preliminary investigation sees fit. This judge is sovereign. He is not obliged to consult anybody or give a reason for whatever he decides. When the teacher is arrested and held without a trial, public opinion is aroused, because it is utterly unusual for someone of her class and background to be jailed. If she is being treated like the illiterate and the poor, then something must be wrong. All over America, people wonder what the courts are up to. Eventually she is brought to trial in secret, in a closed court, and let off with a suspended sentence. Half an hour after the sentence has been passed, the District Attorney, who has received a telephone call from the Department of Health, Education, and Welfare, appeals to a higher court for a stiffer penalty. The object is to make certain that the teacher will have a prison record, thus making it impossible for her to earn her living anywhere in the United States. The teacher kills herself.

Now you must suppose that this case could have such a hold on the public mind that all over America hardly anything else will be talked about; that anyone with access to a typewriter or a microphone—journalists, welfare officers, churchmen, political activists of all persuasions, government officials, magistrates, lawyers, psychiatrists, sociologists, leaders of parents' associations and of student movements—will make passionate statements concerning the law, morality, hypocrisy, preventive detention, discrimination against women, the rights of minors, the need for prison reform, the absurdities of the criminal code, and the abuses of power.

The boy's parents are Communists. The boy is a Maoist. Imagine that major and minor doctrinaire differences on the left could become a subject of excited discussion in the American press, and that readers will know what it is all about and be deeply interested. There will be virtually no news of the case on television, which is government-owned and censored from Washington. However, the *New York Times* and the *Washington Post* will publish letters and even editorials expressing surprise that Communists could behave repressively, and reproaching the parents, both gently and violently, for having coöperated with the bourgeois police.

The teacher's death is an event of national importance. It is brought up at a televised Presidential press conference. The President (a Ph.D. in literature from Yale) will quote, from memory, a poem about a girl martyred by society because she loved the wrong person. The poem is the work of a celebrated American writer, patriot, and member of the Communist Party.

Of course, it sounds hopelessly wrong; this is not an American tragedy. It needs its own context, which is custom-bound, authoritarian, with laws established under Napoleon and a Mediterranean tradition of paterfamilias; it needs a sheltered academic atmosphere where literature is taught as a way of life, almost as a substitute for experience. Given that particular climate, it was easy for someone like Gabrielle Russier, who was intellectually developed but emotionally very young, to become fatally mistaken about possibilities and consequences. The specific sexual situation of the young boy and the older woman is a repeated theme in French novels and plays. She knew it, because she taught Racine and Stendhal, Colette and Radiguet; she grew up in a society where books are revered, but she obviously knew nothing about what that same society would tolerate in practice. She identified herself with Phaedra and Antigone, but she must have forgotten that the same Greeks who called them heroines admired only heroes in real life, a life in which women had no status—none whatever.

She was not at all like other teachers. When she walked into the Lycée Saint-Exupéry in Marseille in October, 1967, to take over three classes in French literature, the students thought she was a new girl. She was thirty, but looked eighteen. She was tiny, just over five feet tall, and weighed about a hundred pounds. Her hair was cropped short, as boys' hair used to be. More than one person shown a picture of her after her love affair became public property thought it was the boy in the case they were seeing, not the woman. In one of her letters she calls herself "an androgynous hippie," which is much the way people were to describe her later on. She was not pretty; her nose was too long and she had the intellectual sheep's profile that for some reason abounds in academic circles. In some photographs she looks like a young Bea Lillie, but she is a sad comedian, grave, or worried, or anxious, or severe. In others she looks like a charming boy, like a head by Piero della Francesca. No one can recall a picture of her smiling. Some people remember her eyes as green, others say no, dark brown. Her students worshipped her. They called her Gatito, which is Spanish for "little cat," and they used the familiar "*tu*" in addressing her.

This is so unusual from pupil to teacher in France that it just touches the implausible. Relations are formal in a lycée. Even young children would be called "*vous*." (Lycées are not high schools; classes start with the equivalent of sixth grade and go on to university level.) One of the complaints students have is that their teachers are remote as planets and that they can never discuss anything with them, not even their work. Gabrielle, on the contrary, wanted to be one of them. She based much of her social life on their movies, their outings, their songs. She invited them to her apartment to talk and listen to records. The students loved this, but their parents were bothered; because she gave her students books by Jean-Paul Sartre and Boris Vian, some parents started a rumor that she was organizing a Communist cell. (She was not a Communist, and she was only vaguely political.) Even her car might have belonged to an adolescent. It was a small red Citroën called a Dyane, decorated with Pop Art flowers. On the rear window she had pasted "MAKE LOVE NOT WAR." Brave advice—she was a French Protestant, daughter of a respectable Parisian lawyer, granddaughter of a clergyman, and anything but an adventuress. One of her lawyers was to describe her as "a Boy Scout," and as a one-person welfare group, "always off to battle for just causes." To her ex-husband she was and remained "morally impeccable."

The red car was important to her; it seemed to play a role in an idea she had of herself. Sometimes she signed her letters "Dyana Rossa," meaning Red Dyane, for its color and make. At thirty, she was divorced from an engineer by the name of Michel Nogues and had custody of their nine-year-old twins, to whom she was an attentive, a scrupulous, but also—to foreign eyes—a severe and unbending mother. She was half American: her mother had come to Paris from Utah in the nineteen-twenties to study music and had married a lawyer she met one night at the Opéra. Raymond Jean, a professor of literature whom Gabrielle studied under at the University of Aix-en-Provence, later published a collection of her letters from prison, and in the preface to this book he said that he never heard her speak a word of English but that he thought her American side had somehow caused her to be "different." If so, she was different on two counts: Protestants are a tight, self-protective minority in France and, like all such minorities, subject to legend. The myth of their supposed sexual puritanism is persistent. A foreigner of Protestant origin finds himself willy-nilly identified with a stern and dismal community whose ideas are said to be dull and virtuous and whose collective temperament is grim and sad. They are not expected to get much fun out of life. (Whether there is a word of truth in any of this is another matter.) Protestants are in no way put down, discriminated against, or oppressed; they are, on the contrary, frequently suspected of being behind banks and commerce and politics—all the hidden mechanisms that worry the ordinary citizen and make him feel the victim of secrets. They do tend to hang together; their home lives and their traditions are not exactly like those of the majority of the French. Gabrielle Russier's "desire to serve, in the Anglo-Saxon sense of the word," as someone close to her put it, may have come out of that background; it may also have accounted for the glacial discipline she imposed on Joël and Valérie, her twins, who spent most of their time in two separate rooms, like two only children. They were not allowed to leave their rooms without permission, or interrupt adults, or even be with them much. They were utterly forbidden to make "unnecessary" noise, or eat between meals, or help themselves to food when they were hungry. Raymond Jean wrote that a stranger entering Gabrielle Russier's apartment would never have known there was a child in it, so profound was the hush. According to Michel del Castillo, who published a book about the *affaire*—*Les Écrous de la Haine*—her daughter, Valérie, once said to a neighbor, "My brother went out of his room without permission. He ate some jam in the kitchen. I think I had better tell my mother. She would be very angry if she knew." To some of us, nine-year-old Valérie might sound like a prig and a busybody, but in France such stories are quite often repeated with the intention of gaining the listener's approval. They speak volumes about a certain idea of education.

Gabrielle Russier had gone back to the University of Aix-en-Provence when her children were still babies to take a degree in French literature. Part of her body of work was a paper on the use of the past tense in contemporary French fiction. With charts, graphs, and diagrams, she described how many times Robbe-Grillet or Nathalie Sarraute had employed the past absolute, the past perfect, or the imperfect when composing their novels. These studies, which are the fleas of literature and the despair of most writers—except those of France, who rather like them—are also important elements in a university career. To Raymond Jean, she had the makings of "a brilliant linguist," and there is no doubt that her progress was impressive, particularly for a young woman looking after two children. She had a government grant amounting to about two hundred dollars a month, in exchange for which she had signed a contract binding her to teach in state schools and universities for ten years. If she had reneged on the agreement, the state could have sued for the total amount of the scholarship.

Actually, this seldom happens. It seems to be a soft and pleasant arrangement. There is little pressure. It can go on for years, and it explains why men and women seem to be students well into middle life—something that often puzzles Americans. She passed the competitive state examinations called the *agrégation* when she was twenty-seven, which everyone agrees is young for that particularly difficult examination. There is no equivalent for the term, or the institution, outside France. As an *agrégée*, Gabrielle Russier acquired enormous academic prestige; she could teach in a lycée or university at a salary higher than that of her colleagues, and she was embarked on a career safe from shocks and setbacks—in theory, at least. An *agrégé* is supposed to know absolutely everything that has ever been written about his subject, and to know it by heart. The examinations, like so much of French education, require a prodigious memory; a candidate in geography was once failed for having forgotten the name of a Polish mountain. But *agrégés* are taught no pedagogic methods whatever, which means they usually go on teaching the way they were taught a generation earlier. After the student riots of 1968, there was talk of abolishing a system some educators consider hopelessly out of date, but the *agrégés* turned out to be a caste with a powerful voice, and the matter was dropped.

Gabrielle Russier did try new methods of teaching, which may have been another reason her pupils' parents suspected her politics. As an *agrégée* assigned to a lycée in a provincial city—Marseille—she probably started at a salary of about three hundred and fifty dollars plus a housing allowance, plus children's allowances. She was studious, hardworking, fair-minded, and persistent. She has also been called "reckless," "all of a piece," and "incapable of compromising" by people who knew her. Raymond Jean has written that Gabrielle "knew what she wanted" and had a great appetite for gaining control over other people. She was expert at setting the stage for emotional scenes and then acting in them. "The result was that life around her was often tense." Some of her qualities seem greatly attractive—her ability to see her students as people and not little parrots, for example. She was wonderfully disinterested—it would be difficult to think of her as ungenerous or mean. She was able to write, from prison, "I am here surrounded by people who ruined their lives for money" with as much wonder as if she had never taught Balzac and Mauriac, and had not herself come out of one of the toughest middle classes in the Western world. But there is also a lack of humor, an absence of humorous grace, even in love. Could anyone but a humorless woman have signed letters "Phèdre" and "Antigone," or compared herself to the nymph Chloë? Calling herself Dyana Rossa is odder still, beyond any conclusions a stranger can come to without impertinence. It is just simply not usual for a grown woman to identify herself with classical heroines or with automobiles. In one letter to a girl she had met in prison, she called herself "Antigone" and Christian—the boy she loved—"Oreste." Why Orestes? Because he killed his mother? And why Antigone? Was she being the faithful daughter, or the girl who defied authority and was sentenced to be buried alive? The name "Antigone" means "in place of a mother." Was that what she was trying to say? As for Phaedra, who fell in love with her stepson and committed suicide, the choice is prophetic, frightening.

"She had the childish side of all those who study too long, who live in books," one of her lawyers said. "Her world was unreal."

FOR A LONG time, the boy was known only as "Christian R.," because of a law that forbids naming a minor involved with the police. However, long before her death everyone came to know that he was Christian Rossi, that he had a younger sister and two younger brothers, that he lived in Marseille, and that his parents were professors *agrégés* at the University of Aix-en-Provence, which is next door to Marseille, a few minutes' drive. He was tall, heavy, "almost stout," and had longish hair and a beard, which inevitably caused him to be compared with every bearded figure in history from Christ to Castro. He was devoted heart and soul to extreme left-wing politics. At fifteen and a half— his age when Gabrielle Russier met him—he could easily have been mistaken for a man of twenty-four. He was serious and sober but had a violent temper. He was unkempt, rather untidy. Because of his appearance Gabrielle called him le métèque, which is a pejorative term for a foreigner, and also the title of a popular song which begins:

> *Avec ma gueule de métèque*
> *de juif errant de pâtre grec*
> *et les cheveux aux quatre vents . . .*

His father was an Italian from Piedmont, his mother a Frenchwoman brought up in a conservative Catholic atmosphere. Both parents were Communists. To a Maoist such as Christian, a Communist is someone stuffy, retrograde, bureaucratic, and suspicious of new ideas. "The quarrel between Christian and his father was really the fight between China and Russia," someone who knew them reported. There was one point of similarity—a coincidence, really—between Christian's mother and Gabrielle Russier: Mme. Rossi had also been considered a brilliant student. She had been one of the youngest *agrégées* of France. She too had taught in a Marseille lycée and had been adored by her students, who had addressed her with the familiar "*tu*."

ONLY TWO PEOPLE ever knew how it came about that Gabrielle Russier, discreet and prudent in her private life, given more easily to comradeship with men than romance, should have finally chosen a lover from among her students. One of the two is dead, and the other, going on twenty, is light-years away from the rebellious son of sixteen and seventeen. So that in a sense there are no witnesses. From the moment their liaison became public, however, theories abounded. It was said that he had fallen in love with an older woman because his mother had not given him all the love he needed. Another theory was the Phaedra story—that she had preferred the son to the father, hence the father's relentlessness. There was nothing to support these fantasies except idiot gossip. In the weekly *Paris-Match*, a well-known writer, winner of the Goncourt Prize, who had never laid eyes on either of the lovers, wrote that Christian was frail and effeminate, a mother's boy, and that Gabrielle was a great amazon of a woman—the very opposite of reality for either one. She was also criticized in print, again by someone who had not met her, for having written to Christian, "You were the only man I ever knew." It was taken for granted that there must have been something not quite normal about her to have written this to an adolescent—this most typical of all infatuated declarations. What no one questioned was just how this letter was made public. Was it stolen from Christian? Was his mail opened and read aloud at a press conference? Did he show it to a reporter? The bandying about of a remark she must have considered deeply intimate was the only thing "wrong" or "not quite normal." The question of what people see in each other still defies analysis. The mystery of what a couple *is*, exactly, is almost the only true mystery still left to us, and when we have come to the end of it there will be no more need for literature—or for love, for that matter.

All anyone knows about this particular mystery is its background—the student riots of May, 1968, when France was either within a breath of armed revolution or merely involved in a vast group-therapy session. For a short time, everyone could act his chosen role, and then the nation elected a conservative government. But for a few weeks young people lived in a fever of rage, hope, idealism, and anticipation that now seems indefinable except as a climate. No person involved with the movement slept at home, if he could help it. Christian's father occupied his college building at Aix-en-Provence, while Christian himself virtually lived in the Lycée Saint-Exupéry. As for Gabrielle—"dragged into politics by Christian," said one of his friends—she was either in the streets demonstrating with her students, or opening her flat to pupils who wouldn't or couldn't go home, or sitting in on endless discussions and committee meetings. Her first date with Christian had a deadly-serious and unwittingly comic side. She asked him to go to a movie with her. He said he was expected at a Maoist meeting. If she would attend the meeting with him, he would go to the movie with her, providing it was all right with his parents. He was still sixteen then. It was Gabrielle who rang the Rossis for permission. She and his parents were quite good friends. She had been a student of theirs. During the transport strikes of May and June, 1968, Gabrielle used to call on the Rossis every morning and drive all four Rossi children to school. Professor Rossi is said to have been delighted when he learned that Christian was in one of her classes. After the movie, she drove her pupil home and stayed to have a drink with his parents.

About five weeks later, without ringing the parents and asking them anything, she and Christian took off for Italy. Christian's parents believed that he was hitchhiking with another boy, a classmate. That other boy did come along, but very soon felt that nobody wanted him. Gabrielle quarrelled violently with him, called him "schizophrenic," and threw some of his luggage out the window of an Italian train. That same summer, Christian's still unsuspecting parents sent him to a family near Bonn to improve his German. Gabrielle turned up in her decorated Citroën, saying she was a cousin who had been sent to fetch him home sooner than expected. They drove back to Marseille and spent three weeks in her apartment. The Rossis, in the same city, knew nothing about it.

The journey to Italy and the clandestine August weeks were about as much as the love affair amounted to. They were sometimes together after that, but wretchedly, furtively, harassed and spied on, in an atmosphere of tension and worry that would have tried lovers of much longer standing. (Perhaps because she foresaw some of it, she tried to lock him out of her apartment even before the trip to Italy, and he broke down the door.) From the end of the summer until her death exactly a year later, Christian was in hiding, or in a psychiatric clinic, or in a home for delinquents, or watched and surveyed by his relatives, while she was in jail, or in a hospital, or in a convalescent home, or followed by plainclothesmen wherever she went. It is not surprising that she once cried to a friend, "I don't want to see him!" when she heard his ring at the door, or that, between the time of her trial and her death, when the same friend said, "Christian still loves you," she looked blank, as if his name suggested nothing whatever.

But at the beginning they wanted to live together forever. (Christian has since declared that he never intended to marry her, because marriage was against his Maoist beliefs—a declaration that is neither here nor there. At that time—the law has since been changed slightly—a girl of fifteen could marry with her father's consent, but a male minor under the age of eighteen required, and still does, the personal permission of the President of the Republic,

which is by no means automatically granted.) Wanting to
live together meant that they presented the Rossis with an
ultimatum: the parents had no face-saving way out. They
could not close their eyes to the affair and call it sentimental education. Christian *looked* adult, but the Rossis
knew he was not, and perhaps to parents no child ever
can be. Even the most selfless and indulgent parents will
seldom grant the right to a private life without a struggle.

At the start of the autumn term, Gabrielle asked Professor Rossi for an interview. She was shattered and astonished when her former professor did not want her to
"make her life over again," as the French expression has
it, with his sixteen-year-old son. He lost his temper and
shouted at her to leave the boy alone, and she came away
sobbing. The only result of the interview was that the
Rossis' home life became a hell of daily quarrels. Sometimes Christian sulked, sometimes he stormed out of the
house and went either to Gabrielle or to family friends
for a few days. After a quarrel with his father, Christian
wrote a letter to his parents breaking off relations with
them—a thing that, at his age, he was not in a position
to do. But the letter turned out to be a serious piece of
evidence in the case against Gabrielle, because Christian
wrote it from her apartment. It is mentioned in the verdict as proof that she was attempting to remove him from
the influence of his parents.

The Rossis still had no real idea of how far the affair
had developed. They told their friends that the boy was
"bewitched" and "under a spell," and they took him to a
doctor. It was a mutual acquaintance in whom Gabrielle

had confided who finally told them about Italy and the departure from Germany with a "cousin." Whether you are a lenient parent or a tyrant, it is insulting to be lied to. They thought that Gabrielle was neurotic and dangerous, a sorceress who had obtained ascendancy over an emotional boy. They also saw the affair in terms of a possible precocious fatherhood and a hampered life. When Gabrielle Russier asked if she could talk to him, Professor Rossi is reported to have said, "My God, what does she want? Is she pregnant?" Christian's parents were not reassured by her promise that she would see to it that he passed his exams; it sounded as if she wanted to take over his upbringing. Gabrielle was in love, and she was sometimes Phaedra, which means "bringer of light," and sometimes Antigone, but the Rossis saw a divorced woman with two children at home; they saw confusion, scandal, and emotional disaster.

As soon as she realized that the Rossis were seriously opposed to the affair and would on no account let Christian come and live with her, Gabrielle Russier suffered what we call loosely a nervous breakdown. She was seized with fits of uncontrollable trembling. She could not speak above a whisper. She could not stop talking about her affair with Christian and the Rossis' reaction to it. At the start of the new term, she asked for three months' sick leave with pay, which she later prolonged. She was too upset to face a classroom. It is extraordinary that it should have been she, the adult of the pair, who collapsed at the very first obstacle they encountered—a parental rebuff that any grown person might have predicted. It was almost

as if at the age of thirty-one she had heard her first "No."
The Rossis' next step was equally predictable: they packed
Christian off to a boarding school in Argelès-Gazost, in
the Pyrenees.

If Gabrielle Russier lived more in books than in life,
Professor Rossi, on the contrary, had forgotten one of
the lessons of literature, and that is the hopeless folly
of trying to separate lovers by force. Christian loathed
his new school. Gabrielle, who came to see him secretly,
wrote a friend, "You wouldn't recognize him; thin, anxious, he hardly knows how to smile anymore." Meeting
outside the school, they were found embracing in her car
and taken to a police station. It must have been thought
serious, for Christian wrote, "They want to put me in a
reformatory." Gabrielle later learned that she had been
followed by police from Marseille. The boy's parents had
already conferred with a judge of the Juvenile Court, and
asked him to open a dossier.

Affairs between teachers and students are more frequent than any of this might make it appear; if they are
discreet, no one takes them seriously. The Ministry of National Education now made a move to impose discretion:
Gabrielle was offered a post at the University of Rennes,
at the other end of France. Gabrielle wanted to let Christian know about the offer. Because his mail was held up at
school, she sent a telegram in Italian signed with a man's
name. The verdict read in court at her trial mentions that
she went to Argelès-Gazost to see him, that she "harassed"
him with letters, and that she "tormented the young man
by letting him know of her nomination to Rennes." Al-

though it was a promotion from lycée to university, she turned it down. Christian was also showing the symptoms of nervous collapse; he had to be put in the school infirmary and given tranquillizers. So far his relegation to this school had produced nothing but more tumult and discord, and in November he added to it by running away. He arrived in Marseille with toothpaste rubbed in his hair, which was supposed to make him look elderly and serve as a disguise. His parents had no idea where he was—he had last been heard of in the school infirmary under sedation. He was not with Gabrielle; she had hidden him with friends.

A runaway minor is a legal matter in most countries. In France, an adult who abets him can be jailed. As the daughter of a lawyer, and a teacher of minors, she certainly knew it. One wonders what either of them meant to do next. Did they think he could hide indefinitely? What she probably never did expect was that the Rossis would take the problem to court. No one expected it. The interest and the astonishment of French public opinion showed how unusual the case was.

THE NAPOLEONIC CODE does not speak of corruption of minors as such. The word used is "*détournement*," which means diversion, deviation, turning away. *Détournement de fonds* is how embezzlement is described, for instance. *Détournement de mineur* specifically means having caused a minor to leave home. Nothing said or written about the case ever made this clear. Most people thought, and probably still think, that Gabrielle Russier was charged with having slept with a boy, or that she had been sued by the Rossis. Actually, their complaint was against X, or John Doe. Under French law, anyone who "by fraud or violence" removes a minor "from the place where he has been put by those in authority over him" can be given a sentence of five to ten years. If no fraud or violence was involved, the sentence can be two to five years, plus a fine. If the minor dies, the penalty is death. Every crime or simple misdemeanor involving a minor is judged in terms of these articles—everything from helping a runaway, to sexual seduction, to inciting to prostitution, to kidnapping. Sometimes the law has to stand on its head: a sixteen-year-old male prostitute was once charged with contributing to the deviation of a minor—that is, of himself.

Cases involving middle-class children are almost always hushed up for fear of scandal. Those that do reach the courts generally have to do with girls from the most dispossessed ranks of society—girls who are wards of the state, whose families have long been shorn of their parental rights. It is extremely rare for a woman to be charged with having deviated a boy. When you read the penal code, in fact, you see that there seems to be no provision for it. But if the charge is laid against a woman, then the law comes down heavily. She is treated more severely than if she were a man who had seduced or deviated a girl. One of Gabrielle Russier's lawyers, Maître Albert Naud, has tried to show this difference by describing a similar case: "The dean of a university faculty seduced one of his students, a girl of seventeen. There was more than thirty years' difference in their ages. They travelled together and stayed in hotels, where she used his wife's name. They exchanged passionate letters, which the wife was able to intercept and so obtain a divorce. It never occurred to anybody that deviation of a minor had taken place, though the girl was only seventeen and the dean fifty. No prosecutor, no magistrate, not even the girl's family mentioned this aspect of the case. Yet if the dean had been a woman and the girl had been a boy, a charge would have been laid at once." Nearly every person who wrote about the Russier affair—even commentators who thought she had behaved foolishly—mentioned this curious twist in the jurisprudence concerning minors. They agreed that part of her punishment came from her being a woman. It seems to be accepted that a girl of any age is asking for trouble, and should know better, while the man, the seducer, is somehow or other her victim. In fact, if a man deviates a girl and the girl is fifteen or more, and if it can be shown without any ambiguity that there was mutual consent, the case is dropped. But the consent of a male minor is not taken into account, although for perfectly evident reasons it must have existed. A man's conduct is considered inevitable and therefore largely innocent, but a woman's thought-out and reprehensible.

It is puzzling in a society where women, on the whole, have a better time of it than women in English-speaking countries. Frenchmen do not seem to resent women or to be afraid of them; they are not bored by feminine company (all-male clubs or outings are rare and considered ridiculous); the war of the sexes scarcely exists. Equal

pay for equal work is the law of the country, and women
often hold more important jobs than do women in America. A woman's intelligence is respected, her professional
status accepted, and as to her personal life, the French
are notorious for an indifference to others that is also a
form of minding one's business. But that is the swim of
life, its ordinary commerce. When you read the law and
when you look closely at specific social situations, you discover that women never have the last word. A woman's
past as well as something called her "soul" weigh in the
balance when she is being judged in court. In the summer
of 1970, in Aix-en-Provence, a woman was sentenced to
twelve years' imprisonment on the suspicion that she had
incited a man to commit murder. (The murderer received
eight years—four less.) There was not a shred of evidence
against the woman except gossip about her morals, including her having slept with a man of forty-seven "when
she was only twenty-two." When she asked in court if it
was a crime for a woman to have lovers, she was told, "The
quantity matters." The formal accusation contained "The
recital of her existence would have tempted the pen of
a Balzac," and the police report included "She seems to
have sold her soul to the Devil." Her private life and her
"soul" replaced facts—something inconceivable if a man
were being judged. A girl accused of having shot her lover
was reproached by the magistrate for her taste in books.
"I have searched through the record for your soul, but I
failed to find it." All this comes under a tradition Maître
Naud has called "*la latinité*"—the Latin attitude toward
men and women. A Don Juan is admired; perhaps God

punishes him, but that is God's affair. Whereas anyone who publicly defended Gabrielle Russier was apt to receive a deluge of letters reminding her defender that Gabrielle was a disgrace to womanhood, as well as a whore, a pervert, and a nymphomaniac. Gabrielle Russier was seven before women were allowed to vote, twenty-eight when married woman could have bank accounts, and thirty before she could legally get advice from a doctor about contraception. She died before women were allowed to enroll their children in kindergarten without the husband's written consent, or have a say in where the family would live. The shocked protest that followed this last piece of legislation was like something preposterous out of the Victorian era. After the Liberation, women who had slept with Germans (prostitutes, mostly) had their hair cut off, while men who had willingly gone to work for the German war effort more often than not got away with it. A woman found guilty of adultery in France can be sent to jail for two years, whereas a man escapes with a fine—and he can be fined only if he was stupid enough to bring his mistress into his home. None of this is to say that if the legal status of women in France were different Gabrielle Russier would have found tolerant magistrates, for Americans do not need to be told at this stage of their social history that you cannot legislate attitudes.

The Rossis had lodged their complaint against X, without naming anyone. Nevertheless, the first person the judge conducting the preliminary investigation asked to see was Gabrielle. He asked her if she knew where Christian was hiding. "Find out for yourself—it's your job," she is reported to have said, and even, "All right then, arrest me!" Talking back to any functionary "in the performance of his duties" is a misdemeanor in most Latin countries. (No similar law protects the public from the clerk in the post office, let alone someone more exalted.) The magistrate is said to have lost patience with her.

One can't help noticing that everyone connected with this case was either irritable or violent. Christian broke Gabrielle's door in; she threw a young boy's luggage out a train window; in one of her letters Gabrielle cautions her ex-husband that it will not help her cause if he blows up at people. As for members of the legal profession, they were at the end of their patience when proceedings were barely under way. Even the Minister of Justice was to explain the case by saying, after her death, that the boy's parents had begun the whole affair because they had lost patience too.

The examining judge did not waste time arguing with her. On December 5, 1968, three weeks after Christian had vanished from school, she was charged and arrested without warning. Four men arrived at her door, the magistrate among them. One heard on the radio that her flat was searched from eight at night until two in the morning—which seems irregular, for no policeman is allowed to enter a private home between sunset and sunrise. The search party may have been looking for drugs as well as for Christian; they conscientiously tasted all the cooking herbs she had in the kitchen, looking for marijuana, and there is an account of a policeman's biting an aspirin in two to see if it tasted peculiar. Because she kept a bottle of Scotch in the house, she was asked if she let her students drink. In her bathroom, the four men came across "feminine articles"—sanitary napkins, from the sound of it—and reproached her for leaving such things where her children might see them. At the end of the search, long after dark, she was taken away. An examining magistrate is not required to notify anyone of an arrest; Gabrielle was not able to get in touch with anyone until the next day. She was photographed and fingerprinted and given a number. One of her fellow-prisoners said later, "The first and worst of the humiliations was being examined entirely naked before the others. Never in her entire life had Gabrielle felt such shame, but no one took the slightest notice." In a textbook issued for prison guardians, specific mention is made of the business of stripping and searching. It is supposed to be a psychological "contest," from which "the prison authority must emerge the victor." It is a known way of breaking morale in all countries. The prisoner is searched coldly, efficiently, silently, and, from his point of view, obscenely. His nakedness among the uniformed makes him seem inferior, helpless, and finally submissive.

How could any of this happen to someone who had never been in trouble with the law, and had never been tried? The answer is the system of preventive detention. If you are arrested for questioning in France, you are taken to the police, then before the examining magistrate. The only information he will have about you is a report called a "telegram." It can be a long list of facts, or a terse statement. The first thing the magistrate can decide, without asking you a single question, is whether to keep you under arrest or not. If you seem to be an educated person, well dressed, living at a respectable address, if the charge against you is not too serious, if you are not likely to run away, then you will most probably be let free until the case comes up. If you have no fixed domicile (perhaps you live in furnished rooms or a hotel), if you are an important witness who might vanish, if you are dangerous to society—*presumed* dangerous, for at that point you have not been tried for anything, let alone judged—then you can be held as long as the magistrate thinks it necessary. Perhaps you are merely what Casamayor (the pseudonym of a distinguished judge, a member of the Court of Appeal, who writes about such matters; he is a contributor to *Le Monde*, for instance) has called "just a poor devil," someone penniless and shabby, of a race considered inferior—Algerian, for example; then your fate may seem to have less meaning. You disappear into prison. No one will ever get up a committee to see what has become of you. The magistrate is not obliged to ask anyone's permission or advice; his signature is all that matters. You may not even be the supposed culprit but just a closemouthed witness. The judge suspects you know more than you intend to say. He is free to hold you until you change your mind. If you turn out to be innocent, you have no recourse against the law. You cannot even sue for the symbolic one franc in damages, though preventive detention may have cost you your job, your domestic equilibrium, and your reputation. When Gabrielle Russier was arrested for the first time, the public suddenly learned that a large section of the prison population was composed of persons awaiting trial, some of whom had been waiting for months.

It was at this point, in December, 1968, that the story, which had circulated for weeks in university circles around Marseille and Aix-en-Provence, became public property. A blurry picture of a tense woman who looked like a boy accompanied the first accounts of the runaway minor and the Communist parents who had not hesitated to turn to the bourgeois courts. One person in five votes for the Communist Pary in France, year in and year out, and so, of course, a large section of the public was directly interested. French news reporters, unless they work for government-owned radio and television stations, are allowed much more personal expression than in the English-speaking world. If Gabrielle Russier was described as a sympathetic figure who had risked all for love, or as a rebel standing up to a repressive structure, the Rossis were criticized left, right, and center. To those who wrote about the *affaire*, it seemed unbelievable that Communist parents could object to free love, or apply middle-class standards of behavior to their children, or make use of a capitalist law machine. Right-wing papers poked fun at the Rossis, orthodox Communist papers had hard words for the government but not the Rossis, while the liberals and the Maoists called their attitude a betrayal. There were long, earnest, and irrelevant discussions in print as to just *how* Communist the Rossis were; whether they were good Communists or bad; what their attitude had been during the Algerian war (which ended when Christian was ten); whether Professor Rossi was not more Maoist than he should be; and how he felt about the Italian Communist Party. One writer assured everyone that the Rossis' reaction to various stands taken by the Italian C.P. had been "positive," whatever that meant. Mme. Rossi was harshly dealt with. "She's fifty, but looks twice her age," it was solemnly announced over the air. There were conjectures as to her motives, her attitude toward her children, her character, her capacity for affection—usually by persons who had never laid eyes on her. A woman who described herself as "a friend of the family" and spoke with a strong Marseille accent undertook (anonymously, of course) to inform millions of radio listeners that Mme. Rossi was "disagreeable . . . a shrew," and that she forced her husband to wash dishes. The scorn in the anonymous voice was indescribably droll. She sounded like a monologue in an old Marcel Pagnol film. "They must be making seven hundred thousand francs a month between the two of them," the family friend went on, as if this were an added grievance. "Seven hundred thousand francs" means seven thousand new francs, or about fourteen hundred dollars. (As professors *agrégés* attached to a university, they might, in fact, have earned more than this.) The suggestion was that a man who earned money and yet washed dishes would be capable of anything. "He was all for sexual liberty," one also heard, "but not for his own wife and children."

If the French Communist view of the bourgeoisie is like the old cartoon symbol of the capitalist with moneybags in his pocket and a top hat on his head, the middle-class fantasy about Communists wallowing in pornography turned out to be just as peculiar. It takes a great stretch of imagination to envision an old-fashioned French Communist, with his earnest conversation, his crumpled, respectable suit, and his fat, comfortable wife, engaged in a sexual orgy. The Victorian primness that prevails in the Soviet Union was never mentioned. Perhaps no one had heard of it. At first, the Rossis said absolutely nothing; then Christian's mother sent a dignified letter to a newspaper. She mentioned the "traumatic effect" the boy's liaison and the discussion it entailed were having on his younger sister and brothers, adolescents too. But what seemed to shock and surprise the public most (and to a foreigner this was most striking of all) was that someone of Gabrielle Russier's class and background should receive the same treatment as a person illiterate or poor. One was made uneasy, finally, at the slant of some of the protest: how could they arrest a university graduate, a professor, an *agrégée*? It was "abnormal and rare," said Casamayor; "unusual for someone of her class and for someone with a legal domicile." It was exactly this "abnormality" that led many liberals to take up her cause: preventive detention was so unaccountable in terms of her station in life that it became suspect. Why was she in jail? Had she really been arrested for having slept with a boy? Was she so dangerous to society that she had to be plucked out of it overnight? Was there more to the charge than anyone knew about? The public was reminded over and over that this was "a professor with an advanced university degree." (Later, she came to dread these press campaigns, thinking they did her more harm than good, and her lawyers would finally beg her friends not to say anything on her behalf.) But here was another contradiction: the fact that she was a "person of quality" turned out to be one of the factors held against her. She was educated, she was a teacher, she should have known better. In other words, had she been an ignorant pauper there might have been no case, and if there had been, the Public Ministry—the French equivalent of the Justice Department or the Attorney General's office—might not have cared as much about getting a conviction. As the Deputy Public Prosecutor was to say later, "If she had been a hairdresser, or if she had slept with a young apprentice, it would have been different."

It was plain to anyone interested in the case, and it must have been clear to her too, that she could be free in a minute by telling where Christian was hiding. This she was unlikely to do. It was up to Christian to give himself up. Before doing so, he asked for assurance from the judge that he would not be arrested too. The magistrate saw him at the Palais de Justice on a Sunday (which is unusual) and so could not sign the court order until the next day. She was released on Tuesday, December 12th. With Gabrielle free, Christian's freedom became a problem, for the two had no intention of parting, and he did not wish to live at home or in a boarding school. His parents took an extreme step—they asked a judge of the Juvenile Court to intervene. No one seemed able to decide whether Christian had fallen in love with a woman of thirty-one because there was something the matter with him or whether he had become unruly and disobedient as a result of the affair. The idea of sexual attraction, or love, or both together, appeared to be so singular that a rational explanation for his behavior had to be discovered and a remedy applied. The judge ordered Christian sent to an examination center for delinquent minors, to see if he was a neurotic requiring treatment. The boy spent Christmas at the center, and was bored and miserable. After a number of tests and interviews, it was decided that he was not deranged but had an intellectual and emotional maturity beyond his years. This can be interpreted in an unfavorable sense, for young persons who seem remarkably mature often have problems, or the groundwork for them. At any rate, no therapy was suggested. Still unconvinced, Christian's parents had him transferred from the center for delinquent minors to a private psychiatric clinic where a course of treatment could be applied. The guardian of a minor has the right to do whatever he thinks best, and no state psychologist or social worker would be likely to question the decision of an educated parent. In the clinic, Christian was kept alone and given tranquillizers. He had no one to talk to and nothing to do. Sometimes he was allowed out of his room, and on one such occasion he managed to escape. He went straight to Gabrielle. He was very thin, and groggy from the drugs he had been given. She opened the door and burst into tears.

The charge against her was still open, but Christian had such a horror of the clinic that she could not bring herself to send him back there. Knowing the risk she was taking, she once more hid him with friends. But the friends could not keep him forever either; they got in touch with the Rossis, who now began their original procedure all over— Christian was again interviewed by the judge of the Juvenile Court and *again* sent to the examination center for delinquent minors. He stayed there three weeks, idle and bored. The psychiatrists at the center did not propose any kind of treatment or therapy. He had become someone nobody knew what to do with. The judge had at first suggested to the parents that they rent a room for Christian in Marseille and try letting him live alone. They were opposed to this. The judge now suggested sending him to a home for boys, near the Saint-Charles railway station. It was not a punitive establishment but a reeducative shelter for minors who had been in trouble with the law. Discipline was relaxed; the boys slept there but went out to work or to school. Christian, enrolled in a new lycée, the Lycée Thiers, discovered that Saturdays and Sundays at the shelter were free. Every Saturday and Sunday, therefore, he appeared on Gabrielle's doorstep. They made no effort to hide but went openly to restaurants and movies and drove about Marseille in her bright-red car, followed by plainclothesmen dressed as students. After three weekends of this, the examining magistrate sent for Gabrielle and gave her a serious warning. He thought that she did not understand the danger she was in, or that the charge against her could lead to prison. Her argument was that she loved Christian and that she had never promised not to see him—but that was no argument. Christian was also summoned for an interview at the Palais de Justice. Later, he said that as he was leaving the building two men, who turned out to be male nurses, seized him by the arms and dragged him to an ambulance parked a few feet away. They were, he said, acting on his father's instructions, and were employed by the private psychiatric clinic from which he had fled earlier that winter. The walls were padded. The only lavatory was a hole in the floor. He stayed there for two months.

Perhaps it did not happen that way. Perhaps Christian went to the clinic willingly, like any patient, but afterward could not remember. On the other hand, perhaps he was dragged to an ambulance from the steps of the Palais de Justice in Marseille and kept in solitary confinement and forced to submit to a drastic form of therapy known as the "sleep cure," whether he needed it or not. Either way, voluntary or forced, medically justified or medically lunatic, his incarceration would have been *perfectly legal.*

The guardian of a minor has not only the law but the full weight of public opinion behind him. Even when Christian's version of the story appeared in print, it was difficult to find anyone except psychiatrists and educators who entirely disapproved: the boy sounded nervous and moody, he was a chronic runaway, doctors must know what they are doing, and a long sleep never did anyone any harm. Actually, no one ever denied Christian's story. The director of the clinic observed a scrupulous professional silence. In France, as in most countries, no doctor will ever criticize another except behind his back. No medical or psychiatric association ever asked for an investigation or even a clarification of the story, perhaps for a reason already mentioned—even if it did happen that way, it was legal.

"Put him to sleep and he will wake up cured" sounds like a fantasy, but the "sleep cure" is, in fact, a form of therapy widely used in France. Because the word "sleep" makes it sound like a rest, it is often sought after by pa-

tients. It is a form of treatment that began in Austria in
the early twenties; it is practiced in Switzerland, and it is
now something of a psychiatric fashion in France, where
rest homes and clinics are equipped for administering
the "cure." In serious hospital therapy, it is thought to be
useful when—for example—a patient is in such a state
of anguish, excitement, or distress that no form of social
contact is at all possible. The psychiatrist will order a sleep
cure of about eight days, on the average. This is supposed
to break the tension and get him out of his environment.
The patient either swallows or has injected large doses
of tranquillizers and barbiturates in their various forms.
He sleeps and dozes and is lost to the world about twenty-three hours out of twenty-four. But the cure is taken
also voluntarily, eagerly, by persons who are nervous, tired,
insomniac, depressed, overworked, in the midst of an unhappy love affair, or up against any of the problems that
make people say, "If I could only sleep until it is all over
. . ." To someone who is not a doctor, this always sounds
chilling, for the suppressed part of the sentence seems to
be "and never wake up." With the sleep cure, you do wake
up; it seems like a harmless, temporary death. (One of
the reasons it is dispensed so lavishly in private clinics is
that, like a course of weight-reducing in similar institutions, it is very expensive.) The sleep-cure patient, exactly
like a failed suicide, comes back to the world physically
weakened, thinner, groggy, horribly depressed, lower in fi-
nances, and unfortunately right back in the same life. The
sleep cure is, moreover, a known cause of melancholia. The
patient is warned about it, and often advised to recover

by getting a little mountain air. He then goes either to a hotel or to a rest home full of other sick persons. The high altitude, the boredom of institutional life, the solitude, the lack of anything interesting to discuss or of any productive work to do, and the company of other neurotics give the final push and turn a temporary depression into something agonizing. The backlash of the sleep cure is, sometimes, suicide.

Christian's parents' reaction may seem extreme, but it is not inexplicable. In a situation where an American might expect a boy of sixteen or seventeen to rebel, a French father is taken aback. France is anything but a matriarchal society; public opinion holds a father responsible for his children and the way they behave even after they grow up. In Paris, the only son of a middle-class family, psychotic and with lower than average intelligence, murdered a prostitute. During the trial, it emerged that his father had been making him an allowance of about two hundred dollars a month. This doesn't seem an excessive sum for a man to give his dim-brained and unemployable adult son, for at least it kept him from stealing, but suddenly the *father* became the accused. Tons of hate and insult fell upon him because of the pocket money. As the father left the court where he had just heard his son sentenced to be beheaded, he was surrounded by a clot of Parisian hags, jeering, cursing him, and shaking their fists. What was his crime? He had not behaved "like a father." "He was not a man." He had failed in his "paternal role," and the paternal role is expected to be authoritative. As you go south, the greater the role of the father. In spite of population shifts

and industrialization and urbanization, the Roman paterfamilias still somehow prevails. The family structure is
almost untouchable. The father represents family law, and
law in general. As he obeys certain traditional social laws,
so he is obeyed in turn by the group, which is his family.
These are not random musings but ideas put forward by
members of the Mediterranean Psychiatric Association at
a meeting in May, 1970.

France is cut into two distinct climatic zones by the
Loire River. South of the Loire, there are fewer divorces,
fewer suicides, and—where the father's authority is stronger—four times *fewer* parricides. Catholicism alone can't
account for it—some of the most important Protestant
communities are in the South. Christian's father, who was
Italian-born, most certainly expected to be obeyed, and he
had a long history of tradition to back him up.

There is also the length of time French children live at
home, for reasons both of custom and of economics. Their
studies seem to go on longer. When they go to university,
it is in the home city, and it would be considered very
strange if they were to move out. Besides, where would
they go? There is an unlimited housing crisis. Strict or not,
French parents are closer to their children. They take their
meals and their holidays together. It is extremely rare to
hear a French person say that he does not like his parents.
Perhaps the admission would be thought undignified, or
perhaps you just accept your family whether you like them
or not. The Russier case nevertheless inspired a number
of French commentators to denounce family life as the
cause of all her troubles, not to mention Christian's. Wil-

helm Reich was quoted more than once, and there were waves of Freud, Marx, and Lenin. Engels' *Origin of the Family* came into vogue with lycée students because of this case, and has remained so. No one mentioned Georg Groddeck's belief that if an element of cruelty were not present in every form of education, not even the most loving mother would lift a finger to teach a child anything. Parents do the most astonishing things, all in the name of love—for in spite of everything that was said and written about the Rossis, nothing led one to believe that the Rossis did not love Christian. "What would you have done in my place?" Mme. Rossi asked a reporter, who replied, "I don't know what I would have done, but I know what I *wouldn't* have done"—which seems to beg the question. Unless parents are certifiably demented, they don't imagine the most damaging, the most irreparably wicked, the most demonic thing they can do and then go ahead and do it; they always do what they think is the right thing. If you ask in whose interest, the parent will answer, "The child's," and that is the only inaccuracy. Dreadful mistakes are made for the sake of safeguarding a problematic, an imaginary future. When Christian's parents told their friends he was "bewitched" and "under a spell," they must have believed it. The modern exorcist is the psychiatrist, and so he was called in to expel the spirit that had taken possession of their son.

Christian has said that he underwent two forced sleep cures, each lasting three weeks. He dozed, drugged, round the clock, and was wakened only for meals, which he ate in a drowsy state. At the end of the first three weeks, he had an interview with his father. It was unsatisfactory, and about a week later he was subjected to a second cure. There was no public medical reaction to this account when it appeared in print, but there was plenty of professional comment in private. And it was to the effect that the treatment could not have killed him but it might have made him very ill, and if he was the nervous, moody person that was suggested, it could have made him afraid of a number of things for life. However, his parents must have had a reason for committing him, and the medical director of a licensed establishment saw no harm in it; otherwise he would have refused. One of the delusions mental patients have sometimes is that they were dragged into clinics and forced to submit to intolerable treatment.

But how ill was Christian Rossi? He had twice been seen by state-appointed specialists, who thought there was nothing the matter with him. Of course, wrote Raymond Jean, Christian was legally a child and had to be protected and defended against himself; but was it really protection to commit him to a home for delinquents or "to a cell in a psychiatric clinic, to deliver him over to injections and sleep cures"?

At any rate, it happened, and the immediate result, after two months of incarceration, was that he said he would do whatever his parents liked. He agreed not to see Gabrielle again, on which he was released from the clinic and sent off to live with a grandmother in Montpellier. Again he was enrolled in a new lycée. As his health and vitality came back, he found being watched and observed and controlled utterly intolerable. Everyone seemed afraid he would break his promise and run away, and finally, in April, that is what he did. He got to Marseille, went to a friend's house, and telephoned Gabrielle. He knew by then, but perhaps did not fully grasp, the meaning of the difficulties this would bring her. He understood that if he went into hiding—his intention now—she would be jailed. "Do whatever you like," she is reported to have told him. They did not see each other. Except for one meeting in a public park, in the presence of another person, they never saw each other again.

After his telephone call, she prepared to be jailed with such resignation—with such self-satisfaction almost—that her friends were aroused. "She was highly intelligent," said one of her colleagues, "but in love she had the sentimentality of a little housemaid fresh from the country." Gabrielle said to her friends, "When I am in jail, Christian's parents will see how much I love him." One can only suppose that she had weighed all the consequences—whether her small twins needed her more than Christian needed a showdown with his parents, for instance. Valérie was at a holiday camp in the mountains. Gabrielle arranged for her cleaning woman to look after Joël, and, remembering the humiliating search of her apartment that had preceded the first arrest, she gave her personal papers to a neighbor. Two days after Christian had vanished from his grandmother's, Gabrielle was committed to the Marseille prison known as the Baumettes.

She was held until mid-June—two months in all. She still had not been convicted of anything. After her death, the Minister of Justice said that her "education" had been taken into account, and that the prison authorities had tried to limit the chances of "contagion" from other prisoners. He also remarked, crossly, that he was tired of hearing about bad conditions in the Baumettes. This prison consisted of three large blocks with barred windows, one block each for men, women, and juvenile offenders. Police dogs roamed the space between buildings and lights were played on the windows at night, as if it were a top-security edifice for criminal lunatics. Although the women were, as a rule, four to a cell, Gabrielle was given certain privileges: she was allowed at first to share a cell with only two women, both accountants, and considered closer to her by education than prostitutes. They were, in fact, a pair of active lesbians, and she loathed being shut up with them. She was horrified by nearly all of the prisoners. For the first time in her life this extreme romantic, the sheltered only child of middle-aged parents, came into contact with the by-products of poverty, prostitution, and thievery. Later, one of the other prisoners, a girl by the name of Muriel, told a reporter that Gabrielle was simply unable to understand or to cope with "the spitefulness, the jealousy, and the vulgarity" that prevail in the penitentiary world. "She had lost even her name. She was nothing more than No. 59,264." Prisoners were allowed out in the walled courtyard between two and four in the afternoon. When Gabrielle first appeared in the yard, none of the other women knew anything about her. "Because her hair was cut very short, like a boy's, the most spiteful of the prisoners put the word around that she was a lesbian." Odious comments and remarks were made in her presence. "Gabrielle, pale as the dead, listened without saying anything. She resembled a frightened little girl brought face to face with the ferocity of adults." In time, she learned to answer her tormentors "gently and intelligently." She infuriated the prison guards by her good manners, and because she never acquired the filth or the slang of prison jargon. She was forced to hear "revolting obscenities" addressed to her by these same guardians. Most of this abuse was about her having slept with an adolescent. One day when Gabrielle was reading in the prison library, one of the guards said to her, "What's the good of that to you? You're nothing but an old rag now. Your life is finished."

And yet in her letters she says that finally she came to prefer the guards to her fellow-prisoners. Her prison friendship with Muriel was a curious one. In a way, this girl, who was eighteen, seems to have become a nonsexual substitute for Christian. Muriel was a heroin addict, serving a sentence for possession of narcotics. Gabrielle took a great interest in her, nicknamed her Satan, and asked to have her as a cellmate. This request was granted. She immediately undertook the girl's education—drew up reading lists, accompanied her to the prison library. When they were parted, Gabrielle wrote her letters that seemed oddly intense, even given the high-keyed friendships people develop when they are shut up together: "Walls separate us, but I know you are somewhere...."

After Gabrielle's death, reporters found Muriel in the Marseille bars where drugs are sold. Her throaty young voice was recorded and widely broadcast. She blamed herself for Gabrielle's death, because she had never made an effort to see her. What seems most likely is that, once out of jail, Muriel had probably forgotten all about her. Remorse and guilt did not prevent Muriel from peddling Gabrielle's letters around. They turned up in a women's magazine; they were read on the radio. A drug addict, especially a minor, was still something of an exotic item in France in 1969. The press attitude toward Muriel became tinged with some of the sentimentality spilled over from the Russier case once Gabrielle was dead. She was invariably described as "Muriel [or Satan], the little addict." These letters were different in tone from any others collected and published. Hearing one of them read by an actress during a radio broadcast, a listener could easily have thought it was a letter to Christian. Described as "poetic," the letters to Muriel were pedantic, flowery, romantic, and pretentious—"literary" in the worst sense of the word. Sometimes Gabrielle seemed to be addressing herself; when she spoke directly to Muriel, she seemed to be composing a love letter. One felt that Gabrielle must have been terribly innocent, and that she had a great desire to be loved and needed by someone young. The actresses chosen to read *any* of her letters invariably adopted pompous Comédie-Française diction thickly iced with sugar, and the real voice of the prisoner who had asked, "Why am I here and what have I done?" remained silent.

Gabrielle suffered enormously from the petty horrors of prison life. Her mail was not just read and stamped by the prison censor but held up by the examining magistrate, who was in no hurry. Some of her letters were lost and may have fallen by mistake into some legal wastepaper basket. Letters to her daughter were not delivered but simply disappeared. A neighbor of Gabrielle's wrote the judge, asking if she might visit Gabrielle in prison. Only relatives are allowed to see prisoners, and Gabrielle had none in Marseille. Her mother was an invalid, paralyzed and in a wheelchair, which meant that it was difficult for Gabrielle's elderly father to leave Paris. The judge never answered the request. If Gabrielle was jaunty at first, and decided to look on her imprisonment as a new experience, she soon fell into the despair that is typical of people who really do not understand why they have been arrested. That is, although she knew that Christian had run away and that she was being held as a hostage, she did not think she had done anything *wrong*. The Dominican nuns who visited her, and whom she liked, advised her to look on herself as a "political"—that is, political prisoner. It was good advice; in the Nazi camps of the Second World War, political prisoners were less likely to slip into despair and had, apparently, a better chance of survival than people who had not done anything to provoke an arrest.

She was also desperately hard up. There was rent to be paid, and legal fees, and income tax, and the loss of Social Security because she was in jail. This was a blow, because it affected her children. She had devoted friends, but it does not sound as if any of them put their hands in their pockets for her—though surely that would be the first thing an imaginative friend would think of. Nevertheless, in terms of what happens to "the humble" of France, her situation as a prisoner was privileged. She was only one of thousands who have been held without trial, with the law creeping along at snail's pace and their lives ruined and broken. Until this happened to an educated French-woman of good family, and for a reason the readers of popular newspapers could grasp and sympathize with—love—these other prisoners might as well have been try-ing to hang themselves in cells in South America. The feeling in France suddenly seemed to be, "If it can happen to her, it can happen to me," whereas what happened to the Algerian street-sweeper would never affect anyone. There is absolutely no doubt that if she had been obscure and "humble" she would never have been heard of and there would never have been an editorial about her on the front page of *Le Figaro*.

Sixteen months before her first arrest, Algerian prisoners rioted in the Santé prison in Paris. It turned out, according to *Le Monde*, that there were twenty-seven hundred "North Africans and other foreigners" in cells each of which had only one small window just under the ceiling and, as sole sanitary installation, "a water closet without a seat, the bowl of which had to serve as a sink for washing their dishes and as a washbasin for their ablutions." When, during a heat wave, these conditions became intolerable, the prisoners began a hunger strike, of which no one took the least no-tice. Then they began singing and banging on the doors and throwing things out the windows. In the confusion that resulted, some of the prisoners said there had been severe beatings and perhaps a death. The prison authorities denied it, and that was that. There was never a word of followup to this story, in *Le Monde* or in any other newspaper, and one never heard it mentioned in private conversations. It was just simply not interesting. The public was never told what these men were in jail for, what their names were, or anything else about them. And yet it is more than possible that half of them, or two-thirds, or even all of them, were held in preventive detention. Now, these conditions are no worse than in some other places and countries, including the State of Arkansas or New York City. But unless a middle-class public can see its own image reflected in someone like Gabrielle Russier, nobody—nobody in the middle class, that is—cares. "People held in preventive detention commit suicide all the time," said Casamayor. "They are humble persons. We never hear of them."

Gabrielle's lawyers had made two demands for "temporary liberty," which were turned down, giving the impression that either the prisoner was dangerous or the charge was very serious indeed. There has been no official explanation to this day why they were refused. The Minister of Justice said later that the question of her parole was "delicate," and that when she was released after her first arrest the examining magistrate had received letters of protest from parents. It was taken for granted by the public now that her imprisonment was a form of pressure on Christian, who was still in hiding. She was not freed, in fact, until the day he gave himself up. He told someone that he had not realized she was still in jail, and perhaps that is true, though the papers were full of it. He was now seventeen. He had never been on his own, except as a runaway, and had never earned his living or been responsible for anyone else. He may have been unable to realize what it means exactly to have a prison record, to be in jail, to be parted from your children, to fall hopelessly into debt, to lose your job, and to be barred from your profession. He has said in an interview that he wrote to Gabrielle twice a week but that she never answered. She seldom mentioned him in letters from prison. Her ex-husband, Michel Nogues, who had been loyal to her throughout, met her as she came out of the prison gates. He was shocked at the change in her. Everyone who saw her in the three weeks between her release and her trial spoke of her altered manner. She trembled, she shrank away as if afraid of a blow, she could barely speak above a whisper—much the symptoms of her nervous breakdown eight months before. She cried almost continually and seemed afraid of scoldings, like a child who has known too much harshness. Raymond Jean, who saw her at this time, said that she was "haggard, pale, undone, thin." She kept looking over her shoulder, as if she was afraid of being spied on, and she seemed to have trouble breathing. A woman friend who saw a great deal of her was convinced that this behavior was an act, and one of her lawyers thought so too. He said that he believed she had "simulated" some of her symptoms, or at least exaggerated them, but that the "breakdown itself was real enough." Her entire conversation was about her life in prison and her terror and apprehension about the trial, which still loomed ahead. Once again Christian was packed off to stay with a relative, and his parents, at their wits' end, even suggested that he join the Navy. There was no contact between Gabrielle and him. They seem to have drifted out of each other's life. A news magazine reproached him in an editorial for having abandoned her, but there was not much he could have done at this point except get in the way. She wore out her friends by repeating the same questions over and over: How strong were the Rossis? What would become of her children? Would she be barred from teaching? Was she the victim of a plot involving the Rossis, the law, and the Ministry of National Education? She felt she had been "crushed by a rock" and that she had wandered into a Kafka world. Between the time of her release from jail in June and her trial in July, she was unable to cook, shop, look after her son Joël—her daughter was still in a holiday camp—or cope with even the simplest domestic situations. Michel del Castillo's book has an account of how a neighbor came into her darkened apartment one night and found Joël alone in his room and supperless, while Gabrielle cowered in an armchair in the living room. The neighbor asked her if the little boy had been given anything at all to eat. (It must be remembered that her children were not allowed to help themselves.) Gabrielle seemed unable to grasp the question or even understand what was being said to her. The kitchen was completely empty of food, as if she had not done any shopping for days.

"Timidly, Joël said, 'There are cornflakes in the cupboard.'

"As though seized by a sudden fit of madness, Gabrielle leaped from her chair and screamed, 'Cornflakes! Cornflakes! I've had enough about cornflakes! I never want to hear about cornflakes! Never again!'"

She then crept behind the refrigerator and crouched on the floor, sobbing. When the neighbor, who had gone back to her own apartment to prepare a meal for the child, returned half an hour later, she found Gabrielle in the same place, still crying. She told the neighbor, "They broke me in prison. There are times when I can't stand my own son or anyone. Yesterday I kicked the cat. I'm finished."

Her symptoms may have been "simulated," but her worries were real. She had been suggested for the post of university lecturer at Aix-en-Provence—something for which she was amply qualified. Twenty professors met June 27th to vote on the appointment, among them Raymond Jean, who argued in her favor, and Christian's father. She was turned down by a vote of eleven to nine. Then, two days before her trial, she received a letter asking her to repay the Ministry of National Education two months of her salary, for the time she had been in prison. It seems harsh and bureaucratic, and as if the Ministry of National Education had somehow been wondering where she was all that time and suddenly found out. Of course, there is another side to it: during the academic year of 1968–69 she had hardly set foot in a classroom, for she had been given a long sick leave, and after her first arrest had been suspended with pay for several months. (The suspension was not punitive; the principal of the lycée was afraid her presence might be "disruptive.") Gabrielle Russier did not pay back the two months' salary and probably couldn't. As the state's claim has never been revoked, this debt has been inherited by her twins. Joël and Valérie owe the Ministry of National Education two months of their late mother's salary, to be paid out of whatever their inheritance amounts to. Shortly before the trial, Gabrielle made an attempt to kill herself by taking barbiturates. She was found in time by a neighbor, who persuaded her to see a psychiatrist. The psychiatrist said there was not much he could do, and he gave her a prescription for more sleeping pills.

In spite of her distraught state of mind, she did not lose her bearings. She pulled herself together enough to write to one of her students—a girl who was both her friend and Christian's—asking her to see if Christian might not be persuaded to appear in court at her trial on July 10th. She thought that if the magistrates could see the tall bearded figure described in the accusation as "a child" it might take some of the opprobrium from the charge. However, he was not called, he did not testify, he made no deposition, and his presence was not considered "useful." Perhaps the testimony of a male minor is not taken into account (though a girl's might have been). What could he have testified? He might have testified that when she wanted to end the affair he broke down the door; that he had instigated the trip to Italy; that he had begged her to fetch him in Germany; that he had threatened to run away from boarding school unless she came to see him (and then ran away anyway); and finally—of capital importance—whether she was the first woman in his life or whether he'd had previous experiences and knew exactly what he was doing. Perhaps the court would have refused his deposition; on the other hand, it might have helped.

A French trial of this sort is a three-cornered affair. There is the accused, Gabrielle, represented by her counsel; the *partie civile*—Christian's family, with *their* counsel;

there is the Public Prosecutor, or his deputy, who, as I have said, represents the Public Ministry, which means society, the people of France. To be more specific, it means the judiciary power of the prosecution in the name of the people of France. (An inexact equivalent of the *partie civile* in Anglo-Saxon law is the "complainant.") Once the Rossis had lodged their complaint against X, the matter was out of their hands—in that they could not have changed their minds and stopped the procedure—and became entirely the affair of the Public Ministry. The Public Prosecutor and his deputies are not ordinary lawyers but high-ranking magistrates. As their titles suggest, they conduct the prosecution, they ask for the sentence they think necessary, and if the jury or the presiding judge does not give the verdict or the sentence they ask for they have the right to appeal. The lawyers representing the *partie civile* also question the witnesses and the defendant, so it seems like two against one. What the complainants—in this case the Rossis—are asking for, as a rule, is damages. The damages can be a large sum or the symbolic one franc, the award of which confirms that the complainants have been harmed morally, or mentally, or in their public stature. One of Gabrielle Russier's lawyers remarked dryly, of the Rossis, "One would have expected [from Communists] a more nonchalant attitude toward bourgeois principles, bourgeois morality, and the bourgeois police." At the Russier trial, the Deputy Public Prosecutor had specific instructions to ask for a thirteen-month suspended sentence. It was of enormous importance, for Georges Pompidou had just become President of the Republic, and the tradition is that a new President declares an amnesty for all sentences of twelve months or less. (All traffic fines still pending are wiped out.) If Gabrielle Russier were to receive a sentence of twelve months or less, she would come under the shelter of this amnesty; she would not have a police record, and there would be no legitimate reason to prevent her from teaching. That was why the prosecutor had received instructions to ask for thirteen months.

On the day of the trial, the Palais de Justice was swarming with photographers and reporters. Gabrielle saw the father of Christian and had a curious exchange with him. As though afraid of being scolded, she told him it was not she who had invited the press. He reassured her. The concierge of the building watched Gabrielle go by and said the equivalent of "dirty bitch" between her teeth. As often happens at a hearing where a minor is involved, the court was cleared. Some of the public who did not know this was customary were left with the impression that the details of her liaison were too filthy and scabrous for delicate ears. When the sentence was announced the next day, Gabrielle was not in court. Because of the reporters, the photographers, and the knot of furious women lying in wait for her, Gabrielle's lawyer had obtained permission from the President of the Court for her to be absent during the reading of the verdict. She learned that she had been fined the equivalent of one hundred dollars and given a suspended sentence of twelve months, and so came under the Presidential amnesty. Her police record, as the French expression quaintly has it, "remained virginal." She shot off telegrams in all directions signed "Antigone" and "Phèdre," including one to her lawyer (signed "Antigone") that said, "Thank you. Long live the sun."

ABOUT THIRTY MINUTES after the sentence had been passed, the Deputy Public Prosecutor came up to Raymond Guy, Gabrielle's counsel, in the Palais de Justice and said, "I am going to appeal *a minima*. I have just received instructions."

The full Latin phrase would have been "*a minima paena*" meaning "from the smallest sentence." This is the appeal that the Public Ministry (in the name of society) brings when the Ministry thinks that a sentence has been too light. It is very rare. One of Gabrielle's lawyers said that between 1932 and 1969 he had known of only ten such appeals, and then in cases involving much more serious matters than the deviation of a sixteen-year-old boy by a woman. On the other hand, perhaps any aspect of public morality is a serious matter in France. In the summer of 1970, there was an appeal by the Public Ministry against the decision of a lower court acquitting a Bordeaux publisher on a charge of distributing pornography. What he had distributed was films intended for health and nudist clubs. The Court of Appeal also acquitted him, stating that the films were innocent. It was a decision that created a precedent: until 1970, the courts had been extremely severe where "reproductions of the human body in its entirety" were concerned. This is merely to point out that Public Ministry appeals may be rare but they are certainly selective. As a rule, if a defendant accepts the verdict of the court the matter ends there. But if he has the impertinence to appeal for a smaller sentence or a lower fine, the office of the Public Prosecutor will lodge a counter-appeal *a minima*, which may make the defendant wish he had accepted what he was given in the first place. Maître Naud, who came into the case at this point and who is a Paris barrister with a high reputation, called it "a sort of dreadful game." What was absolutely without precedent was the speed with which the Public Ministry issued its orders to the Deputy Prosecutor to appeal—within half an hour after the sentence. "In my career of thirty-seven years at the bar, I have never seen an appeal instituted so rapidly," said Maître Naud.

None of this was taking place in secret, but well lighted by the radio and the press, and accompanied by a volume of comment, debate, and protest almost unparalleled in recent French life. Victor Hugo's celebrated remark "The law is a machine that cannot move without crushing someone" was quoted by everyone who could remember it. There was scarcely any area of public life in which Gabrielle Russier's name was not mentioned. What seemed to outrage public opinion now was the disproportion between her offense and the weight of her punishment, and to an onlooker who knew little about the penal code the courts did seem capricious when it came to sentencing. Twelve months seemed severe compared with decisions handed down on charges that were much graver. A woman shot her husband to death because he was politically ambitious, did not want her to meet his friends, had a mistress, and had threatened to leave her. She was acquitted, and as she left the court the omnipresent knot of neighborhood female furies cried, "Bravo Yvonne!" In 1969, a man in a suburb of Paris stabbed a neighbor to death because the neighbor's little girl had been bouncing a ball against his door. First he kicked the child; then he called up the stairs to the child's father, "Come down if you are a man"; then he got a knife and ran it into him. He was given a suspended sentence. In 1970, two grown men, brothers, got in an argument over what to feed their dog. One killed the other. The sentence was two years. In the spring of that same year, a woman killed her husband. Her defense was that he made her life intolerable. She was given a five-year *suspended sentence*. Children are regularly abused and ill-treated and some of them die of their wounds. What are the sentences? Suspended . . . two years . . . eighteen months. Nothing is as irritating to lawyers as comparisons of this kind, for in a French murder trial the jury is not asked to decide if the defendant *did it* but if he is *guilty*. It is absolutely untrue that in France an accused person is considered guilty until proved innocent; it only seems that way, because in French law there is no such thing as a plea of "not guilty." It does not exist. What the prisoner has to prove is that the examining magistrate had no right to indict him—in other words, that the state has no case. He can only protest his innocence, and attempt to prove that he was arrested without reason. If you are arrested for murder but the jury finds extenuating circumstances, you are not guilty of the crime the state has charged you with even if you have caused the victim's death. For all its failings, French law is more lenient and elastic than Anglo-American law on the question of guilt and intention, precisely because of the subtle but distinct separation of the fact from the circumstances.

As the Russier case was heard *in camera*, before a court of three judges, those persons who were present alone can know what was said, or what was held against her. Her sentence showed only that it must be tricky to be a defendant when some ministry or other has decided to make an example of you. In the case of the man who stabbed his neighbor, the court expressed sympathy for persons who live in noisy and jerry-built apartment houses. In the case of dead or battered children, the poverty or the alcoholism or the idiocy of the mother is taken into account. Gabrielle Russier had no such elements in her favor.

The Public Ministry now began to suggest that the appeal was nothing but routine. This gave the impression that the law was a great tidal wave no one knew how to stop. But there were respected lawyers who came forward to say, in public, that the appeal *a minima* was not routine, and that the law was being used as a repressive instrument.

In times of stress and confusion, the public in France relies for information on those radio stations that are not government-owned—Europe 1, Radio-Luxembourg, and, in the South, Radio-Monte-Carlo. Just how "independent" commercial stations are is another matter, but at least they seem to be free of a certain kind of unimaginative censorship. It was over these "peripheral stations," as they are called, that the ordinary public, the more than fifty per cent of the population who never read newspapers, now learned what *a minima* was about, and that the appeal was not routine, and that the law was something mysterious called "*du Kafka*." But Casamayor was also heard, over one of these same stations, and he said that the law was not a Kafka mystery, nor was justice inevitably unjust: "The whole thing was an operation and she was its object." She was not the victim of something dark and compelling but merely of "men with opinions." Who were these men? They were in the Ministry of National Education, said some of her colleagues. Maître Naud, who was preparing to defend her before the Court of Appeal at Aix-en-Provence, had every intention of bringing up the rumor that the Ministry of National Education had asked the Public Ministry to make absolutely certain she could never teach again. There were people who found this idea hard to swallow, at the time. The Ministry of National Education has an enormous budget, an army of persons to deal with; it is responsible for everything from kindergartens to universities, and it seemed unlikely that men at the very top level of public life had nothing better to do than pursue and persecute a woman because she had once hidden a runaway. In time, it began to seem that if she was being hounded it must be for something left out of the penal code—for having had a young lover. The difference in age between Gabrielle and Christian was fifteen years, but she was often talked about as "old enough to have been his mother." Her opponents described her as an aging nymphomaniac in search of her lost youth. This insistence on her age sounded curious in a country where women are considered young much longer than in the English-speaking world. Press accounts of any news event will describe as "a young woman" virtually any person under fifty, and the young boy infatuated with an older or married woman is a favorite subject in novels: *Chéri, Le Diable au Corps, Le Rouge el le Noir, Le Blé en Herbe* come to mind one after the other. Some of Gabrielle Russier's friends thought that she was harassed for having sided with her students during the riots of 1968, and that her trial was really political. But in that case why Gabrielle Russier? Professor Rossi had been an active militant, he was a Communist, and not only was he not being harassed but he was receiving the active assistance of the law. The "men with opinions" Casamayor had spoken of perhaps had opinions about her morals and nothing else. Later, the Deputy Public Prosecutor removed any ambiguity by putting it in the plainest possible language: "An inscription on the police file was needed so as to facilitate disciplinary action and remove her from her post. She deserved it."

It stands to reason that a section of the public thought she deserved it too, for the office of the Public Prosecutor rests on more than the "ideas" of a few men. There were all the parents who had objected when she was freed after her first arrest, for instance. She had women against her—mothers of sons, or just women anxious to let the world know they would never have fallen in love with a minor whatever the circumstances. Letters condemning her continued to arrive at women's magazines long after her death. Reams of similar letters were read aloud over Radio-Monte-Carlo—passion over this case reached an extraordinary pitch in the South—and Gabrielle Russier finally became a subject better not brought up at dinner parties, like the Dreyfus affair several generations before.

One other count against her was the fact that she was divorced. It sounds improbable in a country like France, where divorce is accepted, relatively easy to obtain, and widely practiced. But there exists a prejudice against a divorced woman not just in France but nearly everywhere. It comes to the surface if a private situation becomes a moral issue; then the person involved is not just a woman but a divorcée—though in similar circumstances no one is ever likely to pull a face over a divorced man. Even in the United States, the last place one might expect it, this mental prohibition exists. "He liked the company of thirty-five-year-old blond divorcées" turned up not long ago in *Time*, and what it meant was "He liked the company of sleazy women." Take out the words "blond divorcées" and substitute "unmarried women" and see how the sentence sounds. So that if "divorcée" is journalists' shorthand for "floozie" even in America, what can it be in a country as Catholic and conservative as France? In all that was written about Gabrielle Russier, the phrase "a divorced woman with two children" clanged away like a clock endlessly striking, though her divorce had been the least scandalous imaginable: she and Michel Nogues had discovered they did not want the same kind of life, and they parted amicably. He remained her friend, and stood by her through the trial and after. Each time her status ("divorced") was mentioned in a certain tone of voice, one wondered if things had changed all that much since a pre-1914 French book of etiquette advised, "The divorced woman removes her wedding ring, she resumes her maiden name, and she tries to live a discreet and retired life."

Part of the public also believed that Gabrielle Russier should be made an example; otherwise there would be nothing to stop adolescents from leaving home, disobeying their parents, and starting up love affairs with elderly persons. Probably no Ministry of Education anywhere would want its instructors to keep falling in love with the children they teach. But perhaps not very many would. The French humorist Pierre Daninos has pointed out that whenever one does anything even slightly out of the way in France the response is invariably "But what if *everyone* did that?" There must be millions of students who would not sleep with their professors even if it were legal. Other arguments were more serious: She was a teacher, entrusted with the care of young persons outside their own homes. Replacing Christian's parents, she betrayed the trust they—and all the other parents—had placed in her. Also, as a teacher she was a civil servant and bound by a code demanding respectable behavior. "Gabrielle Russier gave a bad example," said the Deputy Public Prosecutor, "because she scoffed at parental authority. If she had at least made due apology . . ."

It would require a huge volume to record the positions taken and abandoned, the opinions asked for and supplied, the long debates in the form of letters, the speeches, the declarations, the statements of belief. Tracts littered the pavements around universities and lycées, and posters were pasted up in Aix-en-Provence and Marseille accusing society, the Fifth Republic, the teaching system, bourgeois hypocrisy, and Christian's family. Libellous gossip circulated wildly—everyone knew someone who knew that the Rossis had tried to have their son certified insane (they had not) or that they had all sorts of dubious reasons for wanting to break Gabrielle Russier for life. The Rossis had not asked for the appeal *a minima*; once they had Christian at home, that was all they wanted. It became impossible to point this out, because hardly anyone would listen. The voices of officialdom went on saying that the appeal was only a legal routine, and lawyers in private practice continued to retort that it was not. "They always ask for the maximum sentence and we nearly always get less," said one lawyer. "If the prosecutor were to appeal *a minima* each time, it would never end. Every case would go to appeal." When it was no longer necessary to prosecute this particular appeal because the defendant had killed herself, it was the turn of the Minister of Justice to explain, also through a radio station, "It was all legal. Everything was done within the law."

"They have made a mountain out of nothing," Gabrielle Russier wrote despairingly from jail, and that was how it began to seem—for what, exactly, had she done? Unless one accepted a love affair as something criminal, it seemed absurd to refer the case to a court of appeal. She had fallen in love and lost her head; encouraging Christian to lie to his parents was perhaps a mistake, a failure as their friend, but at that point she was neither friend nor teacher. If every weakness and subterfuge for which infatuation is responsible were punishable by law, no prison in the world would be large enough. As an adult involved with a minor, did she introduce him to some advanced form of vice? Did she make him drink? Give him drugs? Unlikely. She was,

if anything, slightly puritanical. Did she make him unhappy, torture him, sequester him, spy on him, and make
his life hell? Did she prevent him from studying? One letter she wrote him must certainly have been the least erotic
message any woman ever sent her lover. It was an outline
for work: Christian was to study Italian, he was to see two
movies a week (one "cultural" and one anything), he was
to read one French novel a week and a few chapters of a
foreign novel and write a weekly composition. . . . As her
ex-husband said, she was a born educator. "The contact
between them was not null," said her counsel, Raymond
Guy. "In fact, it was profitable." He must have meant for
Christian; by that time Gabrielle was dead.

THE SHOCK OF good news—the sentence of twelve months
instead of thirteen—immediately followed by bad would
have unsettled a character much tougher than Gabrielle
Russier's. Her fears and worries about the new trial became so obsessive that a doctor advised a sleep cure, which
she undertook in a hospital. She sent Joël off to a camp,
and on the twentieth of July she left Marseille and went
to a rest home in the Pyrenees "to avoid the depression
that follows a sleep cure." Once again she tried to kill
herself, and once again was found in time. Her letters
spoke of her terrors: her lack of money, rent owing on
her apartment, the fear that her children might become
charges of the state. When she wrote, "I am not drama-
tizing. It is the situation that is dramatic," she was speaking the truth. Even an unimaginative woman would have

felt helpless and beset. She had virtually no one in the world. Her parents were elderly and her mother a helpless invalid. Her ex-husband had done what he could, but he was not wealthy, and he was, after all, a man she had divorced. She had friends, but they were neither rich nor powerful, and she herself, as the product of a hard middle-class society where the expression "Everyone has his own problems" strikes the ear rather frequently, probably did not expect much. She did ask, in one letter, if a public subscription might not be opened in the left-wing weekly *Le Nouvel Observateur*, which shows how desperate she must have been for help and money. The other people in the rest home had "only psychological problems, not real difficulties." But her defenses—like theirs, perhaps—were almost entirely eroded. She wrote "if something should happen to me" on August 1st.

She left the rest home on August 30th and came back to a Marseille that had been emptied by the last weekend of the summer holidays. It was a Saturday night. She was alone. No one met her at the station. The apartment house she lived in was as quiet as the rest of the city— nearly everyone had gone away. It seems incredible that the nurses and doctors and psychiatrists who had been dealing with her let her go off without getting in touch with some member of her family or a close friend. She did not bother to unpack. The next day—Sunday—someone came to see her. She and the visitor had a drink and she made coffee—the cups and the glasses were found. After the unknown guest departed, she sealed the cracks of the doors and windows with clothes and old newspapers, shut off the electric meter to avoid the risk of an explosion, and turned on the gas. She lay down on the bed and swallowed all the sleeping pills she had in the house. Firemen broke down the door on Monday. They found Gabrielle in a blue dressing gown, and the empty glasses and cups. Her visitor has never come forward to say what their last conversation was about. There was no inquest, no autopsy, and no one even took the fingerprints on the cups and glasses.

MAÎTRE NAUD, THE lawyer who was to have represented Gabrielle at the Court of Appeal, received two messages in one day. One was the news that his client was dead, and the other a letter from her ex-husband, written a few days earlier. Michael Nogues was disturbed at the idea of a new trial and over the sort of publicity his ex-wife had been subjected to. He wanted the public to see "her real face," and he spoke of "her high moral worth." Their marriage had failed because of their opposing characters and points of view. Nevertheless, "I consider my ex-wife morally impeccable." She was also "an exceptional mother" and "an educator by vocation." This must have been the letter she had asked him to write on her behalf.

A few days later, Mme. Rossi agreed to be interviewed together with Christian. The outcry against her family was so enormous that she may have wanted to state her side of the affair. A reporter from Radio-Television-Luxembourg was allowed in the house with his recording equipment. Her voice was educated, hard, slightly masculine, and—not surprisingly—slightly emotional. Christian mumbled, and suddenly his mother's voice covered his: "Stop! Stop!" "Christian clenches his fists, stops talking, leaves the room," said the reporter. The next day, he was interviewed by the same person, but without his mother, in a café. He began by saying, "I can't speak, I can't speak." Then, responding to questions, he said that yes, he had been shut up in a psychiatric clinic. "It was traumatic." Why had this been done? "Well—you know—parents are responsible for their children. They have every right." Was it true that he had also been sent to an observation center? And why? "Because I was considered a delinquent minor. By my parents—I think." It had been "their decision." Had he loved Gabrielle? (What a question! Was he likely to say no a few days after her suicide?) "Yes." Had she loved him? "I think so," said Christian, making a careful division of responsibility; for who can say what the other person really thinks and feels? Did he feel to blame for her death? Absolutely not. "Justice" was responsible, he said. "And certainly my parents. I think so. I can't reproach them too much—not for the moment." But then he decided he blamed more than merely "justice" and his parents; there was the appeal *a minima*, and also her sleep cure, "if it is true that she took one"—his uncertainty showing that they had not been in touch before the end, that he had no idea what was happening to her or where she was. "You weren't suicidal after *your* sleep cure? " the reporter asked. "No, because I love life." Also, he was sure he would stay alive: "At least, I hope so!" He laughed, as if he and the interviewer were conspirators—at any rate, both living. He sounded charming and young. "She loved life too," he said quickly, overtaking any impression of carelessness. "But she was desperate. I know people who committed suicide after taking the sleep cure." One wondered what he meant, exactly. How many of his friends had killed themselves? How many had been obliged to undergo such extreme therapy? If it was true that this treatment was such a frequent cause of suicide that a seventeen-year-old had known several cases, wouldn't the law step in, or a medical association? "Every day she saw that the day when we might perhaps live together was farther and farther away," he said, without explaining that, either—for every day brought him nearer his majority and freedom to choose. Apart from their brief and confused love affair when he was sixteen, they had not been together much. One wonders if they had really known each other well. Did Christian accuse anyone *in particular*? "I accuse everything," he said suddenly. "Society. Everything. Society, and judges, and parents. I accuse all reactionary and bourgeois parents." It sounded like a lesson, like memory work. It was not the voice of the person who had laughed a minute earlier and said, "I love life." He sounded like a parrot with a Marseille accent. "My future is my own business," he went on, in a new voice, a normal voice. "I won't forget what happened, but I wish everybody else would."

Two weeks later, he vanished again. He had not run away. "He is exiled," someone who knew the family said, on the radio. Also that the subject of Gabrielle Russier was taboo in the Rossi household, because of the three younger children. Christian was described as "torn" between his loyalty to his family and his rejection of them.

By the spring of 1970, he was living in Paris and was said to have broken with his parents. He was eighteen. His "correspondent," the person appointed by the court to keep an eye on a minor, was the Protestant minister who had married Gabrielle and Michel Nogues and christened her twins. In June, Christian sat for his baccalaureate examinations in his and Gabrielle Russier's old school; then he came back to Paris "to find employment." In a radio interview, his clergyman correspondent said that Christian was in a bad way. "Although I am a Christian, I would have found it hard to forgive my parents had I been in his place," said the minister. He was referring not to what happened to Gabrielle but to Christian's having been committed to the care of a Juvenile Court and to the sleep cure. "He must be left alone, in peace. Anything could happen now. His greatest terror is of being sent back to a psychiatric clinic. He is obsessed with this fear."

He is still living in Paris, and he failed his bac and is preparing for the examinations over again by correspondence course. At the beginning of this year, a film about the *affaire—Mourir d'Aimer*—was released, and in the next two months there was a spate of articles and interviews. A reporter for *France-Soir* said that Christian was working for thirteen hundred and fifty francs a month as an assistant projectionist in a Paris cinema, but two months later, when a reporter for another journal asked him what he was doing, he refused to answer. He is not as kind, or as neutral, about his parents as he was in September, 1969. Last January, in an interview over Radio-Luxembourg, a reporter asked, "Do you think you will ever see your parents again?," and the answer was "I might—you can't avoid seeing people accidentally, sometimes."

And *Le Nouvel Observateur* for March 1–7, 1971, had an interview from which the following exchange is taken:

> Q: Did they [his parents] love you very much?
>
> CHRISTIAN ROSSI: I don't know.
>
> Q: And you, do you love them?
>
> C. R.: No.
>
> Q: Why?
>
> C. R.: Because I haven't all that much in common with them. . . . You don't choose your parents. It seems fine to have parents who say they are on the left, who tell you, "It's the right thing to seize the college, or to occupy the lycée," but when it comes to adapting their ideas to their life or to the life you lead with them, *eh bien, ça ne va plus*.

NOT LONG AFTER Gabrielle Russier's death, President Pompidou held a televised press conference. The last question, a totally unexpected one, was asked by a reporter from Radio-Télévision-Monte-Carlo: What had the President done about the Russier case, and, in view of the outcome, what did he think? "I won't tell you what I did," said the President, "but this is what I think." To those watching, he seemed truly taken aback, as if the question was the last one in the world he expected in a conference devoted to the Common Market and planes for Israel. He hesitated, as though he was deeply moved and trying to control his feelings, and at the same time wanted to be certain that what he said would be the right thing. President Pompidou is an *agrégé* in French literature (as Gabrielle Russier had been) and the editor of an anthology of French poetry. Now he recited the first verse of a poem by Paul Éluard, as though drawing it out of the very back of his memory. This is a poem "about" something, as a story is: about a girl whose hair was cut off after the Liberation, probably because she had slept with Germans, and who was punished to divert attention from real collaborators, the truly guilty. The poet—and the President, apparently—felt "remorse" only for the victim who lay on the pavement "with the look of a lost child," who resembled "the dead" who perished "because they were loved." When poetry is translated, the result is either not faithful, not poetry, or not English. This is the verse that President Pompidou repeated:

> *Comprenne qui voudra*
> *Moi mon remords ce fut*
> *La malheureuse qui resta*
> *Sur le pavé*
> *La victime raisonnable*
> *À la robe déchirée*
> *Au regard d'enfant perdue*
> *Découronnée défigurée*
> *Celle qui ressemble aux morts*
> *Qui sont morts pour être aimés.*

No one knew what the President had meant by "what I did," for he could not have interfered with legal procedure. The Minister of Justice had already explained, in a taped statement read over the radio, that the magistrates of the Public Ministry were not obliged to consult anyone, and each had acted within the law and "according to his conscience." What everyone seized on now were phrases from the Éluard poem: "my remorse," "the reasonable [i.e., well-behaved] victim," and, above all, "dead because they were loved." To a foreigner, it seemed an extraordinary moment for television—a great public figure caught off guard, and the head of a highly literate nation turning to literature in order to explain himself. The effect was somewhat lessened when the reporter from Radio-Télévision-Monte-Carlo said that the question had been planted, and that he had been "approached" and told that if he mentioned the Russier trial no one would object. If true, it is interesting that an independent, peripheral station was used, and not one of the government's own channels. The President of the Republic can't be responsible for every "approach" made in his name. His slight hesitation before replying, his emotion, and his surprise seemed too spontaneous to have been counterfeit. Perhaps he had already wondered what he would say if the question should be asked. Anyway, someone asked it.

BEFORE HER DEATH, Gabrielle Russier wrote, "If only what is happening to me could at least serve for something!" One thing did happen—a law was passed making preventive detention the exception rather than the rule. Some lawyers were still skeptical: they pointed out that under the penal code as it existed it was already supposed to be the exception. The Minister of Justice declared that the new law had nothing whatever to do with Gabrielle Russier. And the brother of a student arrested during a university riot wrote to *Le Monde* in July, 1970, protesting that his brother had been in jail since April and that the examining magistrate had now taken off for a month's vacation in Turkey.

For the rest: Two chalk inscriptions remained for a long time on the door of her apartment—"Z," meaning "She lives," and "Immortal Gatito." Her students had put them there.

Paul Léautaud,
1872–1956

ALL LIVES ARE interesting; no one life is more interesting than another. Its fascination depends on how much is revealed, and in what manner. In the rainy Paris winter of 1950 I heard, by chance, a radio interview that had the tone of natural conversation. Someone I at first took to be an old woman was recalling a 19th-century childhood and a pair of unbelievably disastrous parents. The voice was mocking and lively, the dreadful recital was broken by hoots of sudden laughter. Presently I realized the speaker must be a man, either a writer or an actor.

The name Paul Léautaud meant next to nothing then, nor did it to most French listeners, as it turned out. He *was* an author, but his books were out of print. A critic had prophesied, "He will not be appreciated until he has died and 20 volumes of his journal have been published." Jules Renard had mentioned him once: "the great insulter."

That was all. As for his interviewer, Robert Mallet, one could tell only that he was no ordinary radio hack. (He is now rector of the University of Paris.)

What stopped me was that I had never heard an interview of that quality. The French, I had already discovered, possessed a slightly daft gift for radio which, unfortunately, was not to be carried over to television. Programs were individual, unpunctual, and seemed man-made rather than machine-made. (Among other oddities was a music critic who played the overture to *Der Freischütz* every morning for what seemed a lifetime; he had a widespread and vigilant audience who fought off official attempts to make him change the record.) I doubt if any broadcasting system other than the French would have allotted 10 evening hours to a forgotten writer nearly 80 years of age whose every utterance rubbed against the official grain, or would then have expanded the schedule to 38 hours only because listeners were interested.

The programs went on for months, over two different stations. It was difficult to make any sense of the wavelengths or the timetables. In the provinces one heard an announcer tinkling "Paris vous parle!" as though he had never recovered from the miracle of distant sound. Through a barrage of static, when I was lucky, I heard Léautaud describe his infatuation and lack of audacity with Marguerite Moreno, Colette's actress friend, who finally protested, "Well, Léautaud, I'd like to make love before I'm 60." Or heard him informing the long-suffering Robert Mallet, who was very like a jockey trying to draw rein on a frisky horse, that fatherhood had made an imbecile of him, that he was pretentious, that he had misused the French language. (Léautaud detested new words and would not even allow "intellectual" as a noun.)

He was, and he said so, an atheist in a Catholic context, an unpatriotic citizen during the worst of times—for example, during wars. He never voted, disliked children, relayed unspeakable gossip about his own parents. He was a hedgehog of fixed ideas, a number of them disconcerting: He did not understand why May 8, 1945, should have been declared a holiday. He was mean, slanderous, and cruel; he could also display generosity and great delicacy in his judgments. Even at his most caustic there was a simplicity, an absence of vanity, rare in a writer. He talked about death and love, authors and actors, Paris and poetry, without rambling, without moralizing, without a trace of bitterness for having fallen on hard times. He was sustained, without knowing it, by the French refusal to accept poverty as a sign of failure in an artist. Léautaud, at rock bottom, still had his credentials.

His impact on the young must have been a surprise to him. Of course, he was anti-family, which helped. But he also offered heedless, erratic *opinion*, which made him a rare creature at that time; the prevailing climate then, as it always is after a war, was stagnant and afraid. He had been writing for more than 50 years, and now a generation of grandchildren discovered him. Having discovered, they thought they owned. The mistake was understandable. His best qualities were limited to conversation. In order to listen, one had to approach him. Anyone so foolhardy made a second discovery: He was not a lovable old grump, a mixture of The Misanthrope and Father Christmas, but a literary snapping turtle who bit to wound.

The trouble was that everything Paul Léautaud publicly scorned but privately wanted, such as fame, love and money, came too late to be useful. He had been notorious most of his life, but only in the gossipy, essentially provincial heart of literary Paris. The sudden vogue that brought mail from strangers arrived when he was nearly 80. By then he had become a toothless eccentric—ex-critic, ex-editor, ex-poet and novelist—shuffling through the streets of Fontenay-aux-Roses, near Paris, carrying a string bag full of guts for his cats, scowling at anyone who dared say a word to him. His house was a slum, his garden an animals' graveyard.

Such furniture as he owned had been clawed to the bone by the 24 cats who slept in his bedroom at night. He was still young enough for hopelessly complicated love affairs—at 81 with two jealous women at once, both of whom he left at 82 for a girl of 16—and he was still keeping, by candlelight, with a goose-quill pen, the journal that would turn out to be one of the most remarkable studies of character ever written in French.

He became the object of gifts, solicitude and affection, all of it unwelcome. It is an affection that continued, through the long centenary celebration of his birth. One had only to watch the faces three-deep before an armchair or an inkwell that once belonged to him. Although the French have no more native talent than the rest of us for unrequited love, Léautaud was treated with an indulgence usually reserved for cats and children. Ragged, cutting, certainly ungrateful, he was, he is, a public property, specifically of that Parisian public whose knowledge of a writer's life is untempered by too much familiarity with his work. "Students like him because he never gave in to any system, men because he was a libertine, women because he needed a mother," a librarian explains. Perhaps; but perhaps he also reflected petit-bourgeois crotchets and misjudgments.

His suspicion of foreigners, his mistrust of power and authority, his quarrels with his landlords and his fears of being evicted reflected their own disputes and uncertainties. He was not intimidatingly educated, though he had learned the good grammar that used to be taught in the lower grades. Also—and this is far from the least of it—he was dementedly fond of animals in a country where there are more pets in proportion to population than in Great Britain.

It is typical of Léautaud that even his centenary should have been honored too late, with the anniversary—Jan. 18, 1972—skipped or forgotten. Performances dedicated to him were scheduled at the Comédie Française during a period of strikes, so that no one knew until the last second if the curtain would go up. Books have been appearing since last spring—a new biography, a picture album, his correspondence, someone's memoirs—at a rate unheard of in his lifetime, crowded by the ritual memorial exhibition of photos and letters at the Bibliothèque de l'Arsenal. This memorial was the third of its kind since he died in 1956, and that may be the last we hear of Léautaud until 2006, when his unexpurgated letters and diaries can be read in their full candor and wickedness. By then, the men and women he described and dissected will either have died too, or will be much too ancient to care what Léautaud said about them.

Only one volume of the journals appeared in his lifetime; 18 have been published since he died. They are the faithful notes of a misogynist who could not do without women; of a bachelor who trusted only the dependent love of animals; of a drama critic who thought that seeing a play and then describing it was all nonsense; of an instinctive writer who lacked imagination (he could not write about anything except his father, his mother and himself); of a pitiless observer who craved "nothing but tenderness" in return for sarcasm; of a narrow Parisian who never traveled and still knew that "one's country is one's language," and that "the only country that matters is life itself."

They are also an account of theatrical and literary Paris between 1893 and 1956, wide in scope and full of sharp, biased detail: "I have prejudices I treasure." He would not stand for any form of grandiloquence where writing was concerned, and words such as "inspiration" were shot down rapidly: "When I see my father dying and write about his death I am not inspired, I am describing." Asked why he had been at his dreadful father's deathbed at all, he said, "It was only curiosity. *Cu-ri-o-si-té.*" (Actually, he provided more filial devotion than Léautaud *père* had any right to expect.) Almost to the end he went on teaching himself: "A writer who accepts an award is dishonored." "Never stop simplifying." "Know how to select." He was an old man and could still write, "Écrire! Quelle chose merveilleuse!" It was an almost carnal delight that never left him; nor did his *cu-ri-o-si-té*.

Of course every word of this is contradictory. Léautaud was an almost exact mixture of breadth and smallness, and we prefer writers to be consistent. Like most people who save face with irony, he expected to be understood even when he was dealing in opposites. Léautaud was a young man in his twenties when the Dreyfus case became a national obsession, a matter of blind patriotism vs. justice. His close friend, the poet Paul Valéry, persuaded him to give money to a fund that was being collected by a notoriously anti-Semitic newspaper. Valéry, the prudent conservative, made a small donation and wrote in the contributors' book, "Not without reflection." Léautaud wrote beneath this, "Léautaud—*for* order, *against* justice and truth."

He was furious when the next day's newspaper had it, "for order, for justice and truth." He had expected everyone to understand that he was pro-Dreyfus and had merely written an ironic paraphrase of Goethe's priorities. It took courage to be openly Dreyfusist, and Léautaud was. It was also in him to complain that the heroines of Corneille and Racine were being performed by Jewish actresses with misshapen ears. (The persistent French fantasy about Jewish ears might be worth an anthropologist's attention: they are supposed to stick out, like President Kennedy's, or to be set low on the head, like those of Pope John XXIII, or to have attached earlobes, like Virginia Woolf's.)

At the beginning of this century, Mercure de France was at once a publishing house and the name of an avant-garde review. Léautaud was employed by both, as a sort of vague sub-editor at one, and as drama critic by the other. His editorial salary was about 30 prewar dollars a month. Even given five times the buying power his salary would have now, it was not a sum that allowed much elbow room. His wages were never raised, but actually lowered whenever a pretext came to hand (a war, hard times); once they were cut by two-thirds. He never protested; he seems to have taken poverty for granted.

He was the mainstay of the review. Readers outside the capital, unlikely to see a Paris play, took *Mercure de France* only to read Maurice Boissard (his pseudonym as a critic). He was, someone wrote, "a puppy who had taken theater by the neck," but it was a theater accustomed to praise and flattery, and the puppy made mortal enemies. He hated the pompous Comédie Française delivery and thought nothing of bawling objections in the middle of a classical tirade. If no notice was taken of his protest, he simply went to sleep. When he admired a play, he put off writing about it because he wanted to take time and thought. As a result the best productions were never mentioned. Often he wrote about something else entirely (his most quoted non-review is about the death of a dog called Span) with one dismissive sentence for play and author.

After several years of this, the editor of the magazine was so worn down by complaints from the profession, including those of his wife, who was a writer, that he replaced Léautaud with a tractable critic who is today quite forgotten. Léautaud was immediately claimed by every rival review in Paris. "I am too independent for you," he warned André Gide, who had just offered him twice his old salary and the promise of complete freedom at the *Nouvelle Revue Française*. Gide said independence was just what he wanted, which is what employers are apt to imagine as an abstract principle. *Nouvelles Littéraires* also longed for an unchecked critic, and said so in a comically solemn pledge signed by three editors. Somewhat later Jean Paulhan on the left, then Drieu de la Rochelle on the right (he committed suicide when Germany was defeated) were to give the same promise of noninterference.

Léautaud tried them all in turn. In every case the editor reneged, usually under pressure from political or literary cronies: Léautaud had attacked Jules Romains; he was antimilitary and a dangerous pacifist . . . Jean Paulhan balked after receiving one letter from a Communist intellectual of the thirties. Drieu de la Rochelle read Léautaud's copy but seemed afraid of sending it to the printer. At that point, Léautaud, now in his sixties, gave up. The hounds baying after him were always artists, writers and actors. The reading public adored him, but none of them dined with editors.

All that he had to live on now was his mite of an income from Mercure de France, the publishers; and it was this moment that Jacques Bernard, the director, chose for giving him six days' notice. Bernard assured him he had no professional fault to find: "It is just for the pleasure of not having to see you again." He added, "Even if I have to pay for it out of my own pocket." (He never did.) Léautaud replied that it was only right to pay for pleasure. He went back to his office, packed up decades of paper, and departed without a word of protest.

He was 69. This was during the Occupation, the worst of times. He had been with Mercure de France for most of his adult life. Only once had he ever thought of going, and that was in 1936, when Georges Duhamel became director and committed several sacrilegious acts: he got rid of the gas lamps and had the offices wired for electric light; he installed one telephone, ordered one typewriter and hired one female secretary. Léautaud, who preferred candlelight to any other, was bothered by reforms: "Why change something that suits me?" Something he never changed was his horror of capital punishment or punitive justice of any kind. After the war when Jacques Bernard was tried for collaboration with the Nazis, Léautaud refused to testify; when a subpoena was served on him he pretended to be feeble-minded. All the same, his abrupt dismissal had been a blow, and it was now that he began to slip from sardonic to sour.

A student who had an appointment to meet him was greeted with "I am not in" and a slammed door. When a half brother heard he was in need and sent him money his reaction was, "I would not have done the same for him." During a radio interview he remarked that he had always wanted a pair of checked trousers. A young boy immediately wrote that his father, a tailor, would be glad to make them for nothing. Léautaud took it as an insult and snapped, on the air, "Do these people imagine I go around bare-arsed?" How much of it was misplaced bravado? He was as suspicious of kindness, as defensively insolent, as a street child who has known nothing but horror.

He was, in fact, a product of Paris streets, particularly of the quarter south of Pigalle called Notre-Dame-de-Lo-rette. He was the illegitimate son of a prompter at the Comédie Française and a young actress named Jeanne Forestier. "I was never lucky with women," he wrote. "I was three days old when my mother dumped me." No one brought him up, in any real sense. He had his own house key from the age of 5, and an order from his father not to slam the door. From this father, miserly and brutal, he inherited a passion for the theater, a habit of collecting stray animals and another of making loveless conquests. He once complained that between the ages of 15 and 32 he'd had "only 40 women," 22 of them "only once." "How my father would pity me if he could see these figures."

In adolescence he was made to wear costumes cast off from the Comédie Française wardrobe. He learned to brazen it out and kept a defiant taste for looking peculiar. As a drama critic he would turn up on opening nights wearing indescribable trousers and, as he did not own an overcoat, two jackets. The shorter of the two was the least shabby and so he wore it on top. At night he slept in street clothes, usually one of the jackets. When he was 80, he bought six pairs of shoes, six new hats and two overcoats with the money he earned from his broadcasts. He had to be coaxed to accept the fee: "I am not a mercenary."

Beyond all question it was the absent mother who warped his life. She came to see him for the first time when he was 5 and cried, "God, what a disagreeable child!" After that she sometimes arrived with presents, on visits that filled him with "fear and anxiety." When he was 9, she suddenly sent for him. He found her in bed, half naked, her hair undone. Bored and mischievous, she took the child in her arms and promised him an affection she knew she could not sustain. "Je sentais contre ma joue la douceur de ses seins qui tremblaient en mesure avec les baisers." It sounds like a parody of a Belle Époque novel, but it is Léautaud's memory of the erotic moment that brought him to an impasse. In old age he still spoke of Jeanne's hair, her perfume, her beautiful underclothes.

He never saw her again until he was nearly 30 and had been summoned to Calais where his aunt, Jeanne's sister, was about to die. This aunt was the only relative ever to have shown him kindness. She had been Léautaud *père*'s mistress until Jeanne took her place. Her daughter, Paul's cousin and half-sister, had died in childhood, completely neglected by Paul's father.

At 29 Paul was awkward, and so shabby that his grandmother, a stranger he called "Madame," gave him money for clothes. She warned him not to tell Jeanne, also sent for, that he was her son. She had married in Geneva, and would not want a reminder of her past. His mother was still attractive, "light and quick." He heard her asking, "Who is that young man?" "Paul," said his grandmother, evidently forgetting her own warning. "Who is Paul?" "Why, your son!"

One of Jeanne's first questions of the son she had not seen for 20 years was, "Do you like women?" It was the start of a sensual flirtation that lasted the three days it took for the wretched sister to die. She told Paul how his father had seduced her when she was 18, in her sister's presence, after she had shared a bed with the two and had watched them making love. On the last evening she invited Paul to her room and undressed "until she wore nothing but a transparent chemise." Paul, who had fallen in love with her, asked if he was to spend the night. The question was too blunt. She was shocked, or pretended to be, and sent him away. Fifty years later he was still bemoaning his lack of enterprise—he should have insisted. What he also regretted was the loss of "a splendid subject to write about."

As soon as Jeanne was back in Geneva the game bored her. She was afraid he might come to Switzerland, where she had invited him, but where she had a respectable doctor husband and new children. She wrote affectionately, then coldly, then not at all. Once again she was the childhood mother, bringer of "fear and anxiety." He gave one of her letters to a friend, unopened, asking, "Can I bear this?" The friend read it and said, "No."

If Jeanne had no sane reason for hating the son she had abandoned, he soon provided one. During the three days at Calais he had never stopped taking notes. A year later, Jeanne, if she cared to, could read a great deal about herself in a novel called *Le Petit Ami*. The novel created a scandal. Like the later *In Memoriam*, which dealt with Paul's father, it was a statement that one's mother is not untouchable and that parents are not necessarily noble and good. (Even half a century later Robert Mallet, Léautaud's radio interviewer, kept suggesting that perhaps Jeanne had only been trying to demonstrate "la tendresse d'une maman.") *Le Petit Ami* prompted one remark that became celebrated: "Not just anyone can be the son of a whore." The speaker was a minor authoress named Rachilde, of whom little else has survived.

Of course, he never married. "Marriage makes cuckolds and patriotism creates imbeciles." That is, inevitably. He remained a lifelong seducer of married women, among them a harpy he named "The Scourge." He blamed his stormy love life on the natural inferiority of women, their lack of moral qualities, their inability to give affection. But in his journal he admitted, "The truth is that I never had the women I wanted and now it is too late." The only women he admired were those he never tried to love. Colette was one. Marie Dormoy, his editor and biographer, was another, though friendship did not prevent his demolishing her in his diaries and letting her read his remarks. They lunched together every Sunday for 30 years. The cement of their alliance was a passion for animals, a fondness for poetry, a mutual talent for gossip and a number of shared, or complementary, prejudices.

"I am not anti-Semitic," Mlle. Dormoy said recently, "but I hate Protestants. Also, I don't like Poles." It was suggested that perhaps she simply did not like anything beginning with "p," such as potatoes. "No, I like potatoes," she said. It was all in the same tone, on the same level, rather like Léautaud's saying he was not anti-Jewish "in a social sense" but disliked the Jewish theater—which meant most of the playwrights of his time.

He made Marie Dormoy his heir and literary executor. Actually, she had been trying for years to purchase the still unpublished manuscript of the journals for a private arts foundation of which she was librarian. She once offered him the prewar equivalent of about $200. Léautaud, who had no money sense, consulted André Gide and Paul Valéry. They told him to ask for 10 times the figure, and there the matter rested.

What happened next is not too clear. During the Occupation, after he had been sacked from Mercure de France, Léautaud had nothing to live on. He also became perhaps unduly alarmed when Mlle. Dormoy told him the Germans were destroying private diaries. Mlle. Dormoy, now in her late eighties, sometimes recalls having given an unspecified sum for the journal, but sometimes remembers that no money was involved and that Léautaud wanted her to put the manuscript in a safe place. However it came about, she returned from a visit to Fontenay-aux-Roses with an unwieldy bundle of paper. The journals were written on yellow scraps, on torn foolscap sheets, on the backs of bills, inside the lids of Camembert boxes and on the cardboard of sugar containers, even on toilet paper. The handwriting was small and rather attractive, but virtually impossible to decipher. More, the scraps were unsorted and often without a date.

Mlle. Dormoy selected, separated, dated, transcribed, and by the end of the war had some 12,000 pages typed. Because his frankness could have created "a nest of libel suits," she altered names, initials, addresses, deleted the choicer insults, but left several unkind remarks about herself. How much editorial fiddling went on will be known in 2006, though one wonders if anyone at that point will have enough patience to put the record straight. His correspondence, published a few months ago, has been carefully pruned too, and the result is rather dull, which the journals never are. Actually, Léautaud wrote so many infuriating letters that a great many were probably torn to shreds after one reading.

He wanted to say before he died, "I regret everything,' words, he said, "that will sum up my life." The last thing he did say before dying in his sleep was, "Foutez-moi la paix," which was more typical. After his death Marie Dormoy found a box filled with dust on which was written, "Flowers my mother sent me, 13 November 1901," and, in the breast pocket of the jacket he slept in, the photograph of a woman standing naked in a nondescript room. The woman's long hair has been combed forward so that it covers her face. Behind the picture, in Léautaud's hand, is, "If I should depart [i.e., die] never speak about me. Let no one know or even guess how much I loved you. Keep the memory for yourself, like a secret." There is nothing remotely like this in his published journals. Who was she? "A married woman," says Marie Dormoy, prudently, which is either a secret or a euphemism, and in any case will have to do until 2006.

Introduction to
The War Brides

"Bring back a real English lady."
—*Advice to a Canadian Army private from his father,*
in a short story printed during the war.

DURING THE WAR there began to flourish in Canada a
sort of sub-literature that faded soon after V-E Day
along with the innocent and elderly generation that produced it. Thumpingly patriotic and Empire-minded, its
chief contribution was to render unbridgeable the gap
that already existed between men overseas and the civilian population at home. This gap, or fissure, was as
profoundly psychological as physical for it separated two
kinds of experience, the real from the sentimental. It had
been created in part by the songs and movies dumped in
Canada as second-hand patriotic fodder; by the rather
dainty propaganda issuing from Canadian sources, notably the National Film Board; and by tons of romantic misinformation filed by correspondents operating
abroad. The war had become a myth while it was still
a passage of history; the civilian attitude to the women

Canadian soldiers married overseas has to be seen in the light of this myth-in-progress.

Consider a story about an overseas courtship published during the war. Bud, an inarticulate and not very bright Canadian private, becomes engaged without the least difficulty or opposition or even much effort to the wealthy, young and beautiful Lady Clarissa. Clarissa's father shows no curiosity about Bud or about the future to which he is committing his only child. Instead of asking a pertinent question or two he uncorks champagne and proclaims his faith in the Empire—"building a bridge" is what he calls this alliance. Before the end of the story Bud manages to put a whole sentence together: his father owns half of Canada, including "a railway or two." As Bud was embarking with his regiment, he recalls, his father said, "Bring back a real English lady." Obviously an important segment of society has been missing until now in that rough corner of Empire—refined womanhood; the reader is left with the feeling that Lady Clarissa will be the first in Canada of her kind.

This was a story written by a Canadian, for Canadians, some of whom probably did not find it preposterous simply because it took place within the myth. Bud (the knight who was really a prince) and Clarissa (daughter of a grateful sovereign) meet in a fairy-tale kingdom very far from Canada indeed. Looking for "a real English lady," supreme wartime souvenir, Bud stood for the soldier civilians wanted to see; by stepping over the chasm to a legendary Old Country he became transformed. In the wartime novel *Remember Me* by Edward Meade, two

Canadian privates in England wonder why they cannot find the thatched cottages their English cousins have been sending them on Christmas cards for years and years. How much is allowable fantasy and how much is a lie? True to their generation, the Canadians cannot decide.

That was one aspect of the legend. Another took the form of anecdotes. English girls, avid for marriage, were said to leap on any passing Canadian and drag him into blacked-out doorways for goings-on too shameful to describe—the soldier meanwhile clinging to a lamppost and protesting, "No, no, I'm engaged to a nice girl in Regina!" Torn from his lamppost and his chastity the Canadian, as the expression went, "had to marry her." Stories embroidered on this pattern increased as the number of overseas marriages multiplied. It was widely repeated that the Army encouraged such marriages in order to keep the men docile and to prevent them from deserting or getting drunk and shooting up Aidershot. I doubt if many people at home knew about Canadian Army Routine Order 788 and its bleak reminder, " . . . the general policy is to dissuade members of the Canadian Army from a marriage in foreign lands," or would have believed it if they had been told.

From the beginning of the war unmarried Canadian women were assigned a role: "the girl back home." They were assured they would gather lilacs, that there would be bluebirds and that the absent "you" of the songs would be back. In time it became apparent that lilacs were indeed being gathered, but by someone else. Standards of female conduct were offered as a sop: the insufferable Mrs. Miniver, or the wife of the RN captain in Noel Coward's *In*

Which We Serve who when asked by her husband—who had been posted missing—if she had worried about him replies, "Of course not, I've been much too busy." (Of the unnatural, the fatuous, the witless behaviour that was demanded of women not nearly enough has been said.) A great many women lived lives that were lonely and isolated, affected by the war and yet not part of it, dependent on mail, with real life—as they imagined it—indefinitely postponed. Word drifted back of the superior quality of women *there*; they had suffered, Canadians had not; they were good sports, easy to get along with; they had an advantage said to be lacking in Canadian women—they understood men. Recipients of this news—now assigned a new role, "the girl I used to know"—understood that "wonderful women" would soon be followed by wonderful girl I've met," followed in turn by "married."

A number of somewhat floundering studies tried to explain why these marriages were taking place, and it was here that fact and legend began to fuse. Marriage *there* carried an echo of historical reality, a proof of participation in a war civilians were still inclined to see as romantic. The truth was obviously simpler. A two-liner of the period probably had it pat: "What has she got that I haven't got?" "Nothing, but she's got it here." The girls cast off could only go on hearing descriptions of the pluck and high spirits of those characters of fiction who had turned into real rivals, and continue to accept the harping accusation, with its flavour of inflicted guilt, dished out by war correspondents and returning Canadians: "You people don't know what hardship means." Hardship, like expectation, has its own fever chart. War brides arriving in Canada often wondered what sort of reputation had preceded them. Canadians probably ought to have been wondering what sort of Canada had been offered to them. If it was true that the idea civilians had of the war and of life in Western Europe was miles from the truth of it, men overseas (irritated by civilian obtuseness, as one was frequently reminded) painted for their brides a highly idealized picture of the Canada they had left behind—a picture enhanced by homesickness, youthful memories and the passage of time. How very long that passage was seems to have been forgotten. Europeans still know nothing about it, any more than they realize how large the contingent was in proportion to Canada's small population. In fact, the long dislocation of an entire generation would be disastrous for some of the men and women in it. Canadian men were the first to go, the last to come back, and there were an awful lot of them.

More than forty-one thousand Canadian soldiers married overseas, mostly in Britain. Towards the end of the war their wives—so-called war brides, a term some of them detested—began to arrive in Canada along with some twenty-one thousand children. Even for a nation built on the principle of immigration it was an unusual wave: all one generation, all women, nearly all from the same racial stock. A foreigner reading this volume might be led to think they were also uniformly educated and that they had found themselves, almost to a woman, plunged in a primitive culture that was inferior to anything they had known. Of course something like that did take place;

the accounts provided are eloquent. Most of the brides had grown up in towns and cities and might have been just as daunted by life on an English or Scottish farm, few of which were any more modern or comfortable than those in Saskatchewan. The trouble was that no one had warned them or explained exactly what is contained in the words "prairie winter." To a great many of these women the cultural poverty of their new surroundings was devastating; the wonder was that they stayed. But to make the picture complete and clear it must also be said that there arrived a number of women who were giddy, or silly, or who wanted to get away from home, who were emigrating for a lark, who had married too young and too fast; and there were some whose backgrounds would have seemed limited even by the most humble Canadian standards. The shock for Canadian families receiving them was often very great—as great as that felt by brides who found they had married into families where the only conceivable use for a book was as a doorstop.

The brides were issued with Canadian cookbooks; it would be interesting to know what was in them. The recipe for something more practical than pumpkin pie was probably in order, though there is no real preparation for anything as radically different from Europe as the North American continent. No European except for a Russian can ever take in the size of Canada except by travelling across it, preferably by train. A long plane journey gives some idea, particularly at night when the lights of cities are like rafts in what seems to be the emptiest and darkest of seas. A European's first impression is often of immeasurable physical solitude. I did not know until I had read this book how dirty and uncomfortable Canadian trains seemed to the war brides, or how monotonous the land appeared on the other side of the sooty windows, with its miles of unchanging vegetation and unbroken colour patterns. To this strange, wild, entirely other scenery they were expected to respond at once, and to come up with reactions satisfying to Canadians. Travelling on a special train of war brides from Halifax as a young and ignorant reporter I kept asking them to comment on what they saw. We were in New Brunswick, in a drenching rain. Nearly every aspect of the Canadian landscape struck me as moving and poetic then, for reasons that were historical or literary or had something to do with Canadian painting and which were at a remove from the land itself: a field was not a field—it was a Goodridge Roberts. I foolishly expected a reaction tuned to mine. "What does it look like to you?" I asked tense and exhausted women, many of whom had not travelled much even in England.

"It looks rather like Surrey," said one poor bride, in desperation. Of course, it does not; I could not understand then that she had nothing to match it to.

All emigration is based on misapprehension; so is every welcome. The only German bride I encountered told me much later that she had not been on Canadian soil more than an hour before she was asked, "What do you think of the Canadian way of life?" and of the anxiety she felt, knowing that her future probably depended on the right answer. She also secretly wondered how there could be a way of life in a country whose past was so recent—another common misapprehension, for which newcomers pay dearly. A number of brides got down from their special trains at whistle stops in Quebec. Here, if anywhere, the new arrival wanted more than a cookbook (and in English at that!) while her new family would have needed a stout dose of practical reality and open-mindedness. What was probably required was a meeting of saints. One bride found that although she had lived in France, spoke fluent French and was Roman Catholic it still wasn't enough; another took thirteen years to learn enough French to be understood. The surprise is not that a few marriages cracked, but that most of them survived.

No marriage should begin under the roof of parents-in-law; many of these did. One admires the women for sticking it out. It takes only a small amount of imagination to hear the ominous, That's not how *we* do things *here*," which makes an outsider of the son's wife once and for all. There were factors the bride could not be aware of. Sometimes the husband's parents had to face, cope with and conceal from the bride the fact that their son had thrown over his Canadian girlfriend, the one with whom they had shared his overseas letters and already considered a daughter. For the soldier the matter was settled; his parents were left holding the baby—sometimes literally. Canadians were still close to the Depression; the questions the brides heard shouted by workmen along the railway—"Has your man got a job?" and "Where do you all think you're going to live?"—were urgent and immediate. There was a real fear in 1945 that there were not going to be enough jobs to go round; as for living quarters, the expression of the period was, "They'd begrudge you the room for your own grave." From the moment every one of the brides heard, "Has your man got a job?" a myth was dispelled. The Mrs. Miniver image now seemed commonplace, which was not the fault of the new arrivals, who had never asked for that to begin with. They would not be the first immigrants from England to learn that they were British and splendid until they unwittingly put their foot in it, on which they were shortened to Brit. The returning airman who would not abandon his RAF-style moustache or his service lingo for the next twenty years, the blackout beauty with upswept Betty Grable hair, doing her nails as the Canadian landscape rolled by, were by the summer of 1945 already type-cast and dated, like survivors from a jolly film about the war. Canadian ambivalence to Britain was never more marked than just then, as the tide of sentimentality began to ebb, leaving elderly Anglo-Canadians stranded on prewar memories, unable to place English girls who did not seem English enough, and who brought with them a disconcerting glimpse of a socialist future. It was impossible for some Canadians to understand why Churchill had lost the first election after the war. In a discussion that took place in my presence, a new bride said, "Naturally I voted Labour. What has Churchill got to do with the working class?" If she had been foulmouthed her husband's parents could not have been more upset and horrified. The idea that they had a daughter-in-law who was going to say such things *in Canada* was more than they could live with. The mother-in-law asked me not to write what her son's bride had said about Churchill.

"You can see how we'd feel," she said. "After all, we own our own home."

One of several stories circulating at that time had a war bride taken out on a lake and drowned by her husband's family. Everyone knew someone who knew where it was supposed to have happened and how and why it had been hushed up. A new folklore was created about brides who had believed they were marrying rich men (Bud and Lady Clarissa again, in an imaginary sequel) and who found themselves in slums, cabins, shantytowns, on reservations and even in igloos. "And so she turned around and went right back," these stories concluded. But one doesn't need an igloo for strangeness; a peaceful suburb can be quite enough, given a husband who was one man in uniform and quite another in civilian clothes ("He looked like Al Capone," recalls one ex-bride in this book) and with an idealized Canada falling apart. As for "She went right back," how many could or really wanted to? Only a minority, if figures mean anything. Canada had provided passage one way; not many had families who could afford to send the fare home. Some of these girls, who were very young, knew they might never see their parents again. Cheap and easy air travel was barely imaginable. England was as remote as if they had emigrated by sailing ship, while economic difficulties created a second ocean. Reading the account of the lonely young woman who could not afford a five-cent stamp to write to her mother one feels a stab of shame, as if the whole country had been found wanting. The excuse was this: nobody knew. A few who could not conquer their homesickness did go back, probably to discover that the England they returned to was already not the England they'd left. (No national returning ever finds the situation improved, but is convinced it has gone downhill steadily from the moment he departed.) Some, deeply unhappy, stayed because they did not want to hear their parents say, "I told you so."

Most war brides, I think, were helped and welcomed, but I can remember interviewing one—a grave, quiet, self-possessed girl from Scotland—who had arrived into an atmosphere of such demonic intolerance and hatred that I was actually afraid for her. Her husband, unwilling to choose between his bride and his psychotically possessive family, some of whom actually slept in the same room as the young couple, sat in an armchair, looking defeated, fiddling with the dials of a radio. The next day I went back to see her, uninvited and without a professional excuse. I did not tell anyone what I was doing, for this was known as "getting involved," which was a sin against the Holy Ghost. I talked to her, standing in the dark hall of that haunted, evil flat, and offered to try to borrow the money to get her out of it. She did not reject the offer out of hand, or reproach me for my impertinence, but considered the possibility calmly. The fact that I did not have the money myself but would have to raise it (if, indeed, I could) may have weighed in the balance; but what she told me was that she would never go back on her word—she meant her marriage vows—and that as long as she could stand on her two feet she would manage. She would find a job and she would drag that beaten, jobless husband out of his armchair and into a home of their own if it killed her.

She said, "He's a good boy," the "boy" deciding his civilian status in terms of reality; she had probably met him in officer's uniform, giving orders. I don't know what became of her. She is not in this book, though there are some who sound not unlike her. It is probably to them that it should be dedicated.

Paris: The Taste
of a New Age

IT WAS IN a Rue de Sèvres apartment that the French writer Joris Karl Huysmans, with the assistance of Lucifer, tried to evoke the dead. This was in the 1890s, when there was a craze in Paris for apparitions; it has never quite died down. (Huysmans at the time was occupying the only seat left vacant in French literature, that of Christian pessimism. Inching toward Christian optimism should have kept him out of mischief, but he was easily bored.) He managed to conjure up General Boulanger, who had died in exile after failing to bring off a right-wing coup. The general had nothing helpful to say about immanent justice or French politics.

We do not know whether Huysmans ushered him back to wherever he'd come from (a matter of the right incantation) or left him to drift in a kind of limbo between Rue de Sèvres and Rue du Cherche-Midi. Nothing speaks from the narrow courtyard at No. 11. That section of Paris was largely ecclesiastical territory, no place for fallen angels.

When St. Vincent de Paul died, at the age of seventy-nine, in 1660, his heart was presented to the Daughters of Charity and his body was buried on the Right Bank, where the railway station called St. Lazare now stands. Some 170 years later, the Lazarist Brothers, who had in the meantime been dispossessed by the French Revolution, received the present of a large tract of undeveloped land stretching from Rue du Cherche-Midi, where they built a boundary wall three stories high, to Rue de Sèvres, where they built a small, dim chapel of gentle ugliness. They commissioned a silversmith to fashion a full-length glass and silver reliquary (it won a gold medal at an exhibition in 1827) and with immense difficulty hoisted it to a niche directly over the altar.

Wearing the plainest of vestments and buckled shoes, holding the crucifix he had used for the last rites of Louis XIII, Monsieur Vincent has lain there ever since. His hands and face are modeled in wax, "to lend him a more human aspect," a brochure explains. ("There is a lot of wax in Lenin, too," says a Brother, defensively.) His features undoubtedly were copied after the extraordinary portrait by Simon de Tours, who painted Monsieur Vincent as an old man with white eyebrows—plain, ordinary, mysterious, noble. The work of a lesser artist, the wax image inevitably prettifies him; the further we move along in time, the blander the likeness tends to become. Whispering visitors say he looks asleep. It is pointless to wonder what he might have thought of the costly reliquary. He lived and died poor, warning his followers, "The poor are our masters."

The chapel smells of faded flowers, old incense, burning wax: the scent of chapels before Vatican II. Some churches in Paris now look like post offices and somehow smell like them. From the dark nave, the saint's niche seems to float in a bath of light. Visitors tiptoe up a creaking staircase behind the altar. Sometimes they sit on the guardrail, providing a curious and surreal view of backs high up in the chancel; sometimes they kneel and press their lips to the glass case, careful to rub it afterward with a sleeve or a handkerchief. There are always a few Spanish and Portuguese immigrant workers, praying in whispers. The chapel is left unguarded. Nothing is for sale, except the usual church magazines. A coin dropped in the box thuds in emptiness.

The grey façade on the Rue de Sèvres tells nothing. The Lazarists do little to attract the faithful; they find their own way. The place is small, the wooden steps are worn. It would not survive an invasion. A notice in an adjacent corridor requests the favor of prayers "for the 140,000 people who die in the world each day." A prayer formulated as an intention will earn for the well-wisher 100 days of indulgence—remission from the punishment still due to sin after absolution, a sentence served in Purgatory. A prayer learned by heart and recited completely will earn 300 days. The notice has been there since 1907—the year Huysmans died. In 1907, the difference between 100 and 300 days could be measured out in eternity. About 50 million prayers a year took care of all the dead. Infinity ap-

pears as a manageable dimension. It is the street outside
that seems unreasonable.

In the 1970s, when the value of property in Paris began its heady ascent, the Lazarists sold nearly all that was
left of their land (we may now call it real estate). The sale
resulted in the construction of an undistinguished apartment block, a supermarket, and a shopping arcade. The
arcade is in reality a bleak tunnel of storefronts linking
Rue de Sèvres to Rue du Cherche-Midi. Above the Rue
de Sèvres entrance is its name: "*Passage Commercial.*" For
once, a clear purpose has not been disguised by something like "Pompadour's Pathway." Some of the shops
never found takers; their windows still carry glazier's
chalk marks. Some opened and closed rapidly. There is
always one with a "For Rent" sign in the window. Like so
many of the arbitrary projects foisted on Paris, the arcade
does not work because it was not needed. Urban change,
now, has virtually nothing to do with urban requirements.
A considerable amount of innovation seems to drain the
street of its vitality rather than to infuse it with new energy. It is not blight that is settling in but a new sickness—
new to Paris, at least: architectural anemia.

The mind's eye is unreliable. It will see streets as dark
as they were before André Malraux, in his incarnation
as minister of culture, scraped away the dust and grime
of centuries. Some people will tell you that Malraux
had nothing to do with it, that an obscure police prefect
brought into operation a law that had been shut away in a
drawer for years. No matter; the brightening of Paris will
stick to his name. The mind's eye crosses the Pont des Arts

even though the bridge has been shut for a long time and may never be repaired; it lingers in Place Saint-Sulpice under enormous chestnut trees cut down years ago when the underground parking space was built. The asthmatic voice of French pop music is as consistently frail as it was in the sixties; a continuity of a kind. It suddenly delivers an unexpected line in English: "MacDonald is slipping on the canapé." This is not, as you would be justified in thinking, an incident during the usual wildebeest stampede to the buffet at a Paris cocktail party. It is intended to mean that MacDonald has dozed off on a sofa.

In Paris, churches still attract knots of beggars. Clochards wait outside the Chapel of the Miraculous Medal, in Rue du Bac, where Monsieur Vincent's heart is preserved, and where in 1830 Catherine Labouré found the Holy Virgin seated in an armchair. Some lie sound asleep, curled up on the sidewalk in an effluvium of urine and spilled wine. The mind's eye has registered them once and for all as elderly alcoholics; actually, unemployment has brought a handful of younger recruits. Out-of-town pilgrims give them coins before hurrying across to the Bon Marché department store. St. Vincent de Paul, around the corner, has two visitors, Portuguese. One, who probably works as a cleaner, carries her rolled-up apron.

"My daughter," says a solemn man at a dinner party, "has to go to school with the children of Spanish and Portuguese concierges. In the so-called good neighborhoods"— his offhand way of saying he does not really mind where he lives—"most of the children are sent to private schools now. My daughter has no contact with her own culture."

He is left-leaning and would never object to his daughter's mingling with the foreign children—not aloud, at any rate. He disapproves of private schools in principle; they promote caste, they are usually denominational. Public, secular schools are still associated with the struggle to establish the Third Republic. To the suggestion that culture begins at home he replies that he is afraid his daughter's prolonged contact with Spanish children will affect her French.

This is a recent complaint. The blame for the decline of spoken French, particularly in Paris—its slurring and sloppiness, the intrusion into the language of alien words, nearly always given the wrong meanings—is placed on the number of foreign children now in the lower grades. (This does not mean that "Anglo-Saxon cultural imperialism" has been replaced as principal villain.) How much grasp people have of their native tongue in any culture is debatable. French has certainly been affected by a prime minister who did not pronounce his *t*'s and a garrulous Communist party leader unable to utter a *v*. Slavish emulation of the latter on the Communist left has given *pouwoir* for *pouvoir* and a curious *ourire* for *ouvrir*. (The Party keeps threatening to *ourire* political files that will knock the *pouwoir* sideways.) Meanwhile, speakers in the state-controlled media faithfully imitate the voice of *pouwoir* with *quession* for *question*.

"I hope," says the child's father, "that I do not offend your democratic susceptibilities." It must be borne in mind that no turn of phrase in French conversation is ever meant as a joke. "But the truth is that my daughter is bearing the cost of foreign assimilation."

The name on his place card at this formal table indicates clearly that his family had its start in Germany; a good name-detective could even spot the city. Of course, they have been French for a long time—"forever and ever," descendants of old immigration are apt wildly to say.

FERNAND RAYNAUD WAS a relaxed-sounding, pie-faced comedian who, until his death a few years ago, incarnated the hapless citizen at the stage where he has given up struggling against the system and is simply trying to get round it. Sketches such as the one in which the Parisian tries to call the suburb of Asnières and finds it so hopeless that he finally places the call through New York were within a hairline of possibility. De Gaulle had declared the telephone to be "*un gadget*" (defined in the Petit Robert dictionary as "*objet ménager amusant et nouveau*"), and investment in telephone equipment was out of the question until after his retirement. Raynaud would never have run for office; he was too successful, and much too nice. Only one of his sketches showed an unexpected edge of bitterness. He would come on as a dithering caricature of the low-grade civil servant, with a beret straight across his brow (nothing makes a man look more foolish), muttering, "I'm not idiotic. I can't be. I'm French. I'm a customs officer. I can't be idiotic. I'm a French functionary." The collocation of "I'm not idiotic" and "I'm French" seemed so self-evident that the audience would sit in perplexed stillness, waiting for the joke. Raynaud was playing on the ambiguity of feeling toward the *fonctionnaire*: a mixture of envy (he is the only worker in France with job security), contempt (he probably got his job through pull, and now sits there doing nothing), and simple fear (you never know how long his political reach might be). The silence never broke until Raynaud came to "I'm not idiotic. I'm French. My father was called [say] Grabolinsky and my mother was called [say] Pasticceria." The customs officer's deep imbecility was finally revealed—he only *thought* he was French. Raynaud's joke was on the audience, at the exact point of its laughter.

SPANISH AND PORTUGUESE immigration is still at the working-class level. The men often work in building trades— as construction workers, painters, plasterers, electricians. They perform odd jobs: a Portuguese window-cleaner says, "You would never find a Frenchman to do this." Rush around Paris on a *moto* in all weathers for a few francs, he means. No one bears the cost of his children's assimilation. They were on the way to becoming delinquents in their Paris suburb and he sent them home to be raised in his native village. There is an informal division of labor now: the Portuguese have the concierge business pretty well sewn up. They retain Latin habits, calling from windows. Their children play in the street, though after a few years of French schooling they become stiff and careful. The women are cleaners, seamstresses, maids, waitresses at private dinner parties. A Spanish woman solicited for a few hours' cleaning causes offense by saying she wants to think it over. With a million and a half unemployed, what is there to think about? But she is not unemployed—is not on the labor market, that is. Her husband works, they live on his earnings. *Bonne* ("maid") and *Espagnole* hang together, like *J'suis Française* and *J'suis pas idiot*. She has no business refusing. Women say "*mon Espagnole*," "*ma Portuguaise*"; no one asks, "Your Spanish what?"

The Spanish maid has become a stock character in boulevard theater, in those plays that are sold out from season to season and that die in translation. The ringing white telephone (first sound, first act) used to be answered by a pert maid carrying a feather duster—Adelè, Angèle. Now, the *bonne Espagnole* slouches on, raising the spirits of the audience by having a funny accent. The same setting has been used since the 1920s: ferociously lighted living room, French doors opening into a blazing void, staircase with wrought-iron banisters, loggia from which Monsieur or Madame will overhear the second-act indiscretion. Monsieur is still sleeping, and no wonder—the room is full of empty champagne bottles and shed clothes. Madame has gone out, screams the *Espagnole*, obliging the audience with the story so far, or perhaps Madame simply never came home. Monsieur (striped dressing gown, Charvet ascot) descends the stairs. "Who was it, Concepción?" Her very name reduces the house to sobbing laughter. Out of a torrent of incomprehension emerges a clue about the caller: either Monsieur's mistress's husband or Madame's lover. Since the death of the Third Republic there has been only one change: the *bonne* is *Espagnole*. The displaced person enters the art of the host country as a joke.

FÉLIX POTIN WAS a name that stood for middle-class dinner tables. Wines, butter, coffee, and sugar of superior quality were purchased in Félix Potin stores. The name was a novelist's shortcut: "Far from supposing that Ludovic was at this moment waiting for a train in Dijon, Mme. Sanglot serenely picked her way across the agitated boulevard, on her way to shop at Félix Potin." Now the name means chain stores, shopping carts, reasonably cheap food, though the least of the price tags would seem lunatic to Americans. The women at the check-out counters are often Asian and Black. During holiday weekends, when Parisians—French Parisians—depart to the Alps for spring skiing, shoppers are suddenly Portuguese, North African: the metropolitan residue. Rue de Sèvres shrinks to a chain store, an arcade lined with storefronts, half of them blank, a silent chapel with a saint in it. The store, too, is on land that used to belong to the Lazarists.

For the children it is homely, timeless, reassuring. They will never hear their parents deploring the ruin of Paris, or learn nostalgia at second hand. Some probably never stray out of the neighborhood, but that is a Parisian habit. (There are schoolchildren living in outer *arrondissements* who not only have never crossed the Seine but have never seen it.)

The hub of their world is the Montparnasse tower, at the top of the Rue de Rennes. It has been there forever; the urban litter—the fast-food counters set out along the boulevard, the drifts of greasy sandwich papers on the sidewalk—has no beginning. The old Montparnasse railway station, which the tower replaced, was there some fourteen years ago; there are people still living in the neighborhood who went by it every day. Oddly enough, no one can quite say what it looked like. It was low, it was grey, and, yes, it was dirty and run-down. What else? The wooden floors sloped and creaked. There were always a few pimps hanging about, waiting to catch the Breton village girls as they stepped off the train. No one denies that the station was inefficient and had to be replaced. But a postcard view of it arouses no immediate recognition. It might as well have been torn down sixty years ago. What people do recall is that the streets around the station were not as shabby and anonymous as they seem now. There have been few structural changes apart from the tower, which still makes the older buildings look dwarfed and absurd. The changes it has attracted (pizza parlors instead of family restaurants) seem to blind the mind's eye. The nature of a neighborhood has been so fundamentally altered by a single *unnecessary* structure that collective memory is wiped clean.

THE WINDY LITTLE square on the far side of the Bon Marché department store contains the bust of a forgotten hero—the founder of the store, who donated the land to the city. It belongs not to the annals of Paris but to a sub-plot in a malicious novel by Anatole France. There is also a sandpit and a slide. Nothing remarkable, except that such amenities are well within the generation of under-nines. That children are allowed to crouch in very dirty sand with bucket and spade is in itself a tremendous evolution. Until just a few years ago, a foreign parent inviting a child to play with her own would find on the doorstep a mother and child dressed as though for a formal wedding, expecting a quiet *goûter* and an organdy tablecloth. ("They don't know how to play" was a frequent complaint of English-speaking children.)

Now the children of Paris wear comfortable clothes, and that race of tense, elderly, overdressed young has all but disappeared. It is the children of immigrants who are often set down in the sandpit wearing pale colors, with heavy instructions about keeping clean. That there is little mixing is not necessarily a sign of infant xenophobia: children become Parisian before they become French. They observe one another with the brief, prudent, Parisian appraisal that takes in the unknown without acknowledging it. The very small may communicate to the extent of grabbing a toy. Two mothers negotiating the return of a battered plastic cup call to mind one of those French inheritance tangles where brothers and sisters can fight for eight years, tooth and claw, over a worn-out carpet.

Moslems apart, *immigré* parents are careful to give French-born children French names, often choosing those that Paris fashion has left behind. Parents are no longer bound to a state-imposed list of saints and heroes. Bretons who were brave enough to insist on Celtic names used to find themselves raising families without birth certificates, civil status, or legal existence; the children were barred from schools and ineligible for any form of social security. Now that Gwladys is allowed, one never hears it. The sandboxes are populated with Clotildes and Aymars, Clémences and Cyrilles. Birth notices in *Le Figaro* for some time now have been introducing a generation of Laetitias, Virginies, Valentins, and Valentines. It is usual to have a new birth announced "with immense joy" by brothers and sisters who are probably, in fact, gritting their milk teeth. Not long ago Aurélien and Pernelle reported the arrival of Aymeric, while another troop of siblings introduced Élisabeth-Aliénor-Théophilae. Of the new wave of names, southern immigrants greatly favor Vanessa and Sandra. Otherwise they settle for *petits noms* that sound familiar: Maïté (Marie-Thérèse) and Marilu (Marie-Louise).

A child who has fallen down and hurt himself is set on his feet and smacked. "Do you want your face slapped?" a mother asks two little boys who are doing no more than romping. But a child's wail does not necessarily describe humiliation and shock now. Quite often he is simply being mulish and getting away with it. The voice of infant protest has crossed the Atlantic, a few years after the news about women. Children can even be seen sucking their thumbs in public, or clutching a close friend—a diaper or a small pillowcase. Even two years ago it would have been beyond imagining.

Such consolations are absolutely forbidden to immigrant children, who get soundly whacked for putting their thumbs in their mouths. Mediterranean warmth congeals in the north. The mothers are tired and bewildered, lonely and lost. The maternal hand, raised and threatening, is a gesture against life.

"BAD TASTE LEADS to crime." It has been attributed to Sainte-Beuve, to Stendhal, and to Prosper Mérimée, each of whom quoted it. Actually, it was said by a friend of all three, the Baron de Mareste. He was witty, clever, worldly, cultivated, erudite, elegant, and intelligent—in short, an obsolescent species of Parisian. If he still lived, no writer would bother to quote him. Most would shy off even being seen with him. Laughter is intellectually compromising.

Good taste probably leads to bankruptcy. Because of "the decline of atmosphere," rising costs, and a feeling of saturation, there has been a migration of the affluent to the third and fourth *arrondissements*, on the Right Bank, where the most expensive condominiums in Paris are being built almost as fast as permits can be issued. (Fifteen years ago, apartments could be had in the area for bread and butter.) The new settlers crave the old, lost feeling of the Left Bank, an intangible something to do with art. Art means culture, culture means the past, the past means "our cultural patrimony," which is bound to include some of the stuff in the attic. For an intangible something, it comes pretty high. "Atmosphere is a means of exchange," says a real estate agent, quite seriously. The new residents of the Marais, whose arrival has caused an exodus of artisans and the death of their crafts, want a cracking good investment first, then the cultural jam on the bread. They get both. Atmosphere means a house that looks old, on the site of one authentic and destroyed. Sometimes part of the façade is kept, though "seventeenth century" in an advertisement can mean just a scrap of lintel. A mock vestibule contains a piece of staircase leading nowhere. Behind this eminently useless remnant a door opens into a room that looks like the lobby of a private clinic. There is a receptionist in lieu of a concierge, and 250 mailboxes.

Andrée Jacob, *Le Monde*'s crusading specialist on such matters, was born and raised in the Marais. She knows where every stone was quarried. Tiny, tireless, in her mid-seventies, she reports on irreplaceable buildings allowed to crumble for obscure commercial reasons, on fake and gimcrack reconstruction. Some of her fiery articles would bring down libel suits if the people behind the institutions accused did not know that she has, as she puts it, "the dossiers." And so they wait until the ripple of public indignation settles; it never takes long. "They just let the situation rot," she says. Faithfully read, widely respected, she has managed to prevent no more than four or five demolitions, and then only because there were no great financial interests at stake. She has learned that nothing can be done against a combination of political influence, private corporations, and state-controlled banks.

That mixture of state and private enterprise, of nationalized and private funding, is the elastic tissue of Paris operations. Friendship is the backbone. Men who would not have given one another the time of day twenty years ago are now, if not hand-in-hand, at least seeing things eye-to-eye. There have been odd alliances before: see Balzac; see Zola. It is not so much a new class as a mutation. These are the sleeker, more careful, more soft-spoken men in narrow suits, the trim generation of the Fifth Republic. Ceremonial, partial to rigid etiquette and to thought-out marriages, they give rise to taradiddles about a new aristocracy, a royal dynasty based on urban real estate. It is nonsense, of course. Real royals are generally placid and dowdy. Here, there is a twitchiness beneath the gloss, and the chic of the gloss itself is a giveaway. The mutant carries genes handed on from a tripe-eating, money-counting, land-grabbing Third Republic ancestor, red-faced and coarse, with a napkin tucked under his chin to make sure no one else gets the crumbs.

The unholy mess at Les Halles is their creation. The park and garden promised before the central market was removed to a suburb and the handsome Victor Baltard pavilions were torn down never materialized. It should not have surprised anyone with a memory: a garden was supposed to replace the old Montparnasse railway station. At Les Halles, there is a deep hole in the ground (no one can tell you why it was dug) and a trivial shopping center. The muddle of interests responsible for the Forum, as they dared to call it, was powerful enough to have the inauguration treated in the media as an event on a level with the consecration of Chartres Cathedral. Parisians—a good many—were actually tricked into believing that an insignificant and superfluous commercial structure was part of that greater structure, the cultural patrimony.

My *Guide Michelin* calls the church of Saint-Eustache the most beautiful in Paris after Notre Dame. Its closeness to the Forum has been ammunition for critics: on one hand, the most complete example of Renaissance decoration in Paris, and the trumpery taste of the Fifth Republic on the other. Curiously, both buildings seem stranded, two orphans with nothing in common except their isolation from their surroundings.

Whatever is built in Paris is built in a void. There is no contemporary building to which a new structure can be likened. Critics reach back 400 years to make a point. The point is, inevitably, reactionary. In the Lazarist chapel, visitors kiss a pane of glass. In the Chapel of the Miraculous Medal, busloads of pilgrims line up to kiss the plastic-covered armchair from which the Holy Virgin addressed Catherine Labouré. The first seems moving, the latter somehow disturbing. If it comes down to what substance is being embraced, glass or plastic, then that is a reactionary distinction too. It is like putting one's faith—aesthetic or spiritual, just as you like—in nothing but burnished bronze.

To the tune of publicity that could have been scored for the great organ of Notre Dame, "the most beautiful restaurant in Paris," as no one failed to call it, opened last winter in Rue Saint-Martin, "facing the unspeakable Pompidou's Building [the Beaubourg art center], to which it will serve as an antithesis." That was *Le Monde*'s restaurant critic, writing with even more liveliness than usual—*immonde* ("unspeakable") can also be rendered as "disgusting and foul."

La Ciboulette, hailed rather prematurely as a meeting ground for well-heeled members of the intelligentsia and as the Right Bank equivalent, in spirit, of Brasserie Lipp, occupies the three floors of a seventeenth-century house originally built for a banker. The building is "classified," meaning that it cannot be restored more than it has been already, and that the state will lend a hand should it start to crumble. Actually, Lipp and Ciboulette have not so much as a dessert spoon in common. For one thing, it is distressing at Lipp to be sent upstairs. It means you have missed the dead-on tone of temperate confidence required for getting a table on the ground floor. (The food is the same.) At Ciboulette, it is chic to climb. The higher you go (there is an elevator), the giddier the prices and—in line with the doll-house trend of the seventies, elsewhere starting to decline—the more elfin the servings.

Beaubourg used to be the bankers' quarter. If one considers the sums asked for apartments in the renovated and "classified" buildings nearby, one must conclude that it is surely to bankers that the quarter will return. But then, no banker with an image of soundness to protect would move info a dwelling of such inexorable cuteness. The past belongs to those who can afford to turn it into an urban fairy tale. The present is for the dispossessed, eased out of the city to the concrete ring to the treeless suburbs. That ring of slabs-with-windows surrounds most of the great cities of Europe now. Architects will tell you it can't be helped; there are too many people; too many are in Paris; they have to be put somewhere.

THE BEAUBOURG CENTER itself has been discussed into the ground: being there is like being in a factory; in a refinery; in the airport at Roissy. On those long grey expanses one waits to hear a flight called. To some, it was a delayed, nostalgic tribute to the 1960s, already obsolete by the time

it opened, in 1977. Something went wrong, if one can believe the spate of articles called "The End of a Dream" and
"Goodbye to Utopia" and "Beaubourg Sings the Blues." It
is disorganized, inefficient, with a depressed and dwindled staff putting together shows of steadily diminishing
quality. The high point was the Paris-Berlin exhibition,
in 1978; since then, it has been downhill all the way. It
is difficult to keep in mind that an experience only four
years old is being appraised. "For a time," says a journalist,
"it was like a mayonnaise that took; now, it has curdled."
This suggests what must have been expected: something
smooth that would slip down.

It is true that millions of visitors have been clocked.
Most of them wander about the ground floor, where it
costs nothing. They are often young and unemployed. If
the place has not served its intended purpose, it has at
least become a focal point for people who have nowhere
else to go. They come in from the concrete ring. The
new rapid underground trains bring them to the heart
of the city in fifteen minutes. They seldom see anything
more; Paris *is* Beaubourg. They know less of the city than
immigrants' children who move from park to school to
chain store. They come out of a world entirely remote to
Parisians. It could be a foreign film, a place from another
decade. It is a world where, for the young, there is absolutely nothing to do, nothing to see, nothing to think
about. There are no playgrounds; small children play
at setting fires in garbage cans. Tell some of the older
ones that here there were trees, houses with breathing
space, and watch the look you get: puzzled, then won-

dering, then doubting, then indifferent. Those under ten steal from supermarkets; up to sixteen, anything on two wheels; sixteen and over, cars. They hang about in cellars, scrawling Nazi slogans on the walls. They are not sure what the slogans mean: "*C'est pour faire gueuler.*" But the only adults to roar with rage are building superintendents. (No one else goes down there, except the occasional journalist who takes pictures and sounds as if he had just swum the Congo at the risk of being snapped at by the crocodiles.) The young seldom carry weapons; guns are extremely difficult to get in France. It is less dangerous than that, and simpler and sadder.

Beaubourg is their urban initiation. They sit on the floor, swarm up and down the escalators. Their faces are wary and bright; they give off a feeling of boundless, unused energy, draining away in mischief. One wonders if any society is so rich in youth and strength and vivacity that it can afford such a waste. The subject of endless sociological discussion, written about as if they were lumps of unrefined material that could never be used to make a lasting structure, they are not the subject of art. The novelists of the Fifth Republic, like its filmmakers, stick to minute bourgeois cheese-parings, the mouse-view. The center, at any rate, belongs to the young, with its sloping piazza, the escalators for exercise (they are often stalled), and the spectacular view of an unexplored city growing and spreading as they climb.

Selective disapproval manages to leave out the fact that Beaubourg captures and radiates immense vitality. Rue Saint-Martin breathes the way European cities must have breathed during those bursts of construction between plagues and wars. What is built is one thing and what the street may turn into is something else again. An art center has not attracted art or artists. It draws tourists, to whom it is a Parisian freak; a flow of restless, rootless young; speculators.

Until a year ago there were two art galleries in the block facing the center. They opened with high hopes along with the center, and quietly packed up and moved back to the Left Bank less than three years later. One was replaced by a bookstore with a large discount trade, the other by a beautiful eating place. The seventeenth-century banker's house was decaying quietly as a raincoat factory until five years ago, when it was taken over, restored, and turned into "the most beautiful art gallery in Paris." Then and then only it became "classified."

"THE MOST BEAUTIFUL church in Paris after Notre Dame" was started in 1532 and consecrated, with a piece or two still missing, more than a century later. During those hundred years, taste had changed even more radically than in our own century. The original plans for Saint-Eustache were like a final look at the religious architecture of the Middle Ages. By the time the building was ready to be decorated, the taste of a new age prevailed. The result was a patchwork that a still later age would find lamentable. The 1828 edition of a guide to Paris (*Le Véritable Conduc-teur Parisien*) deplored "the poor taste of the architect" and "the confused mixture of Latin and Greek."

Viollet-le-Duc hated the Renaissance, which explains his loathing of the interior of Saint-Eustache; however, he was not the only person to see it as "badly conceived, badly built, a confused mass of debris borrowed from all sides . . . a kind of Gothic skeleton covered in Roman rags stitched together like a harlequin suit."

By the time Saint-Eustache was completed, in 1642, there was absolutely no one living who could describe what had been there before. In fact, a chapel had stood there for 300 years before it was demolished to make way for a more modern, more imposing church. Conceivably, people in the neighborhood were disturbed to watch it being torn down. They had been christened and married there; their parents had been taken from the chapel to their burial ground. The wiping out of a 300-year-old chapel 450 years ago does not arouse our nostalgia. It does not enter our minds to say that if it still existed Paris would be more attractive or easier to live in. Three hundred years at such a remove seem dwindled, short. The loss of a building 150 years old, closer in time, is the work of vandals. Saint-Eustache now looks not like an architectural patchwork but like a harmonious and splendid reproach to anything built within yards of it. As for the chapel, we can try to imagine what it must have looked like, and we can be sure that it was there, for three shrunken centuries. The danger will be when a whole generation of Parisians, for want of knowing, will answer "What was here before?" with "Nothing."

What Is Style?

I DO NOT reread my own work unless I have to; I fancy no writer does. The reason why, probably, is that during the making of the story every line has been read and rewritten and read again to the point of glut. I am unable to "see" the style of "Baum, Gabriel, 1935–(   )" and "His Mother," and would not recognize its characteristics if they were pointed out to me. Once too close, the stories are already too distant. If I read a passage aloud, I am conscious of a prose rhythm easy for me to follow, that must be near to the way I think and speak. It seems to be my only link with a finished work.

The manner of writing, the thread spun out of the story itself, may with time have grown instinctive. I know that the thread must hold from beginning to end, and that I would like to be invisible. Rereading "Baum, Gabriel" and "His Mother," all I can relate is that they are about loss

and bewilderment, that I cannot imagine the people described living with any degree of willingness anywhere but
in a city—in spite of Gabriel's imaginings about country life—and that a café as a home more congenial than
home appears in both. The atmosphere, particularized, is
of a fading world, though such a thing was far from my
mind when the stories were written. It may be that the
Europe of the nineteen-seventies already secreted the first
dangerous sign of nostalgia, like a pervasive mist: I cannot
say. And it is not what I have been asked to discuss.

Leaving aside the one analysis closed to me, of my own
writing, let me say what style is *not*: it is not a last-minute
addition to prose, a charming and universal slipcover, a
coat of paint used to mask the failings of a structure. Style
is inseparable from structure, part of the conformation
of whatever the author has to say. What he says—this is
what fiction is about—is that something is taking place
and that nothing lasts. Against the sustained tick of a
watch, fiction takes the measure of a life, a season, a look
exchanged, the turning point, desire as brief as a dream,
the grief and terror that after childhood we cease to express. The lie, the look, the grief are without permanence.
The watch continues to tick where the story stops.

A loose, a wavering, a slipshod, an affected, a false way
of transmitting even a fragment of this leaves the reader
suspicious: What is this too elaborate or too simple language hiding? What is the author trying to disguise?
Probably he doesn't know. He has shown the works of the
watch instead of its message. He may be untalented, just
as he may be a gifted author who for some deeply private

reason (doubt, panic, the pressures of a life unsuited to writing) has taken to rearranging the works in increasingly meaningless patterns. All this is to say that content, meaning, intention and form must make up a whole, and must above all have a reason to be.

There are rules of style. By applying them doggedly any literate, ambitious and determined person should be able to write like Somerset Maugham. Maugham was conscious of his limitations and deserves appreciation on that account: "I knew that I had no lyrical quality, I had a small vocabulary . . . I had little gift for metaphors; the original or striking simile seldom occurred to me. Poetic flights and the great imaginative sweep were beyond my powers." He decided, sensibly, to write "as well as my natural defects allowed" and to aim at "lucidity, simplicity and euphony." The chance that some other indispensable quality had been overlooked must have been blanketed by a lifetime of celebrity. Now, of course, first principles are there to be heeded or, at the least, considered with care; but no guided tour of literature, no commitment to the right formula or to good taste (which is changeable anyway), can provide, let alone supplant, the inborn vitality and tension of living prose.

Like every other form of art, literature is no more and nothing less than a matter of life and death. The only question worth asking about a story—or a poem, or a piece of sculpture, or a new concert hall—is, "Is it dead or alive?" If a work of the imagination needs to be coaxed into life, it is better scrapped and forgotten. Working to rule, trying to make a barely breathing work of fiction simpler and more lucid and more euphonious merely injects into the desperate author's voice a tone of suppressed hysteria, the result of what E. M. Forster called "confusing order with orders." And then, how reliable are the rules? Listen to Pablo Picasso's rejection of a fellow-artist: "He looks up at the sky and says, 'Ah, the sky is blue,' and he paints a blue sky. Then he takes another look and says, 'The sky is mauve, too,' and he adds some mauve. The next time he looks he notices a trace of pink, and he adds a little pink." It sounds a proper mess, but Picasso was talking about Pierre Bonnard. As soon as we learn the names, the blues, mauves and pinks acquire a meaning, a reason to be. Picasso was right, but only in theory. In the end, everything depends on the artist himself.

Style in writing, as in painting, is the author's thumbprint, his mark. I do not mean that it establishes him as finer or greater than other writers, though that can happen too. I am thinking now of prose style as a writer's armorial bearings, his name and address. In a privately printed and libellous pamphlet, Colette's first husband, Willy, who had fraudulently signed her early novels, tried to prove she had gone on to plagiarize and plunder different things he had written. As evidence he offered random sentences from work he was supposed to have influenced or inspired. Colette's manner, robust and personal, seems to leap from the page. Willy believed he had taught Colette "everything," and it may have been true—"everything," that is, except her instinct for language, her talent for perceiving the movement of life and a faculty for describing it. He was bound to have influenced her writing; it couldn't be helped. But by the time he chose to print a broadside on the subject, his influence had been absorbed, transmuted and—most humbling for the teacher—had left no visible trace.

There is no such a thing as a writer who has escaped being influenced. I have never heard a professional writer of any quality or standing talk about "pure" style, or say he would not read this or that for fear of corrupting or affecting his own; but I have heard it from would-be writers and amateurs. Corruption—if that is the word—sets in from the moment a child learns to speak and to hear language used and misused. A young person who does not read, and read widely, will never write anything—at least, nothing of interest. From time to time, in France, a novel is published purporting to come from a shepherd whose only influence has been the baaing of lambs on some God-forsaken slope of the Pyrenees. His artless and untampered-with mode of expression arouses the hope that there will be many more like him, but as a rule he is never heard from again. For "influences" I would be inclined to substitute "acquisitions." What they consist of, and amount to, are affected by taste and environment, preferences and upbringing (even, and sometimes particularly, where the latter has been rejected), instinctive selection. The beginning writer has to choose, tear to pieces, spit out, chew up and assimilate as naturally as a young animal—as naturally and as ruthlessly. Style cannot be copied, except by the untalented. It is, finally, the distillation of a lifetime of reading and listening, of selection and rejection. But if it is not a true voice, it is nothing.

Limpid Pessimist:
Marguerite Yourcenar

THE LONG CAREER of Marguerite Yourcenar—she was born in 1903—stands among a litter of flashier reputations as testimony to the substance and clarity of the French language and the purpose and meaning of a writer's life. In an age of slops, she writes the firm, accurate, expressive French that used to be expected in work taken seriously. Critics speak of language carved, etched, chiseled, engraved: simply, a plain and elegant style, the reflection of a strong and original literary intellect. She is a master of her native tongue and an *honnête homme* of French letters—novelist, critic, essayist, biographer, translator of Henry James and Virginia Woolf, interpreter of Constantine Cavafy and Yukio Mishima, and—perhaps less felicitously—poet and playwright. (Without rival, one could add, if it were not for the quiet, continuing career of Julien Gracq, now seventy-five.)

It is a way of writing remote from everyday French discourse, which has become increasingly diffuse, imprecise, and dependent on clichés; some teachers say that outside the traditional *lycées*, with their selected student body, her work can scarcely be grasped or imparted. At the same time, almost any literate Parisian would be likely to recognize Mme. Yourcenar in the street, and regard her with respect and affection: more people have watched the television interviews in which she speaks her mind about the conservation of nature, or the decline of Black culture, or the myths of family life, or other writers (as the French expression puts it, she can show a hard tooth) than have read *Memoirs of Hadrian*, her best known and most widely translated book. National reverence for authors does not necessarily encircle knowledge of their work.

HER MIND, HER manner, the quirks and prejudices that enliven her conclusive opinions, the sense of caste that lends her fiction its stern framework, her respect for usages and precedents, belong to a vanished France. She seems to have come straight out of the seventeenth century, with few stops on the way. Nicolas Poussin is her contemporary, for drama and serenity and a classically ordered world; so is Racine, for form, for unity of vision, for the laws of hierarchy and the penalty for breaking them. To read her books (in particular the fiction, the essays in *The Dark Brain of Piranesi*, and two untranslated works of mingled autobiography and family history, *Souvenirs pieux* and *Archives du nord*) is like moving along a marble corridor in the wake of an imperturbable guide. The temperature varies between cool and freezing. The lighting is dramatic and uneven. Only the calm and dispassionate approach never changes.

What are we told? How the body betrays us. Why we destroy faith and one another. That we can produce art and remain petty. What we can and cannot have entirely. Jealousy, but not envy, is allowed free entry. Reciprocated love is never mentioned and probably does not exist. The high plateau of existence, the relatively few years when our decisions are driven by belief in happiness or an over-whelming sense of purpose are observed, finally, to be "useless chaos." By the time Mme. Yourcenar reached this prospect, the view from old age, her fiction was written. Luckily: that useless chaos is what fiction is about.

The limpid pessimism of the voice speaks from a French tradition of right-wing literature, but even the most pernickety French mania for classification cannot hold her to that side of the line. Her life has been a reflec-tive alliance with the rejected and put-upon, and she never misses a chance in an interview to overhaul racists and bigots of every stripe. Her novel *A Coin in Nine Hands* is specifically anti-Fascist, in plot and spirit, its pivot a failed attempt to assassinate Mussolini. The narrator in *Coup de Grâce*—a brief masterwork, to be classed among European short fiction with Joseph Roth's *Hotel Savoy*— is exactly drawn as an aristocratic bully, an instinctive killer, and a natural anti-Semite, who begins in the Baltic civil wars and ends fighting for Franco. Perhaps because of the accuracy of the portrait, Mme. Yourcenar has been accused, directly and deviously, of harboring some of the same opinions as her creation. These witless indictments stick like burrs. Last August, a critic on the state-owned radio station, France-Culture, announced that Mme. Yourcenar was anti-Semitic, "or at least anti-Judaic," because she finds ritual slaughter cruel. The same floating logic should make her anti-Muslim.

On the evidence of her writing, she knows less about Jews, observed as though they were figures out of the Old Testament, than about anti-Semites. Whenever she is questioned on this subject, Mme. Yourcenar replies that she has a great number of close Jewish friends. Possibly the friends did not enter her early life, which might explain why her viewpoint is consistently literary and historical. Literature and history convey a kind of uneasy respect, bringing one to a halt, perhaps at a distance. (Respect and distance might be welcome today, when the most popular radio station in France is occupied for much of its daytime broadcasting by a teller of scatological and racist jokes. Jews, a constant butt, do not complain, because, apparently, they do not wish to be seen as spoilsports.) It would have been wholly possible for someone of her generation, raised in a sheltered, upper-class, Catholic background, to grow up without contact with Jews, or even without hearing much about them. There was the aftermath of the Dreyfus case, but *pas devant les enfants*.

HER ROOTS ARE in French Flanders. She never knew her mother, who died of puerperal fever. *Maman mystique* is

entrenched in France, in spite of the best efforts of Elis-
abeth Badinter, and Mme. Yourcenar is regularly asked if
she missed having a mother. She invariably answers that
you don't miss what you've never had, which more than
begs the question and does not explain why she reached
the age of thirty-five before asking to be shown her mother's picture. What seems even odder is that none of her
relations had ever offered to show her one. (In her family
chronicles and in her conversations with the critic Matthieu Galey, *With Open Eyes*, all her close relatives get the
back of her hand.)

She was brought up as an only child (a half-brother
was much older) and educated at home by her father,
Michel de Crayencour, twice a widower and no longer
young. He taught her Greek and Latin; tied oranges to
trees to surprise and delight her; had her first poems
printed and devised her pseudonym, a near anagram
of the family name. He also gambled away the family
property and fortune, for which she bore him no grudge.
There is a telling remark in *Memoirs of Hadrian* to the
effect that family ties have no meaning if they are not
strengthened by affection: she has said that she did not
love her father and, until she was grown, did not even
like him. Nevertheless, he remains the presumable influence on her young mind. He was born within the lifetime of Balzac; his grandparents were born before the
French Revolution. Two generations from the Enlight-
enment is a short reach, though it is hard to see where
he took his bearings. He twice deserted the army, once
over a married woman, and for a long time could not

live in France. His first wife and her sister died within hours of each other, in the Crayencour apartment, after "light surgery" performed by a shady doctor. There was no attempt to get serious medical help, and no inquest.

Mme. Yourcenar makes him sound idle, selfish, and, at the least of things, careless. She once heard him shout racial abuse at someone who had done him an injury and concluded in her calm way that she had never known much about him. On some secondary image of her father she modeled the only fully drawn heterosexual male character in her fiction—Henry Maximilian, the sixteenth-century Flemish freebooter in *The Abyss*. He carries a manuscript sheaf of sonnets in his tunic pocket, "from which he had hoped for a little glory," which ends "in the bottom of a ditch, buried with him."

Henry Maximilian is dispatched halfway through the novel, leaving the field to the cold and single-minded Zeno, partly modeled on Erasmus and other noble heretics, and almost a summing-up of Mme. Yourcenar's secretive, bitter, clever, homosexual men. Zeno occupied her imagination from the time she was eighteen, as did the Emperor Hadrian—traveling, one would guess, in separate compartments. She thought and wrote about the two, real and unreal, unalike except in their contempt for women, for decades of her life. She parted, finally, from the manuscript of *Memoirs of Hadrian* (it was published in 1951, and at once established her international reputation), but held on to Zeno and *The Abyss* until she was in her mid-sixties. When she finally had no more excuse to write, change, and rewrite, bereft, in a sense widowed, she held

the completed manuscript in her hands and, she told Galey, repeated the name of Zeno some three hundred times.

IT FOLLOWS THAT in a supreme degree she trusts what
has gone by and has no faith in experiments. She has
rebuked the poets René Char and Yves Bonnefoy, hardly
striplings, for taking liberties with form—an authoritative censure that prompted one critic to say he would
trade all her Alexandrines for a line by Char. Her ex-
pedients are deliberately formal and artificial, from the
epistolary novel to the outright cultural pastiche of *Oriental Tales*. *Hadrian* consists of a 295-page letter from
the emperor to his heir, Marcus Aurelius. The epony-
mous narrator of *Alexis* leaves a letter for his sleeping
wife, explaining why he is deserting her and their infant son for a life of homosexual freedom. In *Coup de
Grâce*, Erick, the narrator, tells his life's story to a group
of people in a railway station. *A Coin in Nine Hands* uses
the trumped-up cinematic design of lives briefly linked
by some casual token—in this case, a coin slipped from
stranger to stranger in a handful of change. Inevitably,
one thinks of Arthur Schnitzler and *Reigen*, but the
ronde set in motion by Mme. Yourcenar is political and
moral. The nineteenth century launched its hypocrisy
and syphilis on the roundabout. By the 1930s, as this cool
and dark story has it, sickness, sex, solitude, hatred, and
terror move round the hub of the police state, to the tune
of its contagious thuggery. Any human tie, even the most
fleeting and fragile, brings nothing but bad, black luck.

At its worst and lowest, luck has to be viewed without a blink. To love eyes closed is to love blindly, Mme. Yourcenar writes in *Fires*, a collection of prose poems about a failure of her own. "Let us try, if we can, to enter into death with open eyes" is the last sentence of *Hadrian*. Marcella, the terrorist gunned down by Mussolini's police in *A Coin in Nine Hands*, stares with open eyes "into the void which is now her whole future." Mme. Yourcenar, who makes a dazzling whole of all religions, would appear to believe wholly in none. Wrenched out of the heart of her work, with the possibility of love, is any hope of redemption. An advantage gained from her early Catholic training, she tells Galey, is that it made her gentle. Gentleness is the last quality one would ascribe to her books, where violence and cruelty are played out against a world that seems immobile, like a painting, or a stage set. The theatrical quality is so strong that one often has the sensation of watching a curtain rise, revealing frozen, Poussin-like figures caught at a moment of incipient horror. When they move, it can only be into mortal danger. A prisoner opens his veins, and calculates his chances of dying before his blood runs under the cell door. A prostitute takes her breast cancer to a doctor for a verdict she already knows. A captured partisan, preparing to be shot by a man she was once in love with, starts to unbutton her tunic, in an instinctive feminine gesture of acceptance. Every shot is missed, just as every act is incomplete: the executioner shoots away half her face, and has to administer the *coup de grâce*.

THE SUBJECT IS not cruelty, but heresy—political, erotic, religious—and her characters are aristocrats, whatever their
natural origin, their penchant for the losing side. They are
immune to guilt, which makes them strangers to a convention of fiction we take for granted. They choose their
sexual acquaintances—one can hardly say lovers, given the
circumstances—but do not care to be chosen. They do not
cringe, or dissemble, or wait with petit-bourgeois fatalism
for the blow to fall. They are seldom hard-up for money,
except by high-minded election, though their metaphys-
ical gnawings can seem as acute as hunger cramps. Their
neuroses are so stable and complete that they encourage
rather than cripple decisions and action. They make devastating choices, taking short-term pleasure over lasting
devotion, solitude over emotional dependency, death over
disappointment. It is probably not surprising that Mme.
Yourcenar felt drawn to Mishima, transposing for the
French stage his modern No plays and publishing a study
of his life and work.

Homosexuality, postulated as a condition of heresy,
thus of moral aristocracy, is rarely named. Zeno calls himself a sodomite and a sorcerer, with the observation that
it does not mean what "the herd" imagines, but *Abyss* was
published in the late Sixties, a period exempt from caution. Earlier books mention tendencies and inclinations:
obviously, contempt for the herd is no protection, if we
set aside the Emperor Hadrian, who does not have to
account to his wife for his private arrangements. (Only
once or twice in his masterly monologue do we hear the
voice of Norman Douglas instead of the tone of Imperial

Rome. There seems to be no manner of describing the extravagant doting of a man on a boy without sounding fatuous.) The plaintive and somewhat sappy Alexis informs his wife that he has found beauty, and leaves it to her to work out his meaning. This exasperating sidestepping has to be seen in its time, when a miasma of Beauty was expected to hang over the evocation of sex, and male homosexuality, in particular, was considered a criminal offense, or a flamboyant form of insanity, or a habit to be cured by the right girl and a vegetarian diet. A story about women might not have had the same resonance, or required the same amount of tact and circumspection. In Colette's Claudine novels, published a generation earlier, Claudine's husband cannot take a female rival seriously, just as Willy professed to be amused rather than outraged by Colette's feminine affairs.

Mme. Yourcenar was twenty-six when she published *Alexis* and an amazing nineteen when she wrote some, most, or all of it—accounts vary. It coolly sets forth a man's escape from wife and child, not for another man, but for the possibilities he imagines contained in a world of men. A situation acceptable from, say, a Proust or a Gide might have appeared totally scandalous from a young woman *de bonne famille*, without a blanketing mist of poetic effect. The least to be said is that Mme. Yourcenar's intentions are miles removed from *boulevardier* nudging or any cheap desire to shock. (According to Matthieu Galey, she believes that authors who write directly about the "mystery and reality of sex" show bad manners—an unexpectedly pinch-mouthed observation from someone so supremely gifted at conveying the mystery and reality of erotic tension.)

PREFACES TO NEW editions and versions of her books are usually straightforward. Mme. Yourcenar is given to rewriting and to second thoughts, not only altering the text but changing her mind about its meaning. Fresh insight offered decades later can contradict the evidence of the work itself: the narrator in *Coup de Grâce*, defended as if he were a figure of history slanderously accused of homosexual and racist conduct, is reestablished as a man who may have liked Jews and loved Sophie, the novel's pathetic heroine. (The only attractive female character in the entire Yourcenar *oeuvre*, Sophie is the narrator's victim, from the moment he lets her fall in love with him until he shoots her to death.)

Mme. Yourcenar has said that one cannot write about women because their lives are filled with secrets. The visible and open aspect of women's lives must surely be the least appealing, if we are to take as just the dismal ranks of scolds, harpies, frigid spouses, sluts, slatterns, humorless fanatics, and avaricious know-nothings who people her work, and who seem to have been created for no other reason than to drive any sane man into close male company. Alexis deserts a wife pallid of mind and character, wanly religious, and so ignorant—she never reads a newspaper—that he cannot be sure if she knows he is a celebrated concert pianist; such a ninny, in short, that the reader can only cheer him on.

Zeno, wondering why he ever bothered to sleep with a woman, decides it was "base conformity to custom." Even in heterosexual men, women arouse no more interest than an occasional need, grudgingly satisfied, followed by boredom and disgust. Henry Maximilian reflects that he will quit his life with the relief he has always felt on leaving a mistress. Alessandro, a doctor, in *A Coin in Nine Hands*, after provoking an anonymous exchange of masturbation with a woman in a darkened cinema is simply "grateful to be able to despise all women in her."

Alessandro seems to sum up the spite and the bitterness of the camouflaged homosexual, though it is not clear even after several readings if this is Mme. Yourcenar's intention. He may be meant as a representation of what men turn into after the hopelessness of trying to live with women. As it happens, his wife has left him. Her grounds for complaint are that he is young, good-looking, intelligent, prominent in his profession, well-to-do, and married her for love. The marriage strikes her as a criminal attachment, "which it was, since those passionate years had sidetracked her from her true vocation; that is, from tragic reality." Reality means the anti-Fascist conspiracy, and a political comrade to whom she feels bound "by common hatred rather than love," and her wild, solitary attempt to assassinate Mussolini.

There is more to it than singleness of purpose: "Wealth, success, pleasure, happiness itself provoked in her a horror analogous to that felt by the Christian for the flesh." We are in François Mauriac country, but without the familiar signposts: Marcella is an atheist martyr; there can be no deliverance, no reclamation. Women, like the coin, transmit death, the void, until they set the final example by dying. They are harbingers of the creeping glacier. Common hatred creates a rot more poisonous than the commonplace debacle of love. The end of the marble corridor is a wall of ice.

EVEN PEOPLE WHO are unfamiliar with her work probably remember the outraged arguments that preceded Mme. Yourcenar's election to the Académie Française, in January 1981. The ceremony took place when the Academy was 346 years old and Mme. Yourcenar going on seventy-eight. Some of her admirers, who see the Academy as an overdue and reactionary institution, were disappointed that she accepted. So were a great many Academy members, few of whom have attained her stature, in any field, but who did not want a woman, any woman, under the dome roof of the Institut. (The Institut is the seventeenth-century monument on Quai de Conti where the old gentlemen hold their sleepy sessions.) One objection, that she held an American passport, collapsed when her French citizenship was restored. (A native of Brussels, Mme. Yourcenar was born a French national, through her father. She moved to France at the age of six weeks, and to the United States at the beginning of World War II. Julien Green, an American citizen born in Paris, was elected to the Academy, with honorary French status, some years ago. Mme. Yourcenar's own comment on her national identity: "What is more important and more objective than these

criteria of blood and language is that I am French by culture. All the rest is folklore.") The opposition had to fall
back on the somewhat offhand argument that the Academy uniform of tight embroidered trousers, cutaway, and
sword would not look becoming.

Hostility was not confined to the established right, as
one might expect, but cut across the political battleground
to whatever passes as left on Quai de Conti. Mme. Yourcenar's champion was the firmly conservative Jean d'Ormesson, novelist, memorialist, and former editor of *Le Figaro*,
his challenger the late, then aged, André Chamson, the
Protestant novelist and a considerable left-wing figure in
intellectual circles at the time of the Popular Front. Joust-
ing had to consist of shouting; many of the doddering
members are stone deaf. M. Chamson lost points for calling the elegant M. d'Ormesson a young ruffian, judged
unsuitable on every count. One reason why the members
finally gave way is that public ridicule was starting to wear
them down.

No Academy business in recent decades had ever
drawn so much outside interest. Parisians who knew
nearly nothing about Mme. Yourcenar, except that she
was highly respected, as well as female, watched the ceremony on television. They saw a plain, slow-moving elderly
woman reading a very long speech about a man most
of them had probably never heard of—the ethnologist
Roger Caillois, whose seat Mme. Yourcenar was taking.
She spoke without hurry, with a curious inflexion, not
quite an accent. A Belgian voice? The effect of so many
years lived in English? Writers who choose domicile in a

foreign place, for whatever reason, usually treat their native language like a delicate timepiece, making certain it runs exactly and that no dust gets inside. Mme. Yourcenar's distinctive and unplaceahle voice carries the precise movement of her finest prose, the well-tended watch.

THERE IS A tendency in France—for that matter, in other places—to turn aging writers into teddy bears, as if it were the only way these unwieldy objects can be grasped. Some—Colette was one—give in and let themselves be hugged. (The danger signal is when "well-loved" starts to precede "writer.") It was clear at first sight that Mme. Yourcenar was unlikely to become anyone's *nounours*. Some of Caillois's friends were puzzled by the mystical element she lent the work of a lifelong agnostic and skeptic, but everyone admired the dignified good faith of a performance carried through in an atmosphere of masculine sulks. Some members seemed to be digesting a bad lunch; some went to sleep. The difficulty about the embroidered trousers had been settled by having Yves Saint-Laurent design a suitable costume. Gowned and hooded in quasi-Oriental modesty, looking for all the world like the mother superior of a Byzantine order of nuns, Mme. Yourcenar brought that off, too; she then returned to her house on Mount Desert Island, and is said not to have attended a meeting of the Academy ever since.

At about that time, French critics and journalists began making the pilgrimage to Petite Plaisance, Mme. Yourcenar's island property. (Matthieu Galey calls her "the good woman of Petite Plaisance," which is probably no good reason for throwing the book across the room.) The United States is divided by the French media into four sections: Manhattan, New Orleans, Dallas, and a place in California called "Owliewood," where Jerry Lewis lives. Maine is an exotic venue, and some visitors may not have known quite where they were. A radio critic, last summer, informed listeners that Mount Desert Island, Maine, was part of Canada. Perhaps because of the strangeness of the surroundings, and the strong mind and character of the subject, who manages to shoo interviewers up and down her favorite streets, everyone comes back with the same bleak and unruffled view of the universe. One journalist confided to friends after his return that he felt as if he had been enchanted by a benevolent witch.

He would not have said it to her: it is impossible to imagine anyone's being familiar, let alone impertinent, though it would probably leave her undisturbed. She did not change her expression, or bother to correct a TV anchorman, last winter, when he introduced her as "Marguerite Duras." (In the subsequent fracas, he was interviewed, and explained he had been so overcome by the honor of meeting her that he hardly knew what he was saying.) Actually, there was every excuse for having "Duras" on the brain: she had won the Goncourt prize, and had also received a sharp professional pinch from Mme. Yourcenar. *Hiroshima mon amour*, said Mme. Yourcenar, in yet another interview, trivializes one of the greatest tragedies of history. The title itself is in appalling taste, as bad as saying "*Auschwitz mon chou*." Asked by French-Canadian television if she meant it, Mme. Yourcenar seemed glad to repeat the opinion. Her long, frank interviews are filled with clues to the inevitable biography—willow wands that in the right hands will bend at the right place, showing the biographer where to dig.

TRANSLATIONS OF HER work into English are usually praised, perhaps because Mme. Yourcenar often works closely with the translator. "In collaboration with the author" carries its own drawbacks, not the least of which is a desire to hold too faithfully to original syntax. None of the books now available in English reveals anything of the quality and clarity of the French. English and French are not negative-positive images of each other, but entirely different instruments. The two languages cannot be made to work in the same way. A French sentence, transcribed exactly as it stands, means an English sentence with five words too many. The poise and tension of French, translated word for word, turns into a length of frayed elastic: "And let us even extinguish the floodlights projecting upon the walls and roofs of old residences a poetry which has its beauty but which is merely the reflection of today superimposed on yesterday, endowing things with a 'lighting' they did not possess." ("Ah, Mon Beau Château," from *The Dark Brain of Piranesi*.)

In *The Little Mermaid*, a play adapted from Hans Christian Andersen, a shoal of mermaids announce in chorus that they are "inflating their divine gills." Surely no actors could read some of the lines in her *Electra* with a straight face: "Don't get so worked up, Electra," or "Yes, you're very kind, you, Theodore." *Hadrian* and *Abyss* suffer from a kind of linguistic fuzziness that could give English-speaking readers the impression Mme. Yourcenar writes like Sir Walter Scott: characters are a-doze, they spy a fair ship, perhaps of venerable antiquity, they cast amorous eyes, and life goes on in such wise. Probably translation should consist of adaptation, with the qualities and advantages of English (a glorious language) in mind; and, probably, it is too much to expect. English speakers have to take it on faith that it is not for the sake of examples quoted here that so many people think it is high time that the committee in Stockholm looked at a woman, and at Marguerite Yourcenar in particular.

PARIS NOTEBOOKS

———

PART TWO: REVIEWS

Jean Giraudoux: The Writer and His Work

By Georges Lemaitre

Lying Woman

By Jean Giraudoux
Translated by Richard Howard

PHOTOGRAPHS OF JEAN Giraudoux went on showing the same aging boyish face and the same round granny glasses for years and years, as if he had come into the world as a bookish diplomat of 50. One splendid young portrait of him exists: he is elegant, handsome, wears an officer's uniform and a monocle, and looks the way Proust must have imagined Saint-Loup. Then there is the Jean Cocteau drawing of him on his deathbed, with the head thrown back, the gaunt profile and long throat, all softness vanished. It is a remarkable work, because he really does look dead and not asleep.

Giradoux was born nine years after Gide and Proust, one year after Picasso, seven before Cocteau and Charlie Chaplin—a mixed bag for any generation. He died in occupied Paris at the age of 61, probably by poisoning; the exact cause is still a mystery. The end was lonely. His only son had joined de Gaulle in London; his stepson—a future Prime Minister of France—had vanished into the maquis; his close friend and ally, Louis Jouvet, was waiting in South America for the end of the war. Giraudoux was on strained terms with his wife—she was a quarrelsome pessimist, as women are apt to become when married to philandering optimists—and he lived, much of the time, alone in a hotel.

He must have been on somewhat easier terms with the political forces then in power, otherwise he could not have moved back and forth between Vichy and Paris quite so easily, or lectured in Switzerland, or had a play—*Sodom and Gomorrah*—produced in 1943, or had the scripts of two movies approved. All this probably isolated him more than ever, for he was, if anyone ever was, the refined essence of everything French.

For years of his life Giraudoux was radiant, successful, admired and loved. He was first in school, first as an athlete, apparently irresistible to women; he conducted an excellent foreign office career, and was praised, as the author of a kind of dragonfly prose that is absolutely unlike any other, by everyone he might have cared about, from Gide to Proust, Colette to Sartre. He was also damned, by critics whose names mean nothing today. Readers who do not remember much about Giraudoux certainly know some of his plays: *Tiger at the Gates, Amphytrion 38, The Madwoman of Chaillot.*

One peculiar mishap in his public life occurred when he was named High Commissioner for Information at the start of World War II. Fastidious Giraudoux was France's answer to Goebbels. Louis Aragon called him *Cassandre à la propagande*. The chaos of the department he only vaguely tried to run is still a legend, and so are his broadcasts to the French nation—these were so witty, so dottily reassuring, so filled with mythological and historical references, that nobody knew what he was talking about. He thought he understood Germans ("the well-meaning Frenchman," Count Harry Kessler called him) and believed the German people would never betray their culture. Unfortunately, they did.

Giraudoux died before the first pictures of death camps stopped a whole generation in its tracks. The war, and what came after, seemed to render obsolete everything about him—his way of thinking, of looking at people, his ravishing prose. It has been his fate to move from modern to old-fashioned without any in-between state of popular identification. He was not taught in French lycées in his lifetime and is not today, unless a professor takes it on himself to introduce one of the plays. They say the students aren't interested in "that sort of thing," that they no longer have the background of mythology needed to understand him, and that his French is too subtle. This in France.

"Who reads Giraudoux now?" would have been a good question for the fifties and sixties. Now, there are faint signs of a revival. *Tiger at the Gates* played to full houses, largely of young people, last season, and when *La Menteuse*, his posthumous novel, was published in 1969 the reviews were ecstatic. Also, the revolutionary left, if you please, is now patting his head and saying he was with them all along. It is hard to say what he would have made of that.

Analyzing Giraudoux is like plucking a hummingbird and sorting out the feathers for color and size. Georges Lemaitre has sorted them into seven clear essays—Giraudoux's life, his novels, his theater, his attempts to merge perfection with reality, and so on. Mr. Lemaitre has tact, patience and taste, and writes without a trace of academic or critical jargon—this is so unusual that it is worth mentioning. There is a good selective bibliography, a list of works in English, and the index that French publishers seldom bother to provide.

Yet I wish something had been done to make the book more appealing to readers who don't know much about Giraudoux and can't read French. I am sure that most of them do not care what the École Normale Supérieure stands for in French intellectual life, and would much rather have a photograph showing what the man looked like. There are no pictures—those I have described are from other sources—and there is not even a map to indicate where Bellac and Châteauroux are situated in relation to Paris. It is like having a biography of Proust without a map of the countryside around Chartres.

I read Mr. Lemaitre's book from start to finish with great pleasure, rereading, along with it, two of Giraudoux's novels and some of his plays; but I am devoted to Giraudoux's writing in the way that some people are Gaullists or vegetarians, and what is more, I have his books in French. Most of the translations of the fiction are out of print. What is the good of having Mr. Lemaitre's appraisal of *Bella* if you don't read French easily and can't find the novel in English?

Mr. Lemaitre has studied Giraudoux's women, in fiction, with as much care as Giraudoux must have lavished on the originals; until now I had taken it for granted they were more or less the same girl—the marcel-waved innocent out of prewar French films, who, from the age of 17 until the age of 50, always looked a flat 34. He is also interesting, and discreet, about the fall from grace that took place in middle life, when Giraudoux began evading the dreariness of reality by repeatedly running away from home. What I fear is that his book will drop into the university circuit and die of oxygen failure; I'm sure it was meant to have a better life.

Lying Woman is a novel Giraudoux wrote in 1936 and never tried to have published. It was found after his death in a folder marked "First Draft of Bella," a book he had written some 10 years earlier, and to which *Lying Woman* bears no resemblance. Giraudoux may have filed his manuscript away because its heroine, a chronic liar named Nelly, was identifiable, and because one of her lovers, Reginald, was quite evidently Giraudoux himself. Mr. Lemaitre suggests another sound reason for its suppression: "Giraudoux was probably aware of the flaws in this book and therefore refrained from publishing it." It is not, in fact, a good novel.

Giraudoux at his wooliest reads like a remote ancestor of Françoise Sagan when she is being lazy. Reginald is a hopelessly high-minded and gassy character, and Nelly is never quite clear. As "trivial" is the word most frequently applied to her life and person, another voice soon begins to whisper to the reader: "It's true." She was probably someone Giraudoux knew intimately but never understood. She seems cunning and stupid, like a cold royal favorite, and it is hard to understand the infatuation of her two lovers, Reginald and Gaston (those names!), neither of whom knows the other exists.

Gaston believes the "Reginald" in her life to be an adulterous child she visits in secret, and goes so far as to try to make him a present of a toy automobile, while Reginald swallows whole the standard female lie, which is that there was only one man before him, a brutal husband. None of the three can be seen, heard or imagined, and one tends to define them by the sound of their names. It is a relief to be told that Gaston is pot-bellied, because it is at least a *fact*.

When Nelly's lies and double-dealing have cost her both her lovers, she ticks over in her mind the names of men who might now help her out. The year is 1936; one of the names is Stalin. However, being a down-to-earth little bourgeoise in spite of her baroque inventions, she quite sensibly forgets about politics and instead marries an elderly aristocrat who has strayed into the second-to-last chapter from some of Giraudoux's earlier works. Her first conversation with him is a cross between Charles Morgan and J. M. Barrie (Nelly confides that one of her lovers has been changed into a succulent plant and the other into a mare), and the reader may want to put the book aside at that point.

However, I would strongly advise him to press on, because the last chapter is glorious Giraudoux—sad and funny, ambiguous without cheating. The confused and bitter little story does have what could be called a happy ending, in that everyone gets what he wants, or can appreciate. Gaston gets amnesia (he can forget Nelly) and a dull wife. Nelly acquires wealth, position and respectability. Fontranges embarks on a life of being *cocu et content*, which must have been what he wanted or he would never have chosen Nelly. As for Reginald, he has the last line in the book.

The translation by Richard Howard manages that conjuring trick of making the novel seem as though it had been written in English in the first place. Translating Giraudoux must be like trying to turn yellow into blue; luckily, Mr. Howard is a poet, and whenever his text differs slightly from the original (which was published as *La Menteuse* in 1969) the changes are on the side of style and sense. Only in passages dealing with the fatuous Reginald does he seem to have given up: "In his vanity and his satisfaction, he was the sole artisan of a revelation which fate might have disdained, judging it insufficiently exalted." It is just as foolish in French, but bear in mind that this was an abandoned manuscript, published over its author's dead body.

Transparent Things

By Vladimir Nabokov

Vladimir Nabokov, having spent his life building the Taj Mahal, has decided at the age of 73—for his own amusement and incidentally for our pleasure—to construct a small mock replica. The miniature is not flawed, no, but the most splendid features of the great model have been just slightly parodied, out of playfulness almost. "You see, the past is something of a joke," he seems to be saying; and those whose professional lives consist of literary detective work are going to be kept busy with *Ada*, *Lolita*, and *The Real Life of Sebastian Knight*, trying to discover if he means it.

Transparent Things stands in the same relation to Mr. Nabokov's work as *The Ordeal of Gilbert Pinfold* did to Evelyn Waugh's; it is short, candid, brutal, and it is a semi-explanation. At the beginning it seems to have been written by its own hero, Hugh Person, as he appears at 22—so freshly and youthfully does the author observe an elderly man trying to shut an umbrella, or a German girl wearing mourning, having her picture taken to see how she looks in grief. (We never hear of her again; she is advance signal that black is to be honored.) Hugh Person—still 22—reads a sign in French, "3 Photos Poses" and makes it "Trois Photos Osées" in his mind. *Tant pis if* the reader fails to get the joke: Mr. Nabokov is impatient now, no one is to be coddled. Hapless, hopeless Hugh Person will be 40, 22, 32, 40 again—quickly, seamlessly; if your eye misses a line you are eight years out of kilter. Time shrinks, stretches, separates and overlaps, while Hugh remains the same Person. He will never be 41; Mr. Nabokov can see no reason for it, and so Hugh Person's death-in-life is established at the beginning, when he returns to the Swiss hotel where he once stayed eight years before. In the meantime he has married and his wife has died. He asks for the hotel manager. The manager has committed suicide; even the hotel records with Hugh's name on them have been destroyed.

"So there is no one who might remember me?" Hugh Person asks. No, and just as he cannot recall where his old room was, or the exact color of the window shutters, it is plain at this start of a story for us, but the end of it for Hugh, that no one remembers anything. Death slips in and gradually takes over; the novella is not the work of a young man after all, but perhaps of another of its characters—a foreign-born naturalized American writer who lives in Switzerland and is known as "Mr. R." Mr. R. writes in English. His prose has "a shapeliness, a richness,

an ostensible dash, that caused some of the less demanding reviewers in his adopted country to call him a master
stylist."

Hugh, employed at an American publishing firm, arrives in Switzerland for a meeting. This time he is age 32.
"To make a story quite short," as Mr. R. says, Hugh has
once been Mr. R.'s stepdaughter's lover, but then so has
Mr. R. Hugh's first conversation with Mr. R. is a diamond
of comic description: "'Anyway—how are you?' asked
Hugh, pressing his disadvantage" is only a part of it. By
the time the lunatic interview takes place, Hugh has fallen
"monstrously in love" with a Belgo-Russian by the name of
Armande, whom he marries and removes from Switzerland to New York. Never a master at that particular game,
Hugh finds himself mated to someone as difficult to bed
down as a female giant panda.

Conjugal life becomes a complex theatrical fantasy—
amour à l'américain in a drawing room accompanied by
small talk. If Pirandello had written sex for the stage, this
would have been the scene. Apart from her grim requirements, Armande is stupid, conceited, cold-hearted, and
she snores like a bulldog. Nothing explains Hugh Person's
affectionate patience. "We shall now discuss love," begins
Chapter 17, but we never do. We discuss an idiot woman
and a fool of a man, and if love can be the opposite of
death sometimes, here it is made to sound like contempt
for the living. The only transparent thing respected, pan-
dered to, propitiated in this strange story will be death.

People that Hugh Person barely knows or simply
hears about are "at present dying in a hot dirty hospital

on Formosa," or are "soon also to die," are "at that time terminally ill," or lie "buried under six feet of snow in Chute, Colorado." His own parents die within a year. All that remains of the mother is a French-Canadian accent Hugh cannot get rid of. When his father dies (of a stroke, in a Swiss shop) he does feel something—"the sense of liberation" that consoles survivors. Death, this time, is a breeze "blowing away life's rot," and he is overjoyed to find three thousand dollars in the dead man's wallet. He at once moves to a better hotel, eats a good dinner, and has his first whore, or tries to: inexperienced at 22, Hugh progresses straight from virginity to impotence, and on to anxiousness. When he does get a girl successfully to bed ("poking and panting" is the best Nabokov can say for the effort) it is in a room where the girl once had a happy love affair with a man who has since been killed in a war. Hugh is undone by this memory of the dead, but without knowing it.

He sees Armande for the first time wearing mourning for her father. Her mother dies soon after. Lying beside his wife, whom we are told he loves, Hugh dreams of death and dying. People who have not yet perished in skiing accidents or from cancer of the liver are disposed of in dreams. A nightmare wipes out at least two women; at the moment of dreaming Hugh's somnambulist's grip tightens on Armande's throat and she dies strangled. A rare survivor will be Julia Moore, "the only child I have ever loved," says Mr. R. (also doomed), who has possessed both Julia and her mother, in a backward insolent glance at "Lolita." But then Hugh (Julia's scarcely successful lover) has seen Julia perish in a dream, so she is as good as dead too. Even a remembered picture in one of his child-hood books, an innocent drawing, waits to catch him with its "rings of blurred color" meant to circle "a dead person or a planet." In a Swiss hotel he waits for love—for Ar-mande; eight years later in the same room the wait for love becomes a wait for death. Love and death, past and present, are one on the other like panes of glass—trans-parent things. (Is there need to say that every sentence of Mr. Nabokov's is also crystal clear? That if anything is loved in this loveless story it is the English language?)

In his impatience to be rid of everyone Mr. Nabokov finally sees through Hugh Person *physically*—through skull, brain and hair, as though nothing must be in the way of annihilation. The fate of Person—of persons—is that of pencil shavings "reduced to atoms of dust whose wide, wide dispersal is panic catching its breath but one should be above it, one gets used to it fairly soon (there are worse terrors)." Are there really? Something wrong here. Perhaps it is that Hugh Person is not "you person," as his wife pronounces it, nor yet you American person, as one suspects he is meant to be. "Frail, lax, merry America" is seen through a telescope; one could observe a tough, tense, somber America and have it right too, from a dis-tance. "I hate life," says Hugh to Armande. "I hate myself." But most Persons love themselves, love life, love love, even manage to love the living.

What death does not get rid of fire will destroy. Fire blazes in dreams, in Armande's fear of being trapped in a hotel. It occurs in a novel by Mr. R., *Figures in a Golden*

Window (watch it—everything means more than itself); it will damage the hotel where Hugh spent his honeymoon, so that he can never see it again, and it will eat up Hugh as well as that other hotel where no one remembered him. This is an evil fire, deliberately set, perhaps by the tireless force that disperses pencil shavings. In the end, death will have been offered every kind of hostage; but of course "every" is still not enough. Death survives, and it is as casual, as unpredictable, as eccentric and as daunting as Mr. Nabokov's genius.

From the Diary of a Snail

By Günter Grass
Translated by Ralph Manheim

IN THE FIRST place, who is the snail? Günter Grass? Apparently not, though he does say, "I am the civilian snail, the snail made man." But when one of his children asks, "What do you mean by snail?" he answers, "The snail is progress." "What's progress?" (Partway through the diary you suspect that a chorus of pliant offspring has been laid on to feed Papa cues.) Progress means "being a little quicker than the snail," says Grass. "Snail" also incarnates the political rise of Willy Brandt. Let us just say here that this snail is too gorged with spleen and Schopenhauer to make a good meal, and that it is probably harmless to gardens. Besides, it would always slither around poison-traps; it is morosely keen on survival.

With that settled, about as much as anything is going to be, who kept the diary? Grass did, for the sake of his children and for "the children of other people." That is, he wrote part of a novel, which is the best part of the diary; a brief history of German socialism; notes while on the road campaigning for Brandt in 1969; thoughts about a lecture on Dürer's *Melencolia,* to be delivered at Nuremberg in 1971; an account of the Jewish community of Danzig and its tragic dispersal under Hitler; bits of dull verse; more about Kashubians (see *The Tin Drum*); an essay on snails and their moods (moral: never do what Thurber did before you); glimpses of family life; the story of the Danzig Jewish high school, popularly called the Rosenbaum school, founded and staffed by volunteers when Jewish children were banned from the public-school system; information about Grass himself—why I am a socialist, a list of things I like. There are even recipes, including one for cow's udder, which his family refuses to eat.

These accounts, recitals, pieces of fiction and reportage have been sliced like a loaf of bread and reassembled in an order that seems random, but that probably was carefully planned. Whatever the intention, one has the feeling of reading a number of short and incomplete magazine pieces, with the page turns gone mad.

A reproduction of *Melencolia* is the frontispiece; it sets a tone. Anyone who did not know that Brandt had, in fact, become Chancellor—he overcame even the handicap of having had intellectuals on his side—would take this to be the journal of a thumping defeat. An unexpected Brandt emerges sometimes—taciturn, unsmiling, letting no one come too close even when he allows the use of his first name, infuriating to Grass because he plays with matches instead of putting his fists up. (It sounds like the seasoned

caution of the old pro against the suicidal exuberance of
the talented amateur.) Who remembers, now, that in private betting the odds against Brandt ran at about five to
three? He faced a coalition of church, industry and popular press, and a nastier one of slander and whispered cal-
umny. German liberals, pessimists by definition, predicted
the downfall of democracy and a London and a Paris soon
to be packed with dissident refugees.

Günter Grass is a sympathetic memory of that year.
There was the picture of him disguised as a newsboy, wav-
ing the party's paper—solid-looking, just past 40 he must
have been, backing Brandt because the Nazi snail-tracks
running through the other parties were repulsive to him.
Not every writer was as selfless. Brandt was too far right
for some persnickety types, and he still seems a raving
Bolshevik to others. Grass, however, had been a prisoner
of war at 17, and the Americans had forced him to look
at Dachau: it is something he mentions when he is interviewed. Occasionally he will say that he broke with his
youthful past at that moment; in this book he says he did
not believe what he saw. Probably both are true. Campaigning for Brandt, he came back to Dachau, this time to
sign the visitors' book. It is an irony too heavy to consider,
but he considers it nonetheless.

Between 1945 and 1969 he has become an artist, then
a writer, has married a Swiss girl, had four children ("the
knot tied in our bed") and, particularly because of the
marvelous *The Tin Drum*, has become respected and celebrated. "Isn't it nice to be rich and famous?" one of his
children asks, rather sensibly. Not really. He finds Fame

(capitalized) disappointing and lonely. He would still rather eat tripe and lentils, when it isn't cow's udder, and he feels insecure. He "would like to crawl into something soft, warm, and damp, which it would be inadequate to characterize as feminine." By whatever adequate name he finally calls it, the Social Democrats are surely no substitute. Writing is no longer part of life, it is a way of testing existence: "Often I write to prove to myself that I exist." With that appetite for lentils? It sounds more French than German, as if a deadly Common Market virus of the intellect had crossed the Rhine.

"What were you like before you were famous?" the children persist. They don't always wait for an answer. Tell us later, they say—right now we want to see "Gunsmoke." They also can respond with a matter-of-fact and perfectly innocent directness that is often shattering to adults. He tells them about Hitler and Jews. They reply, "How did they count them?" and "Did the gas always work?" He may have forgotten what they were bound to ask. Writers nearly always imagine it is easy to be a reporter, not to speak of a moral philosopher. The latter is simpler. One of the hardest things in the world is to describe what happened next.

Perhaps because of this, because his great gift is for fiction, Grass's Germany, the Germany he bravely stumps for Brandt, bringing the good word about old-age pensions, comes out grey and flat. He is doing this for the young, for their own good: the writing takes on a nervous finger-shaking quality, as though he knew perfectly well, under the gloom and goodwill, that it is no use telling children what they are to remember. Also, the children of authors are notoriously indifferent to their parents' work, when not downright hostile. (Only a widow will give her husband's books the attention he craved all his lifetime.)

The result is a knotted-up sort of prose that sometimes makes no sense at all, at least not in English: "Making slight slits as usual when something is hanging in the balance, I succeeded in evacuating the hall." He means that he narrowed his eyes, but you have to go back to the original text to find out, or even have someone explain it, for he has used an image of view-slits in tanks and concrete bunkers, which, later, still in the English version, comes up again, this time as "sight slits." Sight and slight do not mean the same thing in English, but then surrealism in books owes quite a lot to proofreading.

Sometimes a prosy earnestness takes over, leading to what one thinks of (perhaps unfairly) as German inflation and to slightly fatuous statements of position: "I am a Social Democrat because to my mind Socialism is worthless without democracy." Well, of course, and is anyone arguing? He relaxes in fiction, in the story of "Herman Ott, surnamed Doubt," Danzig schoolmaster, expert on snails, Gentile volunteer on the staff of the Rosenbaum school, hounded for it, sheltered finally by a sadistic illiterate, bedded by the man's mute daughter—all of it rich, mad, funny, violent and dreamlike, an echo of someone one wishes the snail would stay away from, Grass-the-writer.

All Said and Done

By Simone de Beauvoir
Translated by Patrick O'Brian

A PORTRAIT ONE might call "The French Intellectual in Majesty" belongs in every reader's imaginary museum. Your intellectual sits enthroned; a few of the saved cluster like cherubim overhead, while the naughty ones who would not listen to Reason writhe beneath his left foot. He wears a decipherable political label, though nothing else may be clear. He has left an account of a doomed world in which he apparently intended to be the sole survivor; he has also provided us with sublimely inaccurate and humorless descriptions of places and societies he was unable to fathom, for the simple reason that he was indifferent to them in the first place. In the fifth volume of her autobiography Simone de Beauvoir lives up to the set criteria.

The book covers the years between 1962 and 1972. During this time, she says, she could detect no change in herself, as if she had been living with the slowed heartbeat of hibernation. She is bored and faintly dissatisfied. She is often idle and hates idleness. After the Stockholm trials (of America, for war crimes) she felt "intense nostalgia," and came home as "from a religious retreat." There had "never been a moment of lost time." In other words, this intense political activity was taking up the slack, as bridge or gardening might for a lesser woman. She is tired of everything and especially of us, her readers. She puts a question to us and to herself: "Being a woman, French, a writer, 64 years old in 1972; what does it mean?" At the end of a book that weighs more than a pound she hasn't said and we still don't know.

Much of *All Said and Done* is a recapitulation of earlier volumes. Readers who are unacquainted with Olga, Zaza, Stépha, Lise or Bianca will find no allowances made for ignorance; Simone de Beauvoir takes it for granted that anyone in orbit around her person is visible to all. Her two extra-Sartre lovers, Algren and Lanzmann, have no past, no future and no first names, while a careless Paris provincialism gives us Leiris, Salacrou, Bataille, Limbour, Herbaud, Lacan and Leibovitz without any further identity, either as friends or as men with professions. (Why is it that her women have only Christian names and her men only surnames?) Her books have never been warm; this one is bloodless.

She accompanied Jean-Paul Sartre to Russia and Israel, Egypt and Japan; she followed with evident sincerity and approval every liberal and liberating movement of the decade she is concerned with. Her reports read like prim diaries, or, unforgivably, like tacked-together newspaper cuttings. There is an absence of vitality, of generosity, even of intellectual coherence. Visiting the Ardennes region of France and Belgium, she believed she was in Shakespeare's Arden. This, as we know, was one scholar's rash conjecture: she provides it as a fact.

The book abounds in misconceptions, in outright mistakes, in pointless exposition: "In 1951 I bought a car and learnt to drive: there was nothing original about this move—the automobile industry was coming to life again and a great many French people wanted a car." We are overwhelmed by bootless travel notes: "My room like all the others in the hotel had a table, a desk, and a bed...." By inane musings: "And what is happening in China? That is a question I really should like to be able to answer." (She can't, as it turns out.) By a bland political simplification that is disconcerting from an intelligent woman: "Stalin had all the Tatars deported to Central Asia for collaborating with the Germans, and a great many of them died there. The Crimea is now inhabited by Ukrainians, and they are but indifferent vine-growers." This, incidentally, is also meant to be an oenological jotting. In short, we are given one trifling fact after the other, in a style that has the dazed, ruminative rhythm of a French schoolgirl chewing gum at a concert in time to Bach.

The French text has been transposed into a new and rapidly-spreading sub-speech called Translator's Word-for-Word. In Word-for-Word, instead of rendering a French word into an English one of equivalent meaning, you choose any English word that *sounds* the same (i.e., *confus* / confused, *original* / original, etc.) but whose meaning is entirely different. The result may have a surreal attraction, but it has nothing to do with English, let alone the original text. Some, but not all, of Simone de Beauvoir's compulsively misspelled proper names have been cleaned up. (As Mary McCarthy once wrote, she can't get an American name right even when she has it in front of her.)

The misspelling bespeaks an attitude; I think it is one of contempt. Her deep resentment of America is personal and political. It began with the Liberation (on the evidence of her books) and became immutable after her long visit in 1948. It is based (again on the evidence of her books) on such fatal inaccuracies that one begins to doubt what she has to say about Cuba and Israel too. In 1972 she found the situation hopeful: "Most" of the Americans she knows had assured her the nation was about to collapse. Of the imminent debacle, and the worldwide disorder that will then ensue, she says, "I do not know whether I shall live long enough to see it, but it is a comforting outlook."

While awaiting this consolation she goes to movies (*The Priest's Wife*, in which Sophia Loren and Mastroianni acted with mischievous subtlety, had some very amusing gags. . . ."); she reads novels (we get other plots, even of books like *Cancer Ward*, as if it were an inaccessible volume none of us had seen), and she records her dreams. Fifteen pages are devoted to her dreams. Jean-Paul Sartre figures in these and seems more real than in her waking life. One sentence, a reference to him, makes poignant reading in 1974: "I have not experienced the death of any-one essential to me and since I was twenty-one I have never been lonely."

Gradually we wonder if the book was not after all written as a conscientious account of 10 years of the late 20th century for a civilization still to come, or for a civilization cut off from the world we take for granted; if it was not planned, in fact, for people who do not know how to read. If so, then it should not be judged as an ordinary autobiography. Last winter Simone de Beauvoir wrote to *Le Monde* protesting the refusal of Syria to give out information about Israeli prisoners. Because the plea ran counter to her known political views, the letter was treated as a news item and boxed on page two. (A rebuttal came promptly from the pro-Arab son of the Jewish former Premier Pierre Mendés-France, which made two surprises.) I mention it only because her letter had more grace, point, purpose and feeling than the entire 463 pages of *All Said and Done*.

André Malraux

By Jean Lacouture
Translated by Alan Sheridan

OF THE SEVERAL André Malraux incarnations available,
current iconography usually offers two: the artist-as-an-
ti-fascist with his Gauloise and trench coat, and the
watchful old man, dead pale, his hair iron-black, his eyes
larger and darker even than in youth. He seems witch-
like, female, a kind of crone. At 74, Malraux still appears
to see in himself the young man Maurice Sachs called
"coldly heroic," and he seldom considers, except dismis-
sively, the Malraux whose political reputation stood bail
for a colonial war or the repressive political figure of May
1968. If as a writer he twice lost part of his audience, he
has found it again now: for today's young 1968 is ancient
history, and they have never known the tamed rebel who
slipped into government ministries made to measure for
him. Malraux's two civil war novels, *Man's Hope* and *Man's
Fate*, are widely read at lycée level, which means that the

creative writer exists and survives where he ought to, as living literature. If with time, and on rereading, his characters seem as they did to Ilya Ehrenburg, impulsive romantics in someone else's revolution, they still reflect and define Malraux's drives and beliefs and perhaps a few of his adventures before 1939—though not many.

Jean Lacouture makes it clear that even today Malraux thinks he lived his heroes' lives. For 40 years now he has let stand a legend that he fought in China. When in a 1933 letter to Edmund Wilson he described himself as "Kuomintang Commissar first in Indochina then in Canton" one cannot suppose he was trying to make a fool of Wilson, for he had no reason to. He must have believed his own fable. He did play a role in Spain, a role Lacouture brings down to reasonable size. The real and the unreal have by now become so enmeshed they will probably never be disentangled, and perhaps it doesn't matter. A woman who knew him young told me, "I never understood half he was saying but it all sounded dazzling." The wonder of France's old men of letters is that they can still either dazzle or infuriate: Sartre, almost blind, nearly paralyzed, is still alarming enough to rate television censorship. His comment, "They would not have done it to Malraux," marks off the accepted intellectual.

Yet each of Malraux's new books, which appear at a cadence one can hardly keep up with, as well as his frequent public statements, are the signal for new reactions, quite often of annoyance. He has succeeded in antagonizing Spanish émigré circles in Paris by remarks they consider ill-founded and 40 years out of date. One of their members, himself a writer, took to the air when Franco tried to castigate *Man's Hope* as a fantasy set in a Spain that never existed except in Malraux's head. Imaginary worlds are a writer's birthright: the trouble only starts when he tries to inhabit both worlds at once. Malraux has done it more successfully than most. Interviewed for this book, he described to Lacouture a conversation with Goebbels that probably never took place, for the one, known, provable fact is that Goebbels refused to see him.

Lacouture recounts this, as he does everything, with great tact. He is not out to dynamite André Malraux but to circumscribe him, using much the method Malraux himself employs in his monologues on art—on objects, rather. Lacouture's Malraux is like broken pottery under glass. Joined, the pieces would certainly constitute something of significance, perhaps a masterpiece; and so he prowls round and round, hoping a change of lighting, a new perspective, will answer the plainest of questions: Real identity (?) Real provenance (?) Real dates (?) And he is as fair and as objective as possible as he sorts out the red herrings, the myths, the outright falsehoods from so-called facts, documentary evidence, and other people's memories, which may be no more reliable than Malraux's own. If, at the end, the pieces seem more fragmented than ever, the fault is not Lacouture's. He is dealing with a brilliant imaginary character who may not want to be labeled. "It is hard being a man," he has Malraux remarking at one point—one of those flattening Malraux statements to which some readers undoubtedly respond with a sighed, "*Eh, oui.*"

Sometimes, perhaps out of discouragement, Lacouture takes off on clouds of that French hyperbole the English language does not accommodate without irony. By this I mean that some of it is unintentionally funny, especially when he decides the subject is so immense that mere words will not suffice. (Why did Malraux write books, for instance? "He has written because action, even when fraternal and collective, gave him neither a response to a certain need for an absolute, nor the fulfilment that conquerors seek. His life is not a pretext, it is an end in itself." It would be hard to imagine anything sillier, though when it comes to gassy profundity it is hard to beat the master himself.) Unfortunately mere words are all a writer has to deal with, and so it is better to settle for them from page one. Judicious skipping leaves one with a patient, careful, draftsman's portrait of someone who seems to be part Hemingway, part d'Annunzio, but who is on the whole more thoughtful than both. His beginnings were in the ugly Paris suburb of Bondy, where he was raised by a mother and grandmother who had a grocery business. (Like Camus, like Sartre, he was brought up by women.) Gifted, ambitious, unshy, already inventing stories—he maintained for years a fable that his father was rich and powerful—he began by pinching books on the Boul' Mich' and selling them back to the shops and went on to more or less stealing parts of temples in Indochina. He never finished school, and it is cheering to think he became Minister of Culture in a degree-conscious, diploma-ridden society such as France.

Lacouture pursues him, True or False, through his wars and his women, his books and his bravado. The mystery of his friendship with General de Gaulle receives a long speculative essay. Lacouture sees de Gaulle as Malraux's father, or simply his craving for one. Well, perhaps—but did de Gaulle ever want his Minister of Culture for a son? On the surface of it, these two rock-like egos did not really need each other, and the marvel of it is that they never collided. There seems to have been a great deal of mutual flattery, but both were too intelligent for that to be enough. Malraux, by his own account, never admired anyone but Mao and de Gaulle, while no one knows if de Gaulle ever admired anyone. Lacouture's persevering digging does find an ideological taproot, in that Malraux once wrote a laudatory preface for a book of Charles Maurras. There was certainly that deep French nationalism in both men, of the sort that can bloom into patriotism or the rankest, ugliest chauvinism. But if Maurras looked on the Vichy government as a "divine surprise," de Gaulle and Malraux never saw it as anything but a man-made disaster; that may have been the end and the beginning of their common vision, enough for a lifetime. No one, Lacouture or his reader, can do any more than guess.

As this book is meant for English-speaking readers something must be said of the translation. It is in a never-never language created by substituting an English word for every French one without regard for meaning, style, or the norms of readable English. Surely no publisher would have accepted this text as it stands had it been submitted as an English original. At its best it is undistinguished, at its worst utter gibberish: "He had gone away half-formed and divided . . ." we are told, as if Malraux had turned into an amoeba. Evidence of a hopeless ignorance of English appears on nearly every page: "An image, in little, of the adventure that was about to begin" is supposed to be a sentence. "In little," that about sums it up.

Céline

By Patrick McCarthy

LOUIS-FERDINAND CÉLINE WAS a great and a unique French novelist whose finest books—*Journey to the End of the Night, Death on the Installment Plan* and *Castle to Castle*—do not easily quit the mind. He belonged to no school, unless Villon and Rabelais are schools, and left no disciples except a few minor authors who, as a rule, share some fragment of his bitterness or his obsessions about Jews but no part whatever of his talent. (What a lot of racist, miserly, backbiting Frenchmen such as Céline have been glorious writers! The seed of genius is blind.) Céline, at odds with himself, was never comfortable with any party or following, but it is undeniable that both upper-and lower-case fascists have always felt comfortable with him.

His world of fiction is like a robust Dickensian creation turned upside down, where the Olivers and Davids learn that no one is good or kind and the Nells and Doras die after blundered abortions. A contemporary of Éluard and Aragon—of Hemingway and Fitzgerald, to fix him in American time—Céline did not begin to write until he was about 38. His first novel, *Journey to the End of the Night,* turned up in his future publisher's office as a bulky paper-wrapped parcel with no return address. It must have been something of an electric storm for its first readers, if one thinks of the Colette and Giraudoux novels being published then like a succession of sunny days. *Journey* used argot as if slang had been approved by the French Academy, punctuation that slid phrases together on a sustained note, and seemed to have rid literary French of its three handicaps, which are rigid syntax, small vocabulary and that compulsive intellectual tidiness that can turn books into filing cabinets.

Tracing the unknown author with some difficulty, the publisher discovered a physician named Destouches practicing medicine in a shabby quarter of Paris. Seemingly indifferent to worldly goods, treating his poorer patients without fee, modestly entrenched behind a pseudonym, the good doctor in no time was grumbling over royalties. Everything about Céline was to be complaint, dissent and contradiction, as this intelligent biography by Patrick McCarthy makes clear. For instance with all the noms de plume in the world to choose from he would take one of his mother's Christian names, a choice certainly not guided by filial devotion—in his second book, *Death on the Installment Plan,* he traced her portrait as a masochistic nitwit for whom he seemed to feel little more than contempt.

Journey was published in 1933, the year of Hitler. Céline's dark nihilism, his use of street language, the undertow of mystery and death that tugs at the novel from start to finish were wildly attractive to both Left and Right: both could read into it a prophecy about collapse, the end of shoddy democracy, the death of sickened Europe. Praised, discussed, sold, translated, *Journey* brought to Céline's middle life the unexpected additions of fame and money. If his native gift was large, some part of his spirit would always be small. Son and grandson of Parisian shopkeepers who were perpetually failed or on the brink, he inherited the prejudices and paranoia, the envy of the rich and contempt for the poor, the floating resentment, the absolutely unrivaled meanness with money of the petit bourgeois, which was probably all they had to leave him. He may well have been the first modern French writer to have concealed his earnings abroad, bearing them in cash and by train to Denmark, decades before his successors started carrying theirs to Switzerland in paper bags.

There was now nothing to prevent Céline from becoming richer and richer and more and more celebrated, from growing old respected and honored, as writers still are in France, interviewed by reverent critics to the very last gasp about morals, politics, society and God. What went wrong? Hatred, mostly. He hated foreigners, hated Jews, hated himself. "Céline attacked Jews because he hated them," says Patrick McCarthy, meeting that particular matter head on. Even Céline's much-vaunted patriotism was simply xenophobia. He seems torn apart by an inner grenade of spleen; all we can do is identify the pieces—

the gifted writer, the kind doctor, the hysterical racist, the restless child of a family clinging for life to the lowest reach of an urban middle-class. He may have been more than a little mad. Though competent in his professions, medicine and writing, he was subject to fits of real delirium that sound like a form of schizophrenia, if it is possible for such an illness to come and go like a common cold.

The young Ferdinand of *Death on the Installment Plan* suffers from the hallucinations that were Céline's. They remind one of those visited on Virginia Woolf, when strange figures appeared and words rushed faster and faster through her head. Céline's notorious anti-Semitic pamphlets contain exactly that lunatic rush: "More Jews than ever in the streets, more Jews than ever in the press ... at the Bar ... at the Sorbonne ... in Medicine ... at the theatre ... at the Opera ... in industry ... in the Banks ..." He wrote this in 1941 when the Jews of France were excluded from medicine, teaching, law, the civil service, the performing arts, the armed forces (there had for years been a Jewish officer caste) and all the liberal professions. The laws hounding the Jews were purely French, the police enforcing them French too. A gang of male writers, baying in one of the world's most civilized tongues, joined the pursuit. Céline was no worse than the rest—merely louder: "Jewish bluffer ... Dirty *con*, layabout ... pimp of the universe ... parasite of all time." Had a French Jew wished to respond to this he could not have done so for Jews were barred from journalism as well.

Today anyone curious about these quotations and their context needs one of two rare books, Céline's *Les Beaux*

Draps, long out of print, or *Une Certaine France*, an anthology of French anti-Semitic prose, 1940–44, which Céline's
widow managed to have seized by court order last May.
A reason invoked for legal action was that Céline would
not have wished to be remembered for his racist pamphlets. Whatever factual evidence exists for this surprising
change of heart has yet to be published. It is true that
Céline considered himself unjustly persecuted. When in
1950 he was tried and found guilty of collaboration (in
absentia, having followed his royalties to Denmark) he
seems not to have grasped what the verdict was about and
to have dismissed from his mind all that he had written
and said when his country was occupied by a foreign army.
His protest, "From the time the Germans arrived I took
no interest in the Jewish question," is so foolish a lie that
we can only suppose that he believed the abundant evidence to the contrary had vanished, perhaps by means of
the Celtic magic that so attracted him most of his life.

All this was a long time ago. Céline, amnestied only
a year after his conviction, died in 1961, embittered and
unrepentant, and, it must be added, in his own home,
in his wife's arms, which is more than can be said for a
great many French Jews of his generation, not to speak
of Frenchmen *tout court*. As Patrick McCarthy points out,
his death drew less notice than Hemingway's, which occurred the same day. Mr. McCarthy must have completed
his book a few years ago, for he speaks of a "self-satisfied
France over which Pompidou now rules" where Céline is
all but forgotten. Actually Céline is now widely read. All
his novels are in print, in standard and paperback editions,

including at least one not mentioned in the bibliography, and with *Journey* quite often sold out. In the autumn the revived *NRF [Nouvelle Revue Frangaise]*, Gide's venerable review, will devote an issue to Céline. It will be interesting to see how his wartime attitude is dealt with in 1976.

Nowadays Céline is read by the young. Occupation arguments bore them. His anti-Semitic writings are suppressed, and only the most diligent and curious readers are likely to pry them out of the Bibliothèque Nationale, an institution not open to everyone. This means that his new wave of admirers do not know exactly what he was charged with or why he and his cronies thought it prudent to flee to Germany when the army and government protecting them pulled out. Young persons are apt to look upon him as a heroic rebel harassed by stuffy authority or "le système," as if all systems are one. The explanation that he was openly racist at a time when Jews were being murdered on his doorstep will quite often draw a blank. The respectability of French anti-Semitism is its longest taproot. The educated and intelligent Robert Brasillach wrote, with pride, "Anti-Semitism is not a German invention, it is French tradition." Every country breeds a virus of racist jokes for amusement; a strain circulating in France for about a year now has been based on puns to do with deportation—this in a city where ghosts of deported children haunt the railway stations; ghosts visible, alas, to fewer and fewer of the living. Part of Céline's personal contradiction is that even now, 15 years after his death, one cannot assess his reputation without taking up the matter of his anti-Semitism. Patrick McCarthy does so scrupulously and at length, but without reaching a conclusion, probably because there is none, but only a question: do we refuse the novels because we disapprove of their author, as Jean-Paul Sartre decided we must, or do we go as far as Patrick McCarthy, who thinks that everything Céline wrote should be in print? (The question remains unanswered in any case, for neither Céline's widow nor, probably, the post-war law forbidding the publication of anything arousing racial hatred would allow *Bagatelles Pour Un Massacre* or *Les Beaux Draps* to reappear.) Rejection is always emotional and capricious. Some people will not listen to Wagner because he disliked Jews, but do the same people shut their eyes when they go by a Degas in a museum? Turning away from the novels of Céline is shutting one's eyes in the museum.

Céline is in the curious position of being known and obscure all at once to English-speaking readers. Mr. McCarthy's bibliography lists only four previous studies. Probably few biographers have wanted to take on an ambiguous figure whose unpleasantness had few redeeming features. One is struck in Paris by the reluctance people have to speak of Céline, and by the use of "personage" or "being" rather than "man"—"a disagreeable being," "a disgusting personage"—as if he had been a character in a novel, perhaps one of his own. Also, as Patrick McCarthy discovered, it was virtually impossible to find out much about his early years. In his lifetime Céline was unhelpful, snapping at would-be biographers who asked for details, "Invent them!" This meant the biographer had to turn to public records, as if dealing with someone in antiquity, or rely on the memories of Céline's contemporaries, inevitably partisan, possibly rendered unreliable by time and the political bitterness that surrounds Céline's memory.

Whatever could be found Patrick McCarthy seems to have discovered, including a number of facts and incidents not known or not mentioned until now. The later life is of course a matter of notoriety, particularly Céline's flight to Germany with the upper and lesser ragtag of collaboration and his subsequent arrest in Denmark. Céline also invented stories about himself, as artists often do: delirium is not required for this—the habit of creation seems to be enough. One, heard more than once in Paris, apparently started by Céline himself, is that he became anti-Semitic because an unpatriotic Jewish doctor pinched Céline's post in a clinic while Céline was bravely fighting in Flanders in 1914. In fact he had not yet begun training in medicine, having enlisted in the cavalry in 1913, aged 19. (It was part of his poisoned gift for making himself miserable to have chosen the cavalry when he had "an innate fear of horses," and although loudly patriotic to have dreamed of deserting his regiment almost from the start.)

Not all of his novels exist in English, which seems scandalous when one considers the perfectly trivial books that cross the ocean. Moreover, Mr. McCarthy has found the first two, the most important, *Journey* and *Death*, to be poorly translated. The vivid style has emerged "uniform and grey" and the punctuation, an integral part of his way of writing, has been standardized. Worse, the text is bowdlerized (by what right and in whose name?) with some passages omitted entirely and others "watered-down."

The dates of the translations, 1966–68, make the cleanup even more mysterious. What, in Céline, can have seemed shocking by 1968? The surge of the prose in these novels is like high tide, carrying humor, slang, foul language, poetry, sex, birth, the facts of dying. No fragment or quotation can illustrate how funny Céline can be. One is forced into the irritating and perhaps impossible advice for many readers, which is to get the original French.

Without some knowledge of the novels much of the point of this biography will be missed, for Mr. McCarthy discusses them interestingly but in a way intelligible only to people who know what he is talking about. *Castle to Castle* has had a better fate in English. Readers curious about Céline can learn much from this feverish vision of Collaboration with a capital C as it sat dreaming of final victory, in a German castle, with the Allies advancing by the hour. There might have been more to say of the French part of these troops than "Leclerc and his dreaded Senegalese" but then that the French "had to be dragged kicking and screaming into war" or that "Petain established his government at Vichy and tried to make the best of an impossible situation" are also legitimate viewpoints, but not this reviewer's. We learn how many *collabos* were shot out of hand at the liberation, but there is no corresponding figure for those other dead.

For the sake of symmetry, when Céline died peacefully at Meudon 16 years after the end of the war there were fewer than 200,000 Jews in all of France.

It is tiresome to mention inaccuracies in a serious work, but Daniel Mayer was never Minister of Justice, or even "the Jewish Minister of Justice," which makes him sound a holder of high office in Jerusalem. Another Mayer, perhaps, but one does not mix up the Wallaces and Kennedys of American politics. Madeleine Jacob, identified only and ironically as "the Pasionaria of the Liberation," is mentioned several times in terms of the jibes she received from one of Céline's apologists. American readers have no way of knowing that because she covered the collaboration trials for a leftist paper she was a favorite target of anti-Semites, and that she was a respected journalist, as the profession is normally practiced.

Finally, the story that Jules Moch was so ignorant and illiterate that he amnestied a "Dr. Destouches" without knowing Destouches was Céline is an old *collabo* chestnut that manages to be anti-Gaullist, anti-Resistance, anti-Socialist, and anti-Semitic all at once. The source this time is Albert Paraz, a forgotten minor polemical writer and friend of Céline. Paraz considered himself Céline's spiritual heir. As de Gaulle once said in another circumstance, "Vaste projet!"

Hearts and Minds:
The Common Journey of
Simone de Beauvoir and
Jean-Paul Sartre

By Axel Madsen

SIMONE DE BEAUVOIR'S tribute to Jean-Paul Sartre—"From the age of twenty-one I have never been lonely"—may be coupled with her modest statement that their long, devoted alliance has been the one success of her life. They met as students in Paris in the summer of 1929—both gifted, earnest, in flight from the middle class, though not the same segment of it—and after that meeting were seldom apart. According to Simone de Beauvoir, only once in nearly 50 years have they ever slept on a quarrel.

Although they maintained separate establishments until old age and blindness made it difficult for Sartre to live alone, they traveled together, worked on their books together, saw each other daily when they were in the same city and, as her memoirs have made clear, thoroughly discussed what Sartre termed their "contingent" love affairs. When they were still in their 20s he offered to marry her; she, sensibly, refused, knowing that he hated the idea of marriage and that the offer had been made for her peace of mind. What she obtained would prove far more binding, for he promised never to leave her. (No reciprocal pledge seems to have been given or expected.)

Their nonmarriage contract stipulated that neither of them would avoid other experience—sexual experience, that is. Sartre embarked on this program soon and steadily, de Beavoir late and less happily. Like most systems that try to channel life, theirs had made no allowance for jealousy and pain, perhaps because Sartre himself was devoid of sexual possessiveness. De Beauvoir, to her own surprise, turned out to be vulnerable. Her two "contingent" love affairs ended miserably. In spite of her fame, her generosity, her poised beauty (there is one particularly stunning photograph by Gisèle Freund in *Hearts and Minds*) and her obvious yearning for romantic passion, part of her life remained thinly populated, and she has never concealed how much she minded.

Axel Madsen, who recently wrote a biography of Malraux, has limited his account of Sartre's affairs to those that de Beauvoir has described or that are a matter of public knowledge. A complete list would have required if not a Leporello at least an extra chapter; the philosopher whose mother had once wept because he was so ugly would be a magnet to young, clever, pretty women for most of his life. The nonmarriage became more respectable in its way and certainly more bourgeois than the goings-on imagined by anxious French parents.

It was not only de Beauvoir who felt the distress that sometimes resulted: If some women accepted her as the untouchable Athena to whom Sartre was pledged, others found themselves in an old, familiar marital dilemma with Sartre representing the husband and de Beauvoir the wife, the children and the lights of home; and when Sartre, on the brink of old age, fell in love with a much younger woman and wanted to marry her, de Beauvoir, like any legal spouse, considered it a violation of their contract. ("He can't do this to me," Madsen quotes her as saying, though we are not told to whom. As he translates another of her remarks into a most unlikely "We've sure had to change our tune," we may simply attribute the lapse to a tin ear.) Sartre kept that last, particular, triangle whole by legally adopting his young mistress; if he could not make her his wife he would make her his daughter and heiress—an arrangement that seemed to suit everyone concerned.

In any long relationship there is bound to be strain (Sartre once testily described de Beauvoir as "a clock in a refrigerator"), but what held them together, finally, were the ties one associates with a long marriage: a common outlook, the habit of years, shared experience, affection and respect.

As writers, they had in each other the rarest of birds, seldom encountered, hard to replace—a trusted reader. Each had complete faith in the other's opinion; Sartre's advice, as quoted by Madsen, is a model of common sense. They shared the ingenuous belief that a couple can live on rules and concepts, with mind and heart receiving their marching orders from the will, and with the will in complete control of the psyche: Sartre, in the grip of a mental breakdown, "suddenly declared he was tired of being crazy and returned to his normal self." They also shared an un-French, perhaps an un-European, attitude toward money, with Sartre a particularly soft touch who has given away nearly every *centime* he ever earned; and they have shown an impressive loyalty to friends who sometimes give the impression of economic and intellectual sponging. Madsen reminds us of how "circles close to Sartre" not so long ago tried to get their hands on the Nobel Prize money he had refused; though Sartre denied having had anything to do with the attempt, he never disowned the "circles."

No one in Europe seems likely to succeed them. Their position as creators of a dangerous philosophy few people knew much about has perhaps gone out of fashion; what we have instead is the spectacle of so many aged Pied Pipers scrambling after the young. Unwilling symbols of a generation once lithe and rebellious, now tamed and fairly thick around the waist, they have survived to become its Darby and Joan, sometimes laughed at but more often respected and, in a way, probably loved. Honors will be heaped on them whether they want them or not; the grandchildren of those vanished, sulky existential adolescents of the 1940s may yet end up playing in sandboxes in an urban landmark called "Square Jean-Paul Sartre, Homme de Lettres et Philosophe."

Hearts and Minds contains an excellent selection of photographs, a bibliography and an index with the usual number of names misspelled. According to the jacket copy, it is about "people who are, in Madsen's fine phrase, 'exegesis made passion.'" This meaningless phrase illustrates the book's language, a kind of bogus English that lurches from careless to pretentious to incomprehensible to barely literate. A writer with so little grasp of idiomatic English would surely have been helped by editing and proofreading, but there is no trace of either. French is repeatedly used as though it were English, English words that resemble words in French are given a French meaning, and in some cases the author has simply invented words of his own that do not exist in any language. French rather than English custom has been followed on matters of punctuation, syntax and the use of italics and capital letters, with results that are sometimes bewildering and sometimes simply foolish. What *has* been rendered, albeit artlessly, is the appalling jargon, the claustrophobia, the humorless self-possession of French intellectual life in the 1970s: "Once Barthes, Foucault and Cie had picked literature apart—and Sartre himself had 'totalized' Flaubert—a certain kind of writer was no more."

Just like that.

Colette:
The Difficulty of Loving

By Margaret Crosland

IT HAS REMAINED to an Englishwoman, Margaret Crosland, to produce the best work to date about Colette.
Miss Crosland must have been thoroughly immersed in
her subject, for the book seems to have been written by
someone thinking in French—not only the occasional
turn of phrase, but the turn of mind. She has, however,
kept a scholar's detachment and has avoided what Janet
Flanner in her introduction calls "the patriotic sentimentality" of French commentators on Colette.

Who reads Colette in France today? Her entire work
is in print, and it is safe to say that anyone with access
to magazines or television or a radio knows who she is—
will know, that is, about the cats, about Gigi, about the
apartment in the Palais-Royal, about Colette's mop of
mauve-tinted hair. Some people actually believe she wrote
for children, others that children must be protected from

the very thought of her. Colette seems so established, so ensconced, so respectable, that American readers may find hard to credit Miss Crosland's statement that "Colette's reputation, distorted by rumor and tinged with scandal, has frightened off many people who, although they have never read her books, assert that they are lesbian and immoral." And yet that is very often the case; women whose mothers would not let them read Colette are apt to pass the same injunction on to their daughters. (Are mothers ever as worried about what their sons read?) It is something of a triumph to have been on a moral blacklist for three generations without going out of style.

This odd, lingering prohibition is true not only of a rigid, nonreading milieu. A young professor of literature told me that he never discussed Colette unless his students asked him to. She was "corrupting" because of a complicity she took for granted with the reader—in other words, she never said, "See how wicked *I* am." Miss Crosland puts it calmly, with a perfect word: Colette had an "impartiality concerning any aspect of sexual morality." This "impartiality" has always worried people.

Miss Crosland's summing-up of Colette's life and work is brief and compact and she has settled for most of the things that matter: how important it was for Colette to escape from her loving, powerful mother; how she wanted happiness without knowing exactly what that meant; how she hated the act of writing and wrote—sometimes 11 hours a day—because she was perpetually hard-up; how fame left her skeptical, if not cold. "If I were famous," she once remarked, "I would know it."

Colette's mother was an extraordinary woman who made her children's lives so happy that they could never deal adequately with other people. She was also an eccentric, who "took her dog to Mass and said that there was no reason why he should not bark during the elevation—it was his duty as a dog," and she was a subtle tyrant who "organized other people's emotions rather as she drew up shopping lists." Colette and her mother wrote each other constantly, but Colette's obsession with Sido developed only in middle-age, and after she herself had produced a daughter. It must have been difficult for someone who had never really stopped being someone's child to reverse the roles. Miss Crosland's great tact towards the living causes her to present Colette's relations with her daughter in idyllic fashion, but Janet Flanner in her introduction puts it plainly: "The deep attachment she had felt for her own mother was not in her nature to feel for her own child."

The person to whom Colette remained a child is someone we hardly know about, for the "Sido" of literature is transformed, half imagined. One of Sido's sons, Léo, was never able to make a life for himself as a man; his mind and emotions remained in childhood, in Sido's garden. After Sido's death her elder son, Colette's half-brother, who was a doctor, burned the 2,000-odd letters Colette had written their mother. Probably the too-loving, too-powerful mother could never be shared. "Sido's domination of the family was the most dangerous of all because it was insidious, not authoritarian," Miss Crosland explains.

Curiously, the Colette-Claudine of the Claudine novels is presented as motherless, rather as Proust suppressed his brother Robert, Françoise Sagan her heroine's mother in her first novel, or as, in the Bergeret novels, Anatole France gave himself the luxury of a life with an ideal daughter. When Sido appears in Colette's books, she *is* Sido, as Colette chose to see her, larger than life.

Her father counted for less. When he died, she realized she had never known him. He was a retired army officer, a graduate of Saint-Cyr, passionate about politics and, apparently, about writing his memoirs. After his death the bound volumes of his manuscripts were found to contain nothing except blank pages; he must have sat alone in a room day after day, dreaming that he was composing a book. Colette, luckily, was not allowed to get off with dreams: her first husband simply shut her up with a pen and a notebook, locked the door when it seemed necessary, and, there being no other distraction, Colette wrote.

Colette's first two husbands are, predictably, cut to ribbons. Willy (Henri Gauthier-Villars) was clever (too clever for his own good), vain, egocentric, an exhibitionist, and a literary crook who signed novels he had not written, including, of course, some of Colette's. But he also backed young writers when they needed it—Apollinaire, for one—and he obliged the stiffly conservative French public to consider Wagner, Fauré, Debussy and Ravel when these were dangerously avant-garde. He was a born editor; the example Colette gives of Willy's editing in *Mes Apprentissages* reveals how much she must have learned from him.

After they parted, each wrote malicious portraits of the other, and Willy never stopped trying to justify himself.

As late as 1920 he was still writing the "truth" about the Claudine books, claiming to be their author, naming the Parisians the characters had been based on, and attacking Colette. Fifty copies of Willy's "truth" were printed in booklet form about 11 years ago. Although descendants of Proust's characters seemed proud or at least complaisant about having relatives identified, the "Claudine" descendants are extremely touchy and the wings of French lawsuits have hovered over the little red book and its fairly silly contents. Willy's defense is, if anything, self-defeating; when he quotes even a sentence of Colette's, in order to demolish her, the contrast between his manner and hers speaks volumes. Willy would not have been capable of writing even the weakest of Colette's books.

Colette's disappointing marriage with Willy was followed by the "Missy" period—the Marquise de Morny. Colette was by then in her thirties, and she probably wanted someone to look after her, which up until then no man had ever done. She left Missy for Henri de Jouvenel, a brilliant, ambitious journalist and co-editor of *Le Matin*. It was evident from the beginning that these two did not want the same kind of life. Colette was bored by politics, and her lack of interest bored Jouvenel. They married after a long and rocky liaison, broken off more than once, when Colette found (to her amazement and some consternation, for she was nearly 40) that she was expecting a child. Jouvenel is too easily written off as a fortune hunter. To say, as Miss Crosland does, that "he preferred a rich one" when it came to wives gives the feeling that money was the chief cause of their separation.

Both Colette's first two husbands instigated the separation from her by putting her in a position where she had no choice. Willy had wanted a literary hostess, Jouvenel a social and political one. Her refusal to be either was exasperating to men of that generation. Colette had no personal or social ambition whatsoever and, as it turned out, she had better things to do than act a part. Playing up a husband's career was something a wife was "supposed" to do, but men were also "supposed" to support their wives, and neither of them quite did: her years of music-hall touring were embarked on mainly for income. Both of these marriage failures were shattering to her. Her letter to a woman friend, about Jouvenel, 'I've been alone for a month. He left without a word while I was on a lecture tour. I'm divorcing," merely means that Jouvenel had forced her to make the next move. He had left or threatened to leave before; one witness still remembers Colette sinking to her knees and asking him not to go.

Colette's admirers are apt to see her only as a victim, but as we depend for information on the faulty or biased or face-saving recollections of survivors it might be prudent to reflect that if an unqualified wife-victim is hard to find, so is an unqualified husband-monster. One French critic has remarked that if Colette always had only one man at a time, it was the better to enslave him; and Paul Léautaud, in another context, observed that her relations with her beloved cats and dogs were those of tamer to tamed. Colette was tolerant of her first two husbands' mistresses with an irony that surpassed resignation, yet she may have felt more cheated than one suspects. In the

1930s, when she was signing her books at an annual ben-
efit sale, she was approached by a stranger who told her
he owned several of her first editions and that he brought
one or two each year to have them autographed. Colette
wrote on the flyleaf of that year's volume, "To the only
faithful man I have known."

The two halves of Colette's face are completely different. If you cover one, then the other, you find a mocking
eye and an inquisitive one; as she grew old half her face
seemed wise and the other half cruel. Miss Crosland is
the only writer I know of who has paid close attention
to the violence in Colette. Read her account of Colette
at a luncheon party, coolly explaining how to kill with a
knife. Cruelty is an element in *La Chatte* and in the (to
me) repulsive *L'Enfant et Les Sortilèges*. It is not a cruelty
to animals, but to people. The duality of her nature, which
Miss Crosland examines with a nice perception, sprang
out of her being unable to decide whether the happiness
she had known in childhood, and which she tried to re-
capture all her life, depended on men, on love, or on some
element she had not discovered: "Whether happiness was
in any way connected with love was one of the problems
that was to preoccupy her most." She was never at ease
with a man until she could get away from a passionate
relationship and make a brother of him.

Even the most indulgent of Colette's critics find the
men in her books nonexistent, or, to Miss Crosland,
"somehow faceless." It was something Colette understood
and admitted as she grew older. She had always loved
"either too little or too much," and it constantly worried

her—or seemed to, for a temperament of that kind usually goes with a streak of sexual ruthlessness. One often has the curious feeling that writing about men made her shy. "Shy" may seem a ludicrous word for such an overwhelming person, but it may have been that the men in her life, far from feeling they were under a microscope (an occasional complaint of persons in relation to writers), may have missed being *seen.* Her men are mirrors, one French critic says, in which women watch themselves loving and growing older. Until she met Maurice Goudeket, who became her third husband, her emotional life had been largely unhappy, and she was then 52.

There is only one reservation one can have about this intelligent book and that is a cautiousness, a laudable desire to spare the feelings of the living, that just touches on genteelism. Colette was a tough character who used tough language. She had three husbands and lovers probably of both sexes. She spent years of her life in music halls and working for newspapers. She was "generous to herself and to others," incapable of penny-pinching to a degree almost unnatural for a provincial Frenchwoman. She had splendid appetites in most of the domains that matter; she was a loyal friend, an uncommon writer; and she was also, by chance, a genius.

Miss Crosland exercises the greatest possible discretion on the subject of Colette's supposed homosexuality. She thinks it may not have been true, and if it is true she seems to wish that it weren't. This runs straight counter to her and to Miss Flanner's assertion that Colette only wrote about what she knew and always knew what she was writing about. *De deux choses l'une*: either she knew what she was talking about or she made the whole thing up.

Long before her friendship with the Marquise de Morny, Colette had described female homosexuality in the Claudine novels. It might have been only the imagination of a young woman dreaming her way out of an unsatisfactory marriage, or it may have been, as Miss Crosland suggests, nothing more than "a sophisticated joke," except for the important and far from silly passage in which Renaud (the husband of Claudine, and an idealized Willy) discovers his wife's lesbian affair and blithely refuses to be jealous. He cannot take women seriously enough to consider his wife unfaithful unless another man is involved. Claudine's reaction of anger and resentment seems more than just intuition on the part of Colette. The affair was obviously not simply "charming," as Renaud puts it, but something of which he should have been jealous. Miss Crosland herself regards Colette as "neither conventional nor unconventional, she was outside convention," and perhaps that settles the matter.

Elizabeth Bowen

By Victoria Glendinning

IN 1959, AT the age of 60, unable to afford the upkeep of Bowen's Court—a 17th-century house standing on land her Anglo-Irish family had owned in County Cork ever since the Cromwell invasion—Elizabeth Bowen sold it to an authentic, unhyphenated Irishman named O'Keefe, believing he would live there and that his children would furnish the continuity she, the last of the Bowens, and childless, could not provide. In less than a year the new owner destroyed the gardens, felled the trees, demolished the house.

Victoria Glendinning begins her excellent biography of Elizabeth Bowen with this account of misadventure. It sounds like sledge-hammer Irish allegory: "The Come-uppance of the Protestant Ascendancy, or Ireland's Revenge." Actually, Bowen's Court—which had escaped being burned down during the Irish struggles—was finally wrecked by prosperity and peace: all Mr. O'Keefe had ever wanted the property for was its timber. The last of the Bowens now lies buried in an abandoned graveyard next to the ruin—a most modest statement of claim.

Elizabeth Bowen considered herself, rather wishfully, as someone in the main current of Irish writing. Irish writers, while admiring her, thought she was somewhere else. The rest of her readers, who did not care one way or another, usually saw her as English. Victoria Glendinning settles it once and for all: "She was Anglo-Irish ... when she died the Anglo-Irish literary tradition died with her." To be a hyphenated writer is no joke; identity swings like a metronome. The writer is not two things at once, but one thing slightly modified. Miss Glendinning likens Elizabeth Bowen, in that respect, to Charles Ritchie, the Anglo-Canadian diplomat who played such an important part in her life (as she in his).

"I am strongly and idiosyncratically Irish in the same way you are Canadian," she once wrote him. "Cagey, recalcitrant, on the run, bristling with reservations and arrogances that one doesn't show." This seems self-conscious; a wholly Irish writer would not have bothered to say it. Her biographer uses the term "self-conscious" about Elizabeth Bowen twice—in the way she wrote about Ireland, and again, surprisingly, about being in love. In its melancholy way, the matter of affinity and identity sounds like part of the sweetness of life before the revolution. Concern about being Anglo-anything became irrelevant long before the destruction of Bowen's Court, while to anyone born in Ireland or Canada after World War II it would be mythology.

"Mythology" comes to mind as one rereads Elizabeth Bowen today. What vanished when she ceased to write was not just a unique vision of streets and seasons, children and lovers, flowers and rooms, but a kind of confidence. Even the inanimate objects a writer would choose to mention now are completely other, while the class-security of her generation has been turned upside down by younger women like Doris Lessing and Margaret Drabble. Drama is seldom played out in the English upper-middle classes; all they supply for fiction now is the occasional character seen as bogus, or useless, or simply absurd.

Quotations from Elizabeth Bowen's work, held between the paragraphs of Miss Glendinning's no-nonsense prose, seem like wisps of autumn smoke without the bonfire. The fact is that she does not stand cutting, that no one sentence gives a hint of the underlying flame. The bonfire is *all The House in Paris, all Mysterious Kôr*. (Miss Glendinning considers *Kôr*, that pure and perfect story, to be the quintessence of her art.)

For a certain generation Elizabeth Bowen was not merely a writer, but part of the bridge one begins to cross at about 13, when fiction and life are still magically fused and books contain an element of prophecy. Readers who once drew on *The Death of the Heart* and *To the North* as fragments of their own experience will be thankful to learn that her writing has not been strung up on the gibbet of methodology, or otherwise tortured, and that the language of the biography is free from critical jargon and cant. (This will not surprise those already familiar with Victoria Glendinning's reviews in *The Times Literary Sup-*

plement.) Not everyone will agree that her work is like Colette's—it is hard, in fact, to imagine two writers more different. Elizabeth Bowen's great admiration for things French was not well requited, by the way. Her death in 1973 went virtually unnoticed in France, except in *Le Monde.* (With its matchless gift for delivering curious information with aplomb, that newspaper announced the passing of an author who had been popular with the masses but not taken seriously by the critics.)

A writer's life stands in relation to his work as a house does to a garden, related but distinct. It is the business of critical biography to make the two overlap—to bring some of the furniture out to the garden, as it were, and spread flowers all over the house. It seldom works except when the biography is, in itself, a mysterious work of art—in which case the problem comes full circle. Elizabeth Bowen's mother died early, her father had bouts of madness: about par for an artist. World War I, and the Irish tragedy, seem to have left her oddly untouched. She married a dull but devoted husband who, when her celebrity began to outdistance him, referred to himself, wryly, as "Albert the Good."

The portrait painstakingly put together gives us someone of no great intellectual depth, unreflective about religion, reactionary in politics, and restless to a degree exhausting even to read about. It is also the portrait of someone warm, impulsive and kind, and a whole-hearted writer who could think, of a soured love affair, "Break my heart if you must, but don't waste my time," who would ask herself, during emotional crises, "What effect is this having on me *as a writer*?" But the puzzle of creation cannot be solved by a life taken in inventory, whatever the competence of the biographer. We shall never know (any more than she herself could have explained) the why and how of her starting to write, why her work began on a high level and proceeded to be better and better and why, by the time she was 30, she would be in a class of her own.

She would have imitators galore; the style seemed irresistible. Imitators do not always lack an original gift, but they invariably lack an essential toughness. The rock-bottom one discovers rereading her work is a foundation of tyranny and victimization, with the innocent character quite often an unwitting tyrant. Her life, as revealed, cannot give up the key; the forced fusion of life-and-work inevitably flies apart. Imagine, for instance, Elizabeth Bowen aged 40-something, a tall woman with a long face, dining at Claridge's with a younger man, looking at him "through half-closed eyes" and saying, "I would like to put you in a novel." It sounds like the most preposterous sort of fiction, invented by someone who has never met a writer; and yet it took place. The author of "Ivy Gripped the Steps" would not have written a word of it; the separation between house and garden is implicit here. Still, the essence of the writing condition is that you can have your emotional cake and eat it. If writing equals neurosis—Miss Glendinning thinks that it does—one can say at least that no other neurosis permits that particular luxury. Chain smoking while dying of lung cancer, Elizabeth Bowen sums up the condition—not romantically, but specifically. She had outlived her husband, and would be buried beside him in Ireland. Thirty years after the scene in Claridge's, it was Charles Ritchie, that other hyphenated fellow-conspirator, "Cagey . . . on the run," who brought her champagne and was with her at the end.

Elizabeth Bowen, greatly recommended on all counts, contains a large selection of photographs, a bibliography, and an index.

The French

By Theodore Zeldin

THE VERY WORDS "The French" provoke a reaction. No publisher would be very likely to promote 538 pages (517 of text, 13 of bibliography, eight of index, 50 cartoons and potted biographies of 30-odd cartoonists) devoted to "The Belgians." But about the French, apparently, no book is too vast. Theodore Zeldin, distinguished British historian, Oxford don, author of the greatly admired *France 1848–1945*, has set out, as though he were dealing with an untidy garden, to grub up the stereotypes and clichés and marshal what's left into proper order.

The French do not wear berets or eat bread as a staple diet. They divorce, don't write to their parents, drink hard, forget to go to church, often perform work that leaves them bored and empty, fret about their sex lives, quarrel with their teen-age children—in short, they behave like men and women in an industrialized Western society. In spite of 1789, they still trip over class lines. The old aristocracy has been replaced by a hereditary "meritocracy" of people from the best schools and in attractive careers, as autocratic and as snobbish as the *Ancien Régime.* (The suggestion that class barriers in Britain are lower may be left to personal experience. A British dinner table of total strangers will spend a lively evening listening to one another's accents; in France, the guests perform a kind of whooping crane courtship dance as they try to establish, without asking directly, which guest is a graduate of which elite school.)

No gardener is better qualified than Mr. Zeldin. As he tells us, he has "devoted my whole adult life to studying the French. When *France 1848–1945* was published, in the Oxford History of Modern Europe series in the '70s, it was accepted as a brilliant and original work, and a classic. Between 1979 and 1981, this hefty opus was reissued by the Oxford University Press as five paperbacks, using for titles some chapter headings from the original: "Taste and Corruption," "Politics and Anger," "Ambition and Love," "Intellect and Pride," "Anxiety and Hypocrisy." For the nonspecialist, the amateur reader, they made up a plausible, intelligent, fascinating account (rather than a political history) of a society (rather than a nation), cut up in segments and packed into stout, neatly labeled sociological hold-alls. The reservations one occasionally heard muttered by historians could easily be put down to academic envy and jealousy. It is unusual for a work not particularly intended *pour le peuple* to receive quite so much popular attention.

Translated as *L'Histoire des Passions Françaises*, it made of Mr. Zeldin something of a minor cult figure in Paris. Everyone seemed either to be reading *Passions* or some part of it, or just to be looking up their ancestors in the index, which is a *Who's Who* of the Second Empire and Third Republic. The French are easily upset by criticism but touchingly grateful for sympathetic attention. Mr. Zeldin's faultless French and his seemingly unflappable temperament made him a natural subject for interviews. He was seen, he was heard, and for a time one could hardly pick up a magazine or a newspaper without finding his name, correctly spelled. The fact that no one could divine where he stood politically—whether he was in the thick of the fray or just hanging over a banister—gave him an advantage that would never be allowed a Frenchman: Praise arrived, in equal doses, from left and right.

WHAT, THEN, WENT wrong with *The French*? One British critic calls it all plums and no pudding. Another, an Oxford colleague of Mr. Zeldin, writes of "failure on a grand scale." It seems a heavy hammer to bring down on a work whose jokey chapter headings about the French ("How to tell them apart," "How to laugh at their jokes," "How to make sense of their language") suggest nothing more serious than a volume of essays collected from *Punch*. The scale, of course, is Mr. Zeldin's achievement and reputation.

Why, after reading a book in which so much is original, sensible and unexpected, does one have the disagreeable feeling of having been conned? Why are statistics and opinion polls used, sometimes, to jack up an idea that may have no other support? Why do so many of the interviews with French people, who seem to have been chosen at random, wander nowhere and tell us nothing? Why is there so little feeling of France or of Frenchness? France, England, West Germany and Italy share the problems and difficulties we all know about, but there are differences, other than language, between Paris, London, Munich and Rome. Why, stumbling over some error, do we have to wonder why the author didn't take 10 minutes to check? Why is there so much that is simply stated but unexplained? Why does the text have so little connection with the chapter headings? At the end of "How they choose their style of life," we are no more enlightened than at the beginning. Why, to basic material culled from "all sorts of erudite monographs, journalism, magazines, memoirs, government publications, statistics," does Mr. Zeldin add opinion polls meant to live no more than a day, limited surveys, faceless interviews mentioned as "assisted autobiography"—a term that makes some readers very wary indeed. Are the welder, the dropout, the bourgeois meant to be typical Frenchmen? If so, of what? Why do they all sound the same?

In his zeal to pull out stereotypes by the roots, Mr. Zeldin has torn up the whole garden. He has not bothered to warn, as an ordinary journalist would, that anonymous interviews are not final statements about anything. He surely cannot claim to be as neutral as his tape recorder.

Sometimes, when he is dealing with the rich and famous, he can sound silly. Of Yves Montand ("What lovers want from each other") we learn: "It is rare for him to find a true partner. His enthusiasm for Marilyn Monroe—which was not an affair—was based on the discovery that they had something in common." In "How to be chic," we receive one more thing to worry about: "That is the mystery which women of all countries try to penetrate: how do the French succeed in capturing this indefinable chic?" Well, how do they? Nobody knows, apparently—not even Mr. Zeldin. Two pages later we get a key of sorts from Loulou de la Falaise, the epitome of everything "elegant, striking, chic." "'My role,' says Loulou, 'is to be a fairy.'" Who's Loulou? She works for, or with, Yves Saint-Laurent, as "chief collaborator and inspirer." Fairyland is not much of a clue for those of us left circling the mystery. How are we to become elegant and striking fairies? Loulou apparently leaves it at that, and Mr. Zeldin won't say.

"Why Women's Liberation moves slowly" begins with the cautionary tale of Françoise Chandernagor, daughter of a Socialist minister in the present Government, a brilliant student who acceded while young to an advanced civil service post, on the strength of her brains and record. "Sabotaged" by her male colleagues, who stayed in the office working until 9:30 at night, forcing her to do the same, she dropped her career and fell back on being a wife and mother. Alas, her husband—another civil servant—turned out to be a saboteur of the home. "He leaves his things all over the floor; he never closes a cupboard door." After a vain attempt to change his habits, she now "has given up; she does not have the energy to fight him." Mr. Zeldin has forgotten to tell the other half of the story:

Françoise Chandernagor is also a writer, the author of a thumping best seller called *L'Allée du Roi*. As frustrated lives go, there've been worse.

SOME OMISSIONS ARE far more serious. There is no mention of French Protestants, not even anonymously. French Jews get two passing references and four pages—the same as the number allotted the designer Paco Rabanne but less than are given to the film director Claude Chabrol (five) or the comedian Guy Bedos (six), while the nameless humbug who "in the space of six years has seduced at least a hundred women" and who now satisfies "eight mistresses simultaneously" is allowed, along with his preposterous wife, to bore us for seven pages. "How they pray" overlooks a remarkable man, the Jewish-born Jean-Marie Cardinal Lustiger, whose nomination as Archbishop of Paris gave rise to the joke "Paris is the only city in the world with a Sephardic Chief Rabbi and an Ashkenazic Archbishop." Surely the Cardinal's biography, even unassisted, would tell us something about France?

"How they treat foreigners and Jews" is a chapter heading that stops one short. Are French Jews considered foreigners? By whom? Why not "Foreigners and lawn mowers," or "Canaries and Jews"? Here Mr. Zeldin drops another of the clinkers that litter his book: Some North African Jews have settled in the working-class Paris suburb of Sarcelles, where, he says, "the Communist-controlled municipality has given them special favors in return for their vote." Mr. Zeldin wanders off without telling us how he knows this, or what the privileges are that a municipal government can bestow on any group, or whether recipients of those favors write "J. for Jewish" on their ballots. He does not explain how the lucky know they will be favored. Does the municipality conduct a house-to-house search for Jews, offering an election deal (that, under law, could lead to a jail sentence)? Does he mean that North African Jews can park their cars where they like, are let off paying the local annual housing tax, given first rights to low-cost Government-funded apartments? Mr. Zeldin should say what he means.

"Most foreign women end up as servants," he writes. What foreign women? Sophia Loren? If he is talking about wives of immigrant workers from poor countries, there is still something the matter with "most." "Most" would run into the hundreds of thousands, reducing what is in fact a tooth-and-claw competition for live-in domestic help. The "assisted biography" of one Spanish maid mentions a starting wage of 300 francs a month. Mr. Zeldin does not bother to tell us *when* she started, but as he translates 300 francs into £30, it must have been fairly recently. (The going rate, in Paris, for a full-time maid, living in, working a five-day week, is between 3,500 and 4,000 francs a month.) There is something wrong with his example, and something unreal about his comment that maids "certainly do sometimes receive treatment that no other profession would tolerate. Occasionally they are beaten. Not infrequently they are given worse food than the dogs, let alone the rest of the family; one household had two sets of plates, one beautiful set for their own use, and another for the dog and the servant." Where did he get this ridiculous information and—more important—why does he pass it on without finding out if it is true? What are we supposed to make of "sometimes" and "occasionally" in this context?

Perhaps we are better off with adverbs, if we consider the occasional use Mr. Zeldin makes of figures: "One of the best known erotic works of the postwar era, the *Story of O*, has sold over four million copies in the United States, but only 800,000 in France." He forgets to point out that the population of the United States is roughly four times the population of France, which might have knocked out his conclusion that readers abroad are "more excited by French naughtiness than are the French themselves."

Mr. Zeldin neglects to answer his own questions, but he does leave his reader curious about unfinished stories. At the age of 16, Paco Rabanne was taken by his father to Moscow, where he saw Stalin plain. "The meeting cured him of Marxism." Why? What did Stalin say to young Paco Rabanne? We shall never know, for we are rushed on to something Mr. Zeldin must have thought more significant: "He believes in reincarnation: in a previous life he was a priest of Tutankhamun, and he can often tell what other people were in a former existence: he told me I was a reincarnation of the eighteenth-century philosopher Diderot."

THE CARTOONIST GEORGES Wolinski's "assisted autobiography" produces this: "His father was a small employer who was killed by his communist workers during the Popular Front of 1936." As the Popular Front was an elected government and not an armed insurrection, and as Mr. Zeldin is a specialist on the period, it is reasonable to wonder why we are not told something about this murder, let alone why Mr. Wolinski, who must have suffered a childhood shock of some dimension, chose to become a cartoonist for the Communist daily *l'Humanité*. Apparently, "there is less struggle for money, for careers," in *l'Humanité*'s offices.

Mr. Zeldin has had the excellent idea of using French cartoons to illustrate his book and to speak for French humor. Except for two each by the masters Grandville and Daumier and one from Roubille, who easily put most of their descendants to shame, they are the work of contemporary artists. The French do not find American cartoons funny, or even comprehensible. Except for some by the barest handful of artists—Bretécher, Sempé, Effel—theirs may strike Americans as being all wag and no wit. Captions defy translation, and it is not Mr. Zeldin's fault if they sometimes seem ham-handed. The translations are into British English, and there is at least one caption that may puzzle American readers: A pretty teacher, facing a class on the first day of term, says, "Good morning. My knickers are pink.... Any other questions?"

None of it says much for modern French humor, at least in cartoon form, but that may be the object lesson Mr. Zeldin had in mind. For the answer to this, and other questions, we shall have to wait for his sequel to *The French*.

Intimate Memoirs, Including Marie-Jo's Book

By Georges Simenon
Translated by Harold J. Salemson

AT 81, GEORGES Simenon is the best-known living author and probably the richest. He has attained a celebrity greater than any fellow citizen since his native Belgium became an independent state. His work is sold in every French-speaking country and translated wherever the book trade exists. He began to write at 16, in his home town, Liège, and stopped abruptly in Lausanne, Switzerland, at 69. Within that span, he wrote uncounted short fictions—he used to finish eight in a day—and 220 novels. Eighty-four of these have as their hero Inspector Maigret of the Paris police, whose fame has surpassed that of Sherlock Holmes. Like Sherlock Holmes, Maigret is perceived by addicted readers as a historical figure rather than a creature of fiction; many others see Simenon and Maigret as one.

They are in fact as opposite as can be. Maigret picks up clues and uses them. He is an optimist, in that he believes

in solutions. He is unassuming and underpaid, he takes
orders and he shows little interest in any woman other
than his wife, a first-class cook and a good listener. She
sounds, in fact, like Simenon's idea of a perfect mate. Trying to account for his two wrecked marriages and his nu-
merous affairs and thousand-and-one casual encounters
(most of his partners were paid) he says: "The goal of my
endless quest, after all, was not a woman, but 'the' woman,
the real one, loving and maternal at the same time, without artifices, without makeup, without ambition, without
concern for tomorrow, without 'status.'" A man who reck-
ons his women like a grocery list usually does not know
what he wants. Simenon, at least, has a formula. Does it
match the memory of his mother? She was a flinty, firmly
moral Roman Catholic of petit-bourgeois stock, who remained, by choice, just above the poverty line all her life.
Although Mme. Simenon makes only four or five appear-
ances in these lengthy memoirs, she is the backbone of the
book, the reason, one feels, for most of his behavior and
the impetus of his peculiar genius. He never could satisfy,
or please, or impress her. "*Mon Dieu,* Georges, how ugly
she is!" she exclaimed, after meeting the girl who was to
become his first wife. On the way home from the wedding, he discussed with his mother the best way to make
French-fried potatoes. Invited to America—Simenon
and his family were living in Connecticut—she stayed a
few days and went back to Europe. Her daughter-in-law,
Simenon's domineering second wife, snooping in the old
lady's room, had found and burned the only corset Mme.
Simenon liked to wear. Years later, in an imposing Swiss

château stuffed with servants (European picture magazines were forever running color features of the place) she
remained in the kitchen, asking the help if they thought
Simenon really owned it. In her old age, she gave him four
silk purses filled with gold coins, one for each of his children. It represented all the money he had ever given her.
Simenon mentions this with admiration and pride. Oddly,
French critics saw it as a calculated insult, and proof that
his mother did not love him.

THEIR MOST SIGNIFICANT meeting took place in Liège,
where Simenon had returned to be honored. In the
shabby house that he remembered with horror, she
opened a bottle of wine and invited him to stay for dinner.
He remained for half an hour and fled; his wife and his
publisher were waiting in a car. Mme. Simenon lived on
her widow's pension; wanted nothing; was, indeed, without artifices, makeup, ambition or status—and she never
understood what his life was about.

Except for a few volumes of reminiscence, of which
Intimate Memoirs is the longest, Simenon has not written
a book for 12 years. That is, he has not published a work
of imagination, a Maigret mystery, or one of the taut, pes-
simistic narratives he calls "my hard novels." His passport
identification has been changed from "Novelist" to "No
Profession." To some writers, this would be as good as a
death sentence; for Simenon, ceasing to write seems to
signify release from a stifling obsession. *The* only thing he
hasn't done in his radical about-face is to call in his books

and burn them. He tells us that he will never touch pencil and typewriter again. He dictates his memoirs and—to judge by their unraveled prose and misspelled proper names—does not bother to read them.

He lives in Switzerland, in a modest house—the château was abandoned, in another of his abrupt secessions—nursed and served by a devoted Italian woman who was once his wife's personal maid; plagued by ailments—he dwells on every twinge, symptom, diagnosis and palliative, when there is one; haunted by the suicide of his beloved daughter, Marie-Georges, *dite* Marie-Jo; still suspecting that to be rich and famous means one can never be loved. (One of the reasons he trusts his present companion is that she has not asked him for marriage or to be mentioned in his will.) The grey morality of his novels has tinged his old age. Achievement is meaningless (*The President*). A grudge can cement a marriage, beyond any reasonable breaking point (*The Cat*). A young and beautiful woman can decide to stop living—just like that (*The Disappearance of Odile*).

Reading Simenon's autobiography, it is important to remember his work; he barely mentions it except, like his women, in terms of statistics—three novels written in December, only one in January. European critics followed his lead and made exact tabulations of so many women, so many books. He is stuck with his legend (a novel finished in three days, and his shirt soaked through after every chapter, the shattering effect of an interruption, the endless cups of tea) and, unfortunately, so are we.

The English version of *Mémoires Intimes* has several advantages over the French. For one thing, it is shorter, but still not short enough. Readers who are familiar with his finest work, and who find themselves tripping up in the endless tangle of loose paragraphs, must take it on faith that Simenon was once a master of frugal prose. In the English version names are substituted for needlessly mysterious initials, with an exception: His second wife, Denise Ouimet, with whom he remains locked in endless litigation, is still "D". The surrealist French spelling of American names has been cleaned up. (One rather misses Grand-Mamma Mosses, the painter, and the Plazza Hotel.) Some, but not nearly enough, of the garrulous repetitions have disappeared, as well as specimens of European inflation that, for American readers, would require a footnote—for example, a Swiss psychiatrist's opinion that Simenon's daughter's suicide was admirable, lucid and even sublime. Ten years in North America did not diminish his acceptance of sublime hot air from doctors.

What remains is an 815-page barrage against discussion of his work. He gives us endless filler ("I went in for golf, canoeing, volleyball"), leads us around his private purgatories (his appalling second marriage, the tragedy of Marie-Jo) and introduces us to the moneyed and celebrated. That can't be helped; he was in his 20s when his first novels and stories brought him financial security and mail by the sackload. Unfortunately, the story of his life seems to lose momentum after he leaves Liège, which he describes admirably, and his brief, early poverty in Montmartre. Probably only youth and hope and the climb—the initiation—are compelling. We are kept so busy watching episodes of sex *à trois*, adultery, neurotic fixations of every sort and marital furor that we barely notice the novels that are being produced behind the scenes. Simenon mentions them in passing; they sound not so much composed as spat out. By turning us into voyeurs, he manages to divert our attention from his deepest secret, his creativity. We have to be content with a sex life out of Casanova, domestic hysteria from Strindberg and a father who would have done better if he had remained in the pages of J. M. Barrie, but could not.

A writer's visible life and the root of imagination do not connect above ground. Which of the two is public property? This book is not a long interview. Simenon dictated its contents, by choice. He has chosen to give us—for instance—his wife's faked orgasms. We discover exactly when and where each of his four children was conceived, we follow each pregnancy to term, learn how the baby emerged and what the nurse said and find out what to do when the mother cannot breast-feed. It is a long testimony for the defense: He was a generous husband, a doting father. The truth remains that every artist causes absent-minded destruction and that a writer totally unselfish would never get anything done. In 1978, his second wife, Denise Ouimet, published her view of the marital wreck, *Un Oiseau Pour le Chat* (*A Bird for the Cat*). French critics trounced it as shabby and vengeful, but Simenon was hurt. The *Memoirs* are, in part, his case. His wife was, at the very least, an eccentric. She bore three of his children, managed his affairs rather more than he wanted, chose his casual mistresses and showed jealousy where instinct told her it mattered: toward his mother, his put-upon first wife, and a Belgian servant who made her life over to Simenon. No matter how much evidence is produced, she will go on seeing herself as bird to his cat and he to hers.

The victim was probably Marie-Jo, a pathetic figure, introduced to sex by her mother at 13, hopelessly in love with a father who wanted nothing but a "tiny little girl" in small sprigged frocks. Fifty years lay between them; no wonder he saw her as "tiny." The trouble was, he went on saying it too long. At 8, she asked for a wedding ring and he was foolish enough to place one on her finger. She never removed it except to have it enlarged and he would put it back on her hand. In her 20s, after years of breakdowns and psychiatric clinics (she was once treated in the same establishment as her mother) and unhappy love affairs, an unsuccessful part-time actress, haunted by an anxiety she called *Madame Angoisse,* she challenged Simenon to fulfill the promise of the ring: "Why not me?" Simenon, established with his present companion, pointed to his bed and explained that the woman shared *all* of his life. Marie-Jo pointed to the ring. "I opened an almost unlimited bank account for her," he says, but he is talking about banks and money. To the confused and pathetic young woman, the ring was a dud check. In her last message, she asked to be cremated wearing it.

Simenon has addressed his memoirs to his children— the three adult sons and Marie-Jo, who shot herself at the age of 25. In her Champs-Élysées apartment, an older brother discovered her notes and unmailed letters, most of them to her father, and cassettes into which she wept and talked and sang, in French and half-coherent English. Simenon has used these in an appendix he calls "Marie-Jo's Book." He speaks to his sons and to her ashes, which are sprinkled in the garden of his house in Lausanne. Even if she could hear (the reader suspects he knows she cannot) she would learn nothing. The crucial revelation—that there had been a traumatic incident between the child and her mother—came from her. Simenon, hearing a cassette monologue after Marie-Jo's death, discovered something he had suspected all along, but dreaded having to know.

The translation of *Mémoires Intimes* is slipshod; it lurches from undistinguished English to near-gibberish. Judging by its fatal tendency to stick to word-for-word, it must have been done in a tearing hurry. Unfortunately, words lined up in French are not lined up in the same way in English. "The distance is more distant than anywhere else" is just silly, and "it will cause certain fibers to vibrate" is a French cliché that has no business in English. The original French is not good Simenon, but he deserves better than this.

SOURCE NOTES

"The Events in May: A Paris Notebook—I" was published in *The New Yorker*, September 14, 1968.

"The Events in May: A Paris Notebook—II" was published in *The New Yorker*, September 21, 1968.

"Immortal Gatito" was published in *The New Yorker*, June 26, 1971.

"Paul Léautaud, 1872–1956" was published in *The New York Times Book Review* (*NYTBR*), September 9, 1973.

Introduction to *The War Brides*, edited by Joyce Hibbert. Toronto: *PMA*, 1978.

"Paris: The Taste of a New Age" was published in *The Atlantic*, April 1981.

"What Is Style?" was published in *The Canadian Forum*, September 1982.

"Limpid Pessimist" was published in *The New York Review of Books*, December 5, 1985.

Review of *Jean Giraudoux: The Writer and His Work* by Georges Lemaitre (New York: Frederick Ungar, 1971) and *Lying Woman* by

Jean Giraudoux, translated by Richard Howard (New York: Winter House, 1971), was published in the *NYTBR*, January 30, 1972.

Review of *Transparent Things* by Vladimir Nabokov (New York: McGraw-Hill, 1972) was published in the *NYTBR*, November 19, 1972.

Review of *From the Diary of a Snail* by Günter Grass, translated by Ralph Manheim (New York: Harcourt Brace Jovanovich, 1973), was published in the *NYTBR*, September 30, 1973.

Review of *All Said and Done* by Simone de Beauvoir, translated by Patrick O'Brian (New York: G. P. Putnam's Sons, 1974), was published in the *NYTBR*, July 21, 1974.

Review of *André Malraux* by Jean Lacouture, translated by Alan Sheridan (New York: Pantheon Books, 1976), was published in the *NYTBR*, January 11, 1976.

Review of *Céline* by Patrick McCarthy (New York: Viking, 1976) was published in the *NYTBR*, July 18, 1976.

Review of *Hearts and Minds: The Common Journey of Simone de Beauvoir and Jean-Paul Sartre* by Axel Madsen (New York: William Morrow & Co., 1977) was published in the *NYTBR*, September 18, 1977.

Review of *Colette: The Difficulty of Loving* by Margaret Crosland (New York: Bobbs-Merrill, 1973) was published in the *NYTBR*, December 9, 1973.

Review of *Elizabeth Bowen* by Victoria Glendinning (New York: Alfred A. Knopf, 1978) was published in the *NYTBR*, January 15, 1978.

Review of *The French* by Theodore Zeldin (New York: Pantheon Books, 1983) was published in the *NYTBR*, March 20, 1983.

Review of *Intimate Memoirs, Including Marie-Jo's Book* by Georges Simenon (San Diego: Harcourt Brace Jovanovich, 1984) was published in the *NYTBR*, July 1, 1984.

Mavis Gallant was born in Montreal, where she worked as a journalist before moving to Europe to devote herself to writing fiction. Gallant settled in Paris in 1950 and lived there for the rest of her life. She published more than one hundred stories and dispatches in *The New Yorker*. In 1981, she received the Order of Canada for her contribution to Canadian letters and the Governor General's Award. In 2002, she received the Rea Award for the Short Story and in 2004, the PEN/Nabokov Award for lifetime achievement. Gallant died in 2014.

Hermione Lee is a biographer and critic whose work includes biographies of Virginia Woolf, Edith Wharton, Penelope Fitzgerald, and Tom Stoppard. She was awarded the Biographers' Club Prize for Exceptional Contribution to Biography in 2018. In 2003, Lee was made a CBE, in 2013 she was made a Dame for services to literary scholarship, and in 2023 she was made GBE (Dame Grand Cross of the Order of the British Empire) for services to English Literature.

A NOTE ON THE TYPE

Paris Notebooks has been set in Caslon. This modern version is based on the early-eighteenth-century roman designs of the British printer William Caslon I, whose typefaces were so popular that they were employed for the first setting of the Declaration of Independence, in 1776. Eric Gill's humanist typeface Gill Sans, from 1928, has been used for display.

Book Design & Composition by Tammy Ackerman

GODINE NONPAREIL
Celebrating the joy of discovery with books bound to be classics.

Godine's Nonpareil paperback series features essential works by great authors—
from stand-alone books of nonfiction and fiction to collections of essays, stories,
interviews, and letters—introduced by celebrated contemporary voices who have
deep connections to the featured authors and their trove of work.

ANN BEATTIE More to Say: Essays & Appreciations
Selected and Introduced by the author

GUY DAVENPORT The Geography of the Imagination: Forty Essays
Introduction by John Jeremiah Sullivan

ANDRE DUBUS The Lieutenant: A Novel
Afterword by Andre Dubus III

MAVIS GALLANT Paris Notebooks: Essays & Reviews
Foreword by Hermione Lee

WILLIAM MAXWELL The Writer as Illusionist: Uncollected & Unpublished Work
Selected and Introduced by Alec Wilkinson

JAMES ALAN MCPHERSON On Becoming an American Writer: Nonfiction & Essays
Selected and Introduced by Anthony Walton

BHARATI MUKHERJEE Darkness: Stories
Introduction by the author and Afterword by Clark Blaise

ADELE CROCKETT ROBERTSON The Orchard: A Memoir
Foreword by Betsy Robertson Cramer and Afterword by Jane Brox

ALISON ROSE Better Than Sane: Tales from a Dangling Girl
Introduction by Porochista Khakpour

ALEC WILKINSON Midnights: A Year with the Wellfleet Police
Foreword by William Maxwell and Afterword by the author

MONICA WOOD Any Bitter Thing: A Novel
Introduction by Cathie Pelletier